The First Fifteen

The First Fifteen

~

How Asian American Women
Became Federal Judges

SUSAN OKI MOLLWAY

Rutgers University Press

New Brunswick, Camden, and Newark, New Jersey, and London

Library of Congress Cataloging-in-Publication Data

Names: Mollway, Susan Oki, 1950– author.
Title: The first fifteen : how Asian American women became federal judges / Susan Oki Mollway.
Description: New Brunswick, NJ : Rutgers University Press, [2022] | Includes bibliographical references and index.
Identifiers: LCCN 2020054464 | ISBN 9781978824515 (hardcover) | ISBN 9781978824522 (epub) | ISBN 9781978824539 (mobi) | ISBN 9781978824546 (pdf)
Subjects: LCSH: Women judges—United States—Biography. | Asian American women—United States—Biography.
Classification: LCC KF372 .M65 2022 | DDC 347.73/1409252—dc23
LC record available at https://lccn.loc.gov/2020054464

A British Cataloging-in-Publication record for this book is available from the British Library.

♾ The paper used in this publication meets the requirements of the American National Standard for Information Sciences—Permanence of Paper for Printed Library Materials, ANSI Z39.48-1992.

www.rutgersuniversitypress.org

Manufactured in the United States of America

References to internet websites (URLs) were accurate at the time of writing. Neither the author nor Rutgers University Press is responsible for URLs that may have expired or changed since the manuscript was prepared.

For my late mother, Nobuko Shimazu Oki

Contents

Abbreviations

AABANY	Asian American Bar Association of New York
ABA	American Bar Association
ACLU	American Civil Liberties Union
APABA SV	Asian Pacific American Bar Association of Silicon Valley
AUSA	Assistant U.S. Attorney
FJC	Federal Judicial Center
JD	Juris Doctor or Doctor of Jurisprudence degree
LLB	Bachelor of Laws degree (old designation for JD)
LLM	Master of Laws degree
NAPABA	National Asian Pacific American Bar Association
OIRA	Office of Information and Regulatory Affairs

The First Fifteen

Introduction

In 1998, when I joined the bench in the U.S. District Court for the District of Hawaii, I became the first Asian woman to get a lifetime appointment as a federal judge. While several judges and attorneys expressed disbelief that, as late as the end of the twentieth century, no Asian woman had ever before received such an appointment, it turned out that I remained the only such judge for the next decade. But after that, over a dozen more Asian women got lifetime appointments as federal judges. This is the story of the first fifteen of us.

The idea of telling the stories of the first fifteen came to me while I was a student in Duke University School of Law's Master of Laws program.[1] The program specialized in what it called "judicial studies." That is, it was designed for students who were already sitting judges. A thesis was a degree requirement. I chose a thesis subject I not only was interested in but also knew something about. What was once a thesis has now become this book. My focus is on why the number of Asian women serving as federal judges has grown in recent years and on how Asian women have made their way through the nomination and confirmation processes.

I begin by defining two terms.

First, these stories focus on a particular category of federal judges: Article III judges. Article III of the U.S. Constitution provides for judges "both of the supreme and inferior Courts" who "hold their Offices during good Behaviour," which usually means for life or until a judge chooses to step down. Article III judges include Supreme Court justices, judges on the federal circuit courts of appeals, and federal district judges (other than judges in the territorial district courts).

Of course, Article III judges are not the only federal judges. Magistrate judges, for example, are appointed by district judges for renewable eight-year terms. Bankruptcy judges are appointed by courts of appeals for renewable fourteen-year terms. Judges on the Court of Federal Claims, like the territorial district judges for Guam, the Commonwealth of the Northern Mariana Islands, and the Virgin Islands, are nominated by the president and confirmed by the Senate, with the Court of Federal Claims judges receiving renewable fifteen-year terms and the territorial district judges receiving renewable ten-year terms. By contrast, federal district judges in Puerto Rico are Article III judges.

Presidentially appointed non–Article III judges go through a process similar to that faced by Article III judges, but I do not review the experiences of those non–Article III judges. My premise is that, among other things, lifetime appointments introduce heightened scrutiny of applicants by political decision makers. In addition, the political decision makers may differ. The non–Article III territorial judges, for example, do not have their own senators to rely on (although that is also true of two of the Article III judges I do discuss here—a DC Circuit judge and a Court of International Trade judge). My focus on Article III judges reflects my own history, current position, and academic interest. But non–Article III judges are very much worthy of study. In fact, I am keenly aware of how interesting many of my non–Article III colleagues are!

For example, I recognize that Marilyn Go preceded me by five years when, in 1993, she became a magistrate judge in the Eastern District of New York. She grew up in Hawaii, where she and I met when we participated in interscholastic high school debate competitions. We reconnected in November 1998, at the annual convention of the National Asian Pacific American Bar Association (NAPABA) in New York City, when I was brand new on the bench and she already had years under her belt. I have spent time with her at numerous NAPABA functions after that. She is a guiding light among Asian judges. She was instrumental in fostering NAPABA's Judicial Council, which includes state and federal judges who are members of NAPABA. She has nurtured that group of judges, keeping membership records and minutes of meetings and making sure the group remains engaged and active. She has been an inspiration for me.

Just as there are Asian women who are magistrate judges, there are other non–Article III judges such as Brenda Rhoades, appointed in 2003 in the Eastern District of Texas, who is the first Asian woman to become a bankruptcy judge.[2]

That the ranks of magistrate judges and bankruptcy judges are not more diverse[3] is particularly troubling because the problem can be addressed by Article III judges themselves. After all, under 28 U.S.C. § 631, federal district judges choose magistrate judges, and under 28 U.S.C. § 152, circuit judges choose bankruptcy judges.

I also recognize that Frances Tydingco-Gatewood, chief district judge in the District of Guam, and Ramona Manglona, chief district judge in the District of the Commonwealth of the Northern Mariana Islands, have intriguing biographies that I am leaving out of this book. Tydingco-Gatewood is primarily Chamorro, but her background also includes both Asian and Caucasian threads.[4] Manglona is Chamorro, Carolinian, Spanish, and non-Latina Caucasian.[5] I considered expanding my focus to include the Article IV Pacific Islander women who are federal judges but ultimately decided I had a big enough job sharing the stories of the Article III judges in this book.

Other non–Article III judges whom I am leaving out are the judges on the District of Columbia's local courts (federal courts that are the equivalent of state courts), although those judges are nominated by the president and confirmed by the Senate. Three Asian women now sit on the District of Columbia's superior court, with the first of those, Florence Pan, having been appointed in 2009.

Asian is the second word that deserves definition at the outset. I use the term *Asian* rather than *Asian American*. Given how often I refer to Asians in this book, I have dropped *American* for the sake of brevity except in the title. Unless the context clearly indicates otherwise, the references to Asians are to American citizens of Asian descent. All the federal judges I discuss, whether Article III or non–Article III, are American citizens, although the Constitution and federal statutes do not actually require that federal judges be American citizens. In fact, there is not even a constitutional or statutory requirement that federal judges have been lawyers, although I am not aware of a federal judge serving today who was not an attorney.

I also included judges listed as Asian in the directory of judges maintained by the Federal Judicial Center (FJC). The FJC, which I refer to often in this book, is the educational arm of the federal judiciary. Long before I had any thought of gathering the stories I tell here, I communicated with staff at the FJC about how the demographic information about judges was collected. I was told that with respect to race or ethnicity, the FJC relied on self-identification by judges. The FJC's listing of Asian judges includes South Asian judges, and I include them in my study. Notably, NAPABA counts numerous South Asians among its members.

My primary method of discovering why and how Asian women became Article III judges was interviews. When I preliminarily reached out to them, I was surprised by how varied the judges' responses were. Most of the judges knew me, and many readily and enthusiastically agreed to share their stories. One judge who at the time was only an acquaintance said unhesitatingly, "Anything for you." But another judge wanted to know whether her story would end up forgotten in a dusty law library. If that was likely, she was all in. If not, she cringed at the prospect of unsolicited attention to her personal history. Yet another judge wanted to know whether she could speak freely to me but then retain the ability to object to the inclusion of some details after reading whatever I wrote about her. I told her that was not feasible from my point of view. And another judge wondered whether I might have my work blessed by the FJC, a prospect that I declined.

I have interviewed fourteen Asian women who are Article III judges, the most recent of whom took office in March 2019. When I add myself, we total fifteen. In August 2019, a sixteenth Asian woman became an Article III judge—Martha Pacold of the Northern District of Illinois. Unfortunately, although we had convivial telephone conversations and exchanged multiple email messages, we were unable to reach a quick resolution as to whether Pacold would participate in sharing her story. This was a matter of timing; in her first few months after becoming a judge, she was understandably very busy, while I was staring down my own deadlines and eager to move forward. That I was unable to include Pacold in my book is a disappointment for me. But I realized that, even as I decided to move forward without including her, there might be other Asian women whom I would have to leave out as well. At the time, there were Asian women who had been nominated and were awaiting Senate confirmation. Indeed, Diane Gujarati of the Eastern District of New York and Regina Rodriguez of the District of Colorado were also confirmed too late for me to interview them. Others may be confirmed as this book nears completion.

Some of the judges who agreed to be interviewed by me confirmed that they remained free to decline questions they might be uncomfortable answering. That some judges were hesitant made me, of course, all the more curious about what my interviews might uncover. Federal judicial appointments unfold in a largely public context. If there is opposition, that is usually voiced by various groups in the media, and senators not from the same political party as the nominating president typically are not shy about expressing concerns about a nominee. Still, the most interesting details are likely to be nonpublic, either because they involve behind-the-scenes maneuvering or because they involve unannounced personal connections with people in positions of power. Judges may be sensitive about exposing these matters, although Article III judges are often quick to concede that they are the products of a political process, not one that is exclusively merit-based. Politics may always be at play, not just at a partisan level, but also at a personal level.

In addition, I interviewed some individuals who have helped Asian women become Article III judges. These influential people are members of NAPABA, which appears to me to have become a particularly important player in the federal judicial nomination and confirmation processes in the last decade or so, a role that coincided with President Barack Obama's desire to diversify the federal judiciary.

From the outset, I told the judges that I did not intend to focus on their performances as federal judges. I look at them up to the point when they started their federal judicial careers. My thought was that particular rulings would be discussed only to the extent that they affected judicial nominations or confirmations (e.g., when a federal magistrate judge was nominated to a federal district court position).

This book has three main sections. Part 1 includes background information in two respects. First, it provides an overview of the makeup of the federal judiciary, with particular attention paid to Asians and their growth in the law. I compare increases in the different groups of people who have become Article III judges. These numbers (including even the number of Asian women who are Article III judges) are, of course, always in flux, making the figures I cite already outdated. I hope the numbers nevertheless provide a helpful overview. Following that overview, part 1 looks at how the stories I tell relate to and expand on the existing scholarship.

Part 2, the longest section, discusses, one by one, each of the first fifteen Asian women who became Article III judges, detailing each individual's path to an Article III judgeship. Because my purpose is to trace growth and recognize patterns, I have arranged the judges chronologically by the dates they were commissioned as judges. Part 2 thus starts with my own story. I obviously have considerable information about my own appointment, so that account is detailed, even if my own experience can hardly qualify as the most important or most interesting.

Part 2 relies on information I have gathered from written materials (Senate Judiciary Committee questionnaires, the FJC's website, speeches by the judges, etc.) and personal interviews of the judges themselves and of others instrumental in their progress. I decided not to videotape or record the interviews. I can write things down verbatim at a fairly good speed, and especially after the mixed reactions I got to the interview process at the outset, I thought note-taking would be less off-putting than recording devices.

The judges have provided photographs, some of which are current, but some are from years ago—sometimes from the year that a judge became a federal judge (meaning that my photograph will be the most outdated). The years the photographs were taken are noted. That some of the photographs are dated is not a reflection of a desire by the judges to appear younger than they are today. For some, it results from the common practice of judges having official photographs taken when they become judges. These photographs are used when news organizations request photos or when judges are asked for photos to be included in programs for events at which they are speaking. Frequently, the judges simply do not bother to take new photographs. Also, while some judges submitted current photographs they took themselves, others who wanted up-to-date professional photographs were stymied by the closure of photography studios required by the coronavirus pandemic that was ongoing as this book was being prepared for publication.

In part 3, I look for trends, patterns, and reasons for the growth in the number of Asian women in Article III ranks. I track similarities and differences in the judges' paths, looking at, for example, their ethnicities, the influence of having immigrant parents, and the impact of prior government service. Some of the judges were federal magistrate judges before they became Article III judges, some were assistant U.S. attorneys, and some were state court judges. One of the two federal circuit judges was elevated to that position from a federal district judgeship. Some, like me, came from private practice, had no judicial record to point to, and had been free to engage in activities that, once they were nominated, were identified as controversial.

In part 3, I also look at why a number of Asian women who appear to have been likely candidates for Article III judgeships have not become Article III judges. Some of these women were encouraged to seek Article III judgeships but declined, while others sought Article III judgeships but did not complete the process.

This section cannot pretend to be comprehensive, as there is no complete list of such women. Nor can I claim to have a statistically random or defensibly representative sample. But these are women who, having come to my attention, serve as a counterpoint to the fifteen Article III judges. Why the women in part 3 are not Article III judges today sheds some light on those who are Article III judges.

The increase in the number of Asian women judges reflects NAPABA's growth. By the time President Obama was elected, NAPABA had attorneys assigned to the task of shepherding applicants through the federal process. These attorneys studied the judicial landscape year-round. They kept in close contact with friends who had joined the Obama administration and were able to feed progress reports to anxious would-be nominees or those awaiting confirmation. They looked ahead as well, identifying anticipated judicial vacancies for interested candidates. Ten of the Asian women who have become Article III judges were nominated by President Obama. They actually represent eleven appointments because one woman was confirmed first to the district court, which is the federal trial court, and then elevated to the court of appeals (which I sometimes refer to as a circuit court), the level immediately below the U.S. Supreme Court. NAPABA is a nonpartisan bar association, and its experiences during the Obama administration have guided it during the Trump administration.

I hope that what I have written is inherently interesting to a general audience. I also hope that it will be useful in future efforts to diversify the judiciary—not only for Asian women but also for other groups trying to increase their presence in the federal judiciary.

This seems to be a particularly good time to look back. Over two decades after Asian women's first appearance in those ranks, we are a group, not a single person. Why and how that has happened is the story I tell.

PART I

Context

Diversity in the Federal Judiciary

The addition of Asian women to Article III ranks is best understood in the context of their place in the population. Around the time I became a federal judge in 1998, the U.S. population was 270,248,000, rounded to the nearest thousand, with more women (51.14 percent, or 138,218,000) than men (48.86 percent, or 132,030,000).[1] By 2018, the total population in the United States had risen to about 327,167,000. There were still slightly more women (about 50.8 percent, or 166,049,000) than men (about 49.2 percent, or 161,646,000).[2] In 2018, Asian women in the United States made up 51.97 percent (about 11,752,000 people) of the total Asian population of about 22,613,000. Asian men made up about 48.03 percent (about 10,861,000).[3]

In 2018, non-Latino Whites (about 203,857,000) made up about 62 percent of the population. Asians were between 6 and 7 percent, African Americans were about 14 percent, and Latinos were about 19 percent.[4]

The changes in the numbers of lawyers in the last few decades are notable. As of 2018, women made up 37.4 percent of the lawyers in the United States, and one source puts Asians (male and female) at 4.9 percent of lawyers.[5]

Women first entered the federal judiciary less than a century ago. Florence Ellinwood Allen became the first woman to become an Article III judge when she joined the Court of Appeals for the Sixth Circuit in 1934.[6] She had been preceded by two non–Article III federal judges: Kathryn Sellers, appointed by President Woodrow Wilson to lead the juvenile court of the District of Columbia in 1918,[7] and Genevieve R. Cline, appointed by President

Calvin Coolidge to the U.S. Customs Court in 1928.[8] In 1949, Burnita Shelton Matthews was a recess appointee to the U.S. District Court for the District of Columbia, nominated and confirmed by the Senate the following year to a lifetime district court position.[9] These women were all White.

Examining the Asian women who have become Article III judges as well as their African American and Latina counterparts illustrates the difficulties non-White women have had breaking into Article III ranks. I am conscious that groups such as Native American judges have had even greater problems in that regard. Diane Humetawa of the District of Arizona, nominated by President Barack Obama, became the first Native American woman to become an Article III judge when she assumed office in 2014, followed in 2019 by Ada Elene Brown, nominated by President Donald Trump to the Northern District of Texas.[10] Two Native American men preceded them: Frank Howell Sealy joined the Eastern District of Oklahoma in 1979 and is now on inactive senior status, which means he is not handling cases, and Billy Michael Burrage of the Eastern, Northern, and Western Districts of Oklahoma served from 1994 until his resignation in 2001.[11]

As of July 2019, 217 African Americans had become Article III judges in the entire history of the United States, a little more than a quarter of them women.[12] By the end of 1998, only 20 African American women had become Article III judges; the first was Constance Baker Motley in 1966, and the second was Mary Johnson Lowe in 1978. Motley's appointment was five years after the first African American man, James Benton Parsons,[13] became an Article III judge in 1961. Three African American women—Amalya Kearse, Anna Taylor, and Anne Thompson—became Article III judges in 1979, making that a banner year at the time. Indeed, the federal judiciary looks at 1979 as a landmark year for women Article III judges in general, noting that twenty-three women were appointed that year. You can find a series of profiles about these women at the website of the Administrative Office of the U.S. Courts.[14]

For African American women, 1979 was topped by 1994, when seven African American women became Article III judges, and again by 2010, when six African American women joined them, and yet again by 2014, when their number increased by five.[15] If one considers the period ending in July 2019 (roughly the period in which Asian women have gone from one Article III judge to fifteen) the number of African American women who are Article III judges has nearly tripled, to fifty-eight. These raw numbers represent the number of individuals who have become Article III judges, not those who are now serving as Article III judges, and they do not reflect multiple federal judicial appointments for some individuals (Bernice Donald, Johnnie Rawlinson, and Anne Williams, who were first appointed as district judges, then were elevated to courts of appeals). One woman who is an Article III judge (Analisa Torres) is listed by the FJC as both African American and (to use the term the FJC uses) Hispanic.[16]

By 1994, twenty-eight years after Motley became the first African American woman to become an Article III judge, the number of African American women who were Article III judges had grown to seventeen.[17] With the confirmation of Diane Gujarati in September 2020, the number of Asian women as Article III judges grew to seventeen at the twenty-two-year mark.

The FJC's website indicates that, by the end of 1998, eight Latinas had become Article III judges—the first, Carmen Consuelo Cerezo, in 1980, and the second, Lenore Carrero Nesbitt, in 1983.[18] The nineteen-year gap between the appointment of the first Latino, Reynolds Guerra Garza, in 1961[19] and Cerezo's appointment in 1980 was considerably longer than the five-year gap between the first African American male and female Article III judges. The third Latina was not appointed until 1991, when Sonia Sotomayor was confirmed to the Southern District of New York.[20] As of July 1, 2019, thirty-two Latinas had become Article III judges, about quadruple the number from about twenty years earlier. This figure represents the raw number of Latinas who have become Article III judges, not subtracting those who are deceased or retired. Nor does the figure account for multiple federal judicial appointments for a single individual (e.g., Sotomayor, who served in the Southern District of New York and then on the Court of Appeals for the Second

Circuit, now sits on the Supreme Court). The thirty-two Latinas who had become Article III judges as of July 2019 made up about a quarter of the total number of Latinos (129) who had become Article III judges by that time.[21] That is, about three times as many men are in that group. One Latina (Cathy Bissoon) is also Asian.[22]

I note by way of comparison with the rate of growth of Asian women that, with four additions in 2003, twenty-three years after Cerezo became the first Latina Article III judge, the number of Latinas grew to sixteen Article III judges.[23]

My own appointment in 1998 represented a twenty-seven-year gap from when the first Asian man joined Article III ranks. The first Asian man was Herbert Choy, nominated by President Richard Nixon, who joined the Ninth Circuit in 1971.[24] Like me, he was from Hawaii. The second Asian man was also from Hawaii. That was Shiro Kashiwa, who was confirmed in late 1971 but did not receive his commission until the start of 1972.[25] He joined the Court of Claims, which at that time was an Article III court.[26] Kashiwa was reassigned to the Federal Circuit when it was formed in 1982. Robert Takasugi followed in 1976, named by President Gerald Ford in 1976 to the Central District of California.[27] Nominated by President Jimmy Carter, Thomas Tang from Arizona joined the Ninth Circuit in 1977.[28] As of July 2019, a total of thirty Asian men[29] had been appointed to Article III positions—double the number of Asian women appointed as of that time.

Between my appointment in 1998 and July 2019, the number of White women who had become Article III judges more than doubled (from 160 to 332). The number of African American women was closer to tripling than to doubling (from 22 to 58), and the number of Latinas quadrupled (from 8 to 32). The increase for Asian women (from 1 to 15) represented an even greater percentage increase, with the rate of increase obviously reflecting the existence of only a single judge in the group in 1998.[30] As women of color were increasing within Article III ranks, women in general were seeing a rise, but they still failed to match their proportion in the population. The total number of women appointed to Article III positions in the history of this country stood at 436 as of July 31,

2019, with 3,245 men having been appointed as Article III judges by that time.[31]

Three of the Asian women judges I interviewed were appointed to Article III positions by President Trump. As of July 2019, Asian women made up a little more than 4 percent of sitting Article III women judges, with fourteen active judges and one senior judge (me).[32]

A review of the FJC's website shows that, by the summer of 2019, President Trump had named four Asian men to Article III positions and had also elevated a fifth Asian man from a district court to a court of appeals. President Trump then appointed one Asian man to a district court and one to a circuit court in December 2019. Although President Trump has appointed a handful of male Article III judges who are either African American or Latino, there was a considerable gap in his naming of African American women or Latinas. In March 2019, he nominated his first African American women to Article III positions—Stephanie Dawkins Davis to the Eastern District of Michigan[33] and Ada Elene Brown (who is also Native American) to the Northern District of Texas.[34] Both were confirmed in December 2019.[35]

I naturally wondered whether there might be some other group not designated by gender, race, or ethnicity that might have experienced an increase parallel to that experienced by Asian women in the past two decades. The difficulty in determining whether such a group exists is that the FJC does not track judges by characteristics such as religion or sexual orientation.

However, other entities do track Article III judges by sexual orientation, mostly for the purposes of evaluating what kinds of people different presidents have selected. It appears that Article III judges who are openly LGBTQ have come close to achieving the kind of increase that Asian women have experienced in the past two decades or so.

Counting LGBTQ Article III judges usually means tracking those who are openly LGBTQ rather than including those thought to be LGBTQ but who do not openly identify themselves as such. President George H. W. Bush appointed Vaughn Walker to the Northern District of California in 1989, but Walker, who later became open about being gay, "was not openly gay at the time of his appointment."[36] There were and are likely other Article III judges who have not been open about their LGBTQ status. In 1994, President William Clinton appointed Deborah Batts, who is openly lesbian, to the Southern District of New York.[37] Batts is African American.[38]

President Obama then appointed eleven openly LGBTQ judges, six women and five men.[39] One of them, Pamela Chen, was the first Asian woman who is openly gay to become an Article III judge.[40] Another, Nitza Quinones Alejandro, was the first openly gay Latina Article III judge.[41] By 2016, these eleven judges, added to Batts, brought the total of sitting openly LGBTQ Article III judges to twelve. (Walker retired in 2011.) In 2019, President Trump brought the total to fourteen with Judge Mary Rowland of the Northern District of Illinois[42] and Patrick Bumatay[43] of the Ninth Circuit.

Women in general, and non-White women in particular, remain underrepresented among Article III judges. Although more than half the population of this country is female, women make up only about 27 percent (363 of 1,349) of the active and senior Article III judges in office as of July 2019. Over the history of the United States, less than 12 percent of the Article III judges that have been appointed have been women.[44] Looking at today's federal bench, a recent study concludes, "Today, more than 73 percent of sitting federal judges are men and 80 percent are white."[45] African American women and Latinas, in particular, have seen a disproportionately low rate of appointment to Article III judgeships.

Asian women and LGBTQ groups continue to seek further growth in this realm. If proportional with the population, Asian women would occupy more than double the number of Article III judgeships that they occupy today. This is so even if one disregards senior judges and looks only at the number of active Article III judgeships authorized by Congress.[46] Thus the recent increase does not confer parity, and from a statistical standpoint, it cannot be said that there are now "enough" Asian women who are Article III judges.

Bridging the Gap

In telling the stories of the first fifteen Asian women to become Article III judges, I am adding to existing research in two respects. First, Asian women who are Article III judges have received very little attention as a group. Second, I tell the story about *becoming* a judge, not about *being* a judge. I do not refer simply to the mechanics of the process; those are readily discernible not only from materials online but also directly from any attorney in the Office of Legal Policy or the White House Counsel's Office, from the staff of the Senate Judiciary Committee, or from any Article III judge. I look instead at how specific individuals have been able to navigate through that process.

Studying how one becomes a judge means studying the gap between life before one becomes an Article III judge and life after one becomes an Article III judge. Much has already been written about how outsiders try to fit into the mainstream, as well as about how minority judges rule in their cases. Those studies focus on different sides of the gap that I examine. I focus on the intersection of those sides of the gap, and I try to tell the story of bridging that gap.

Every judge has a unique and dramatic tale about her challenges—of how a judge managed to be nominated, of what a particular senator asked the judge in a hearing, of how the judge tried to get information about the political process surrounding her confirmation, and so on. Judges frequently tell their "bridging" stories to each other. One Article III judge years ago likened these stories to the way people talk about the birth of their children. The stories may also remind one of how people regale each other in conversations about crises that arose on their wedding days. And just as this kind of discussion is commonplace among judges, it is often the stuff of panel discussions and speeches, especially at bar conventions. Individual judges (including myself) have given entire speeches or written entire articles about their individual bridging experiences. Here, I collect such stories from a defined group of judges. Sometimes, especially when a nominee runs into difficulty getting confirmed, the press follows that judge's attempts to bridge the gap. Sometimes advocacy groups write articles, op-eds, and blog posts about whether a lower court nominee should or should not be confirmed.[47] My focus, by contrast, is not on *whether* individuals should or should not be judges but on *how* they became judges.

Scholarship about "bridging the gap" has tended to focus on Supreme Court justices. The controversies surrounding Robert Bork, Clarence Thomas, and Brett Kavanaugh, for example, have given rise not only to contemporaneous press reports but also to articles and books, and contentious Supreme Court nominations have triggered scholarship that has sometimes looked beyond a single justice's story.[48] Controversial Supreme Court nominations also sometimes generate calls to reform the process,[49] something I do not delve into. Instead, I take the spotlight off the Supreme Court[50] and look instead at a set of lower court judges, viewing them not just individually but also as a group. The experiences of the Asian women who have become Article III judges have, up to now, mainly been discussed only anecdotally. I intend here to assemble their bridging stories and to identify themes and distinctions among them.

The stories I tell clearly have echoes of the "outsider" experience. Any Asian woman who is now an Article III judge has been part of a profession in which Asian women have never been the majority. Asian women lawyers functioning in public service, private practice, or any other environment had to participate in groups with "dominants" who were not Asian women. This was so even for me, practicing in Hawaii, where Asians are such a significant percentage of the bar that many feel no need to join the local chapter of the National Asian Pacific American Bar Association (NAPABA). Most of the lawyers I have dealt with, both before and after I became a judge, have not been Asian women, and only a small minority of the judges whom I appeared before were Asian women.

Asian women were, at least in their efforts to become judges, not actually functioning within any real group at all, whether or not they were being dominated by others. They were, instead, trying to leap from one group to another.

There is a rich body of scholarship on how individuals break into and function within groups dominated by people who are different from them. My starting point was Rosabeth Moss Kanter's 1977 book *Men and Women of the Corporation*, which was highly influential in this area. Kanter reviewed the experiences of women sales managers at a large company. Her theory was that the women would function only as "tokens" and feel like outsiders until at least 15 percent of the group became women. Some later scholars challenged Kanter's focus on the effect of the number of women in a group, noting that when men are the tokens in a woman-dominated profession, they do not experience the same marginalization,[51] but other scholars view that approach as reading her work too narrowly.[52] Still others have built on Kanter's research, adding considerations of race,[53] including within the legal profession.[54]

With "outsider" studies examining one side of the gap, on the other side[55] are studies about how women and racial minorities do or (in some commentators' eyes) should function as Article III judges.[56] Amber Fricke and Angela Onwuachi-Wittig argue that, especially with respect to women judges of color, no one has the luxury of being picky about which women of color get appointed. They say, "The strongest argument for increasing the number of women of color in the judiciary is symbolism. For women of color, 'first' appointments to the bench are essential, regardless of political affiliation."[57] They acknowledge that their position is subject to challenge, with some advocating that "the focus should be on

getting women who are concerned about women on the bench"—
that is, not on putting women who are "firsts" on the bench, but
"on getting the 'right' women on the courts."[58] This view, they
posit, assumes that there is some definable, essential female experience, which they question. Their point is that, particularly with
women of color, raw numbers on the bench still matter.[59] Whether
one should ignore ideology is clearly debatable. One does not hear
elected officials who participate in selecting Article III judges
saying that ideology is irrelevant, and advocacy groups vigorously
argue otherwise.[60] But whether one accepts or rejects the position
taken by Fricke and Onwuachi-Wittig, one can hear in it echoes
of Kanter's conclusion that women cease to be mere "tokens" when
they constitute at least 15 percent of an organization.

One final area of scholarship is worth mentioning here. Quite
apart from studies about both sides of the gap, there have been
discussions that specifically examine Asians in the law. Putting
aside profiles of individual Asian judges, this body of scholarship
is relatively small. I mention it specifically because it provided me
with a helpful foundation.

A number of scholars, including California Associate Supreme
Court Justice Goodwin Liu, worked with Yale Law School and
NAPABA to produce *A Portrait of Asian Americans in the Law*,
released in 2017.[61] This study surveys Asian participation in law
schools, judicial clerkships, law firms, prosecutorial and public
defender offices, other government offices, state and federal judi-
ciaries, and legal academia. Consistent with the demographic summary that I begin this book with, Justice Liu's study notes, "The
number of Asian Americans on the federal bench has increased
over the past decade, but remains small."[62] Moreover, "Asian Americans are less well represented among state judges than among
federal judges," and "Hawaii and California have the most Asian
American judges."[63] The study says that over three-quarters of
Hawaii's state judges are Asian American, while, as of 2015, "108
(or 6.5%) of California's 1,674 judges were Asian American."[64]

NAPABA, besides periodically distributing lists of anticipated Article III vacancies to interested members, also posts

easily digested summaries of statistics relating to Asian Article III judges.[65]

In 2003, Edward M. Chen, then a magistrate judge in the District of Northern California (but now a district judge on the same court), described his experience as the first Asian federal judge in a district that includes San Francisco with its large Asian population and that sits in a state that Chen noted was 11 percent Asian.[66] His comments are memorable:

> When I am asked what it is like to hold this position, I explain that there are a number of advantages. First, there is no one with whom I can be confused, at least while I am wearing a robe. Second, it is easy to organize Asian Pacific American jurists. I was able to organize the Asian Pacific American Federal Judges Association of the Northern District of California within a short time. Not only was I elected president, I was also elected vice president, secretary, treasurer, and director!
>
> Seriously, though, the appointment of the first Asian Pacific American to the federal bench for the Northern District of California is noteworthy, given the historical and geographical centrality this district has played in the lives of Asian Pacific Americans. The San Francisco Bay Area has long been the point of entry for millions of Asian immigrants, and it has served as the home to numerous ethnic communities. It is no coincidence that landmark cases such as *Yick Wo v. Hopkins*, *Korematsu v. United States*, and *Lau v. Nichols* originated in this district. And yet until my appointment last year, there had never been an Asian Pacific American judicial officer on this bench in its 150-year history.
>
> The fact that I am the first Asian Pacific American to be appointed to this bench (there is still no Asian Pacific American Article III judge on this court) says more about the appalling lack of diversity on the bench than it does about my personal credentials. While a great deal of progress has been made since the Civil Rights Movement thirty-five years ago, minorities, including Asian Pacific Americans, remain vastly underrepresented in the legal profession, especially in the judiciary.[67]

Chen was certainly not the first judge to note that California, with its large Asian population, lacked Asian judges proportional to that population. In 1997, California Supreme Court Associate Justice Ming W. Chin had decried the lack of diversity on California's state courts and had urged Asian lawyers to "actively pursue judgeships and help in efforts to develop a pool of qualified candidates from different racial and ethnic groups."[68] For at least one position, his call was heeded: California's chief justice is now an Asian woman, Tani Cantil-Sakauye.

Pat K. Chew and Luke T. Kelley-Chew have studied "how the lack of Asian American judges may have affected the poor success rate of Asian American plaintiffs in federal workplace racial harassment cases."[69] In a separate attempt to trace the effect of increasing Asian judges, Josh Hsu explored "whether being Asian American affects how a judge analyzes and interprets the law, and if so, whether this difference justifies the pursuit of a more diverse judiciary."[70]

Grounded in my review of scholarship about both sides of the gap, I turn now to the gap itself.

PART II

The Asian Women Article III Judges

Part 2 focuses on the stories that the judges in this study share about becoming Article III judges. Their stories are arranged in chronological order based on the dates that the judges' commissions to be Article III judges were signed by the respective nominating presidents. These stories form the heart of this book.

All the judges who are profiled are included in the Federal Judicial Center (FJC) list of Asian federal judges. Some women judges appear to have been born with Asian-sounding names, but if they are not listed as Asian by the FJC, I have not included them in my study. Other women judges have taken Asian names in marriage but are not themselves Asian. Thus, for example, I have been asked about Marilyn Patel of the Northern District of California. She took her husband's name in marriage and is not herself Asian. The same goes for Sandra Segal Ikuta of the Ninth Circuit.

The basic demographic information was obtained from publicly available sources, including the FJC's website, the U.S. Senate's website, and, for American Bar Association (ABA) ratings, the ABA website. This information was supplemented by various written and video materials when available. Many of those written sources that were consulted only for background and not relied on for specific facts are not expressly cited for several reasons. First, every judge, being a public figure, has a wealth of information about her in the public domain. Second, some of the materials consulted for background include personal information (sometimes about family members) that some judges preferred not be repeated for privacy or security reasons.

The Asian women judges' interview comments are the primary bases for the stories I tell. The judges occasionally asked that they be allowed to tell me things confidentially, and I respected all such requests. The matters they spoke about in this off-the-record manner usually did not raise privacy or security issues; their concern was instead that they did not want to be viewed as discussing politically sensitive issues. In those instances, if I obtained the same information from another credited source, I included that information with attribution to that source. Of course, this does not mean that anything I attribute to a source other than a judge was something the judge did not want attributed to her. In fact, attribution to other sources occurs most commonly either because I like the phrasing the other sources used or because the other sources had information that the judges themselves did not have or did not impart in their interviews. It was not unusual, for example, for a judge to say that she was not sure what had occurred behind the scenes with respect to something particular in her process of becoming a judge, but someone else may have been able to enlighten me.

I obtained supplemental information from some of the judges after they were interviewed, either in conversation or via email. When this occurred, it was because I contacted a judge for additional information after an interview or a judge reached out to me on her own initiative to supplement her interview comments.

Each judge's story begins with a profile that contains some basic information from the FJC's website.[1] Each profile also notes the judge's rating from the ABA's Standing Committee on the Federal Judiciary, a committee of fifteen attorneys that evaluates all Article III nominees and assigns a rating of "well qualified," "qualified," or "not qualified": "Unanimous committee ratings appear as a single rating. In other situations, the rating from the majority or substantial majority (constituting ten to thirteen votes) of the Committee is recorded first, followed by the rating or ratings of a minority of the Committee. The majority rating is the rating of the committee."[2] Although the member of the ABA Standing Committee on the Federal Judiciary who interviews a judge may indicate why the person should anticipate a particular rating from the full committee, in most cases the rating is given with no explanation.[3] Over the course of several years, the National Asian Pacific American Bar Association (NAPABA) joined a number of other groups to challenge the way that the ABA was rating women and people of color.[4]

The timing of the ABA rating may differ by presidential administration. Presidents William Clinton and Barack Obama sought the ratings before nominating candidates so that, in the event a rating was unfavorable, the nomination could be shelved with no publicity. Presidents George W. Bush and Donald Trump did not submit their candidates' names to the ABA for evaluation before nomination, so the ratings occurred after the nominations had been publicly announced by the White House.[5] In early 2021, President Joseph Biden became the first Democratic president to announce that, like Bush and Trump, both Republicans, he would not seek ABA ratings before nominating judicial candidates.[6] Some candidates may also have been rated by local bar associations or other entities, but those evaluations tended to exert far less influence on the candidate's prospects than the ABA rating, largely because the ABA rating, a common thread for all nominees, allowed easy comparison, and because few local entities had the resources to do as thorough an inquiry as the ABA.

Also included in each judge's profile is the nature of any Senate vote. A confirmation vote may take one of three forms. First, a senator can move for approval of a nominee by unanimous consent. If no opposition is raised, the request is granted, and the nominee is confirmed without any actual vote. Second, a confirmation may occur by voice vote, in which voting is done orally en masse, with all "yea" votes voiced together, and all "nay" votes declared collectively. No actual count is taken of "yeas" or "nays," and, because abstentions are not noted, it is not possible to say that all present voted "yea" even if no "nay" vote is heard. Third, a confirmation may take place with a roll call vote, with each vote individually recorded along with the senator's name, creating a record of who voted "yea" and who voted "nay," as well as of who abstained.

The story I tell of each judge discusses only a narrow slice of her life. The judges' paths differ in many ways, but they all share a common trait: every judge is a "first" of some kind. Yet there are gaps waiting to be filled by more "firsts." For example, various Asian ethnicities have yet to see a woman become an Article III judge, and entire circuits, let alone dozens of district courts, have not yet had a single Asian woman appointed to an Article III judgeship. Judges with certain legal specialties are not yet represented in the group either. For example, no Asian woman who spent most of her legal career with a private, nonprofit organization has become an Article III judge.

Some judges are discussed at more length than others. This is in no way an indication that they are more worthy of discussion. I have simply used as much space as I needed to discuss the influences on their decisions to seek judgeships, as well as their experiences getting through the nomination and confirmation processes. Some judges faced more obstacles or had to be nominated more than once, so their stories are longer. For some, I simply had more information. My own story, for example, was easily accessible to me, and of course I included a great deal of detail, notwithstanding my own recognition that others had more interesting stories. Several of the judges I interviewed also figured in the narratives of other judges I interviewed. In short, the length of any particular judge's story is not indicative of how interesting or how important she is.

Every judge had to go through at least three steps: being nominated by the president, having a hearing before the Senate Judiciary Committee, and getting confirmed by the full Senate. The paths to nomination often differed, as different jurisdictions, different levels of court, different senators, different presidents, and different time periods meant that processes differed. For that reason, I spend time in each profile addressing the process each judge went through to get nominated. Many of the judges had to go through screening by merit selection committees organized by senators in their jurisdictions. These committees were designed to advise the senators and to minimize assertions that unqualified applicants were being recommended by senators to presidents for political reasons. Nomination was routinely preceded by a meeting with attorneys in the president's administration. Because all judges had such meetings, I do not dwell on them unless something unusual occurred.

All the judges also had to fill out voluminous forms, usually with the help of attorneys in the Department of Justice's Office of Legal Policy (or its predecessor, the Office of Policy Development) and/or attorneys with the White House Counsel's Office. Again, I do not dwell on the difficulty of completing those forms because every judge faced that difficulty. The government attorneys provided invaluable advice and information, and the judges I interviewed repeatedly expressed appreciation for their help. Without in any way intending to diminish the value of that help, I do not detail it because it was largely similar for every judge. The same is true for most of the help that home state senators' staff provided. I detail that only when it involved matters interesting to a specific judge's progress.

Questioning at Senate Judiciary Committee hearings is sometimes very brief and anodyne, or sometimes challenging or even hostile. It is the latter situation that I spend time discussing. In short, I focus on the unusual or unique.

In addition to discussing the judges themselves, I discuss a number of individuals who appear in many of the judges' stories because they helped them become Article III judges. Karen Narasaki, who has led several influential Asian/Pacific Islander advocacy groups, is one such notable person. Especially for Obama appointees, the three men whose names appear most often are lawyers who, as NAPABA members, became particularly active in assisting judicial nominees. Their efforts to diversify the federal bench continue today. They are Vincent Eng, John Yang, and Chris Kang.

Vincent Eng once served as the legal director of the National Asian Pacific American Legal Consortium, where he interacted with a number of Asian federal judicial nominees. After he joined the Raben Group, a lobbying and policy firm created by Robert Raben, who had been with the Department of Justice, Eng became known for having an encyclopedic knowledge about judicial vacancies and the progress of every potential and actual Article III nominee. Nominees absorbed the information he could provide, and sitting judges eager to know when vacancies on their courts might be filled consulted Eng routinely. His expertise was not limited to Asian nominees. I recall introducing Eng to a judge from a district other than my own who wanted information about the status of nominees to her court, none of whom was Asian, and Eng willingly shared the information he had. Eng continues to be a resource that nominees look to, as he makes it his business to track the status of Article III positions. I was fortunate that Eng agreed to be interviewed.[7]

John Yang works closely with Eng. Now the president and executive director of Asian Americans Advancing Justice, Yang co-chairs NAPABA's Judiciary and Executive Nominations and Appointments Committee. At NAPABA conventions, Yang conducts what he calls a "Judicial Roundtable," at which he brings individuals thinking about seeking Article III judgeships together with Article III judges in attendance, so that the potential candidates can ask questions and get some insight from Article III judges about how to proceed. As a supplement to the invaluable information that Eng provides, Yang adds introductions to influential attorneys and state court judges who may be involved with filling judgeships at the local level. Some of them sit on senatorial merit selection committees. Along with Eng, Yang is also always on the lookout for individuals who are not even thinking about Article III judgeships but who might be good nominees. Yang reaches out to them to explore their interest. Even during the years he had relocated to Shanghai as part of his private practice, Yang stayed involved with Article III judgeships. I recall that, after I had been on the bench awhile, I talked to him on the phone about a judicial vacancy while he was in Shanghai.

Chris Kang worked with Senator Richard Durbin of Illinois and was active in NAPABA's efforts concerning federal judges, especially because Senator Durbin, now the chair of the Senate Judiciary Committee, was a longtime committee member. After President Barack Obama's election, Kang joined the Office of Legislative Affairs, where he had what he calls a "secondary role" in working on judicial nominations. At that time, Susan Davies in the White House Counsel's Office was instrumental in working to diversify the federal judiciary and in assisting Obama's early appointees. Kang joined the White House Counsel's Office in mid-2011 and was put in charge of judicial nominations until he left in the fall of 2015 to join the National Council of Asian Pacific Americans.[8] Part of why Yang and Eng became so influential was because of their relationship with Kang, although Yang and Eng also worked with Kang's predecessors and with Kang's successors, like Margaret Whitney in the Obama administration. By now, Yang and Eng are confident that they can work with influencers in any administration, and they readily collaborate with NAPABA members of different political parties.

To help the judges whose stories I tell, other NAPABA members garnered support for them behind the scenes, often by soliciting letters of support. One person involved in those efforts told me that bar associations were often the first to be solicited. NAPABA also studied candidates' records to determine who else appeared likely to lend support. If a candidate appeared to need shoring up in some respect, NAPABA identified entities or individuals who could do exactly that. When a candidate with an entirely civil background, for example, needed support from a law enforcement organization, NAPABA worked its contacts to get that. NAPABA also endeavored to meet the candidates' needs by offering help from members with connections to powerful politicians, adjusting which contacts to draw on as political changes occurred in the country. It turns out that, in telling the judges' stories, I have necessarily also tracked NAPABA's growth in influence and sophistication.

1

Susan Oki Mollway

(D. Haw.) (1998)

Born 1950 in Honolulu, Hawaii

Federal Judicial Service:
Judge, U.S. District Court for the District of Hawaii
Nominated by William J. Clinton on January 7, 1997, to a seat
    vacated by Harold M. Fong. Confirmed by the Senate on June 22,
    1998, and received commission on June 23, 1998. Served as chief
    judge, 2009–2015. Assumed senior status on November 6, 2015.

Education:
University of Hawaii, BA, 1971
University of Hawaii, MA, 1973
Harvard Law School, JD, 1981

Professional Career:
Private practice, Honolulu, Hawaii, 1981–1998
Adjunct professor of law, University of Hawaii School of Law,
    1988–1989

Other Nominations/Recess Appointments:
Nominated to U.S. District Court for the District of Hawaii,
    December 21, 1995; no Senate vote[9]

When I decided to seek a judgeship, being the first Asian woman
Article III judge did not enter my mind. Not only did I lack any
confidence I would actually be selected, but I had no thought that
any Asian woman selected to fill the Hawaii vacancy might be

the "first" of anything in the nation. Growing up in Hawaii, with its large Asian population, I was accustomed to seeing Asians in high offices. I had appeared before a few Asian women judges in state court, and before Asian men who were judges in both state and federal court. I had not grown up seeing myself as part of a minority. When I became a federal district judge in 1998, not only was I the first Asian woman to become an Article III judge, but I was the first Asian, man or woman, to fill an Article III seat vacated by another Asian judge (Harold Fong).[10] In 2009, I became the first Asian woman to become the chief judge of an Article III court,[11] and, in 2015, I became the first Asian woman to take Article III senior status, which is sometimes viewed as a kind of semiretired status for Article III judges.

My parents, both of Japanese ancestry, were born in Hawaii. Three of my grandparents had moved to Hawaii from Japan at a time when sugarcane and pineapple plantations were drawing laborers from abroad. Both of my grandfathers came to do manual labor; my mother's mother came to marry a man from Japan whom she knew only from a photograph. Neither of my mother's parents ever learned English. My father's mother was born in Hawaii and spoke English but often communicated in Japanese; my father's father was less fluent in English. My parents went to high school together on Maui. My father's Japanese-language skills were not as good as my mother's, and they spoke English to each other and to their children.

A little more than a year after Pearl Harbor was bombed, my father turned eighteen and left high school to join the U.S. Army. Hawaii was not yet a state; it had a large population of people of Japanese ancestry, but only a few of them (not including my parents or their families) were forced into relocation camps. My father joined the 442nd Regimental Combat Team, made up of Japanese American soldiers led by White commissioned officers. The highly decorated 442nd fought in Europe, suffering enormous casualties as the soldiers tried to prove their loyalty while their country imprisoned Japanese Americans.

After World War II ended, my parents got married and completed college in Hawaii. My father had decided that he wanted to go to law school, but at the time, Hawaii had no in-state law school. He went to Massachusetts to attend Harvard Law School, using GI benefits, while my mother stayed in Hawaii because it was close to my anticipated birth. She later took me and my older sister to join my father. My family returned to Hawaii after my father completed his schooling, and I grew up in Honolulu, the second of six children. My father practiced law, and my mother worked for the State of Hawaii, for a time focusing on certifying aliens for work visas, a task that the federal government had delegated to the state.

I did not go straight to law school after finishing college. I earned a master's degree in English literature and then taught English to undergraduates. I left for Japan with my husband, Daniel Mollway,[12] where I worked as a book editor for a publishing company that specialized in books in English about Asia and the Pacific. We did not intend to live in Japan permanently, and my thought was that, after an adventure in Japan, we would return to the United States and I would get a PhD in English literature from some university. However, while in Japan, I read an article warning that only a third of Americans with doctorates in English literature ultimately ended up working in jobs that used their advanced degree. Worried that I might not end up in the lucky third, or that even if I did, I might need to live in a place I would not otherwise have chosen, I decided to join my husband and a close friend in their plan to apply to law school. I went through law school on savings, loans, and summer earnings, always thinking that I could return to English literature if law did not suit me. I carried that idea with me even as I began practicing law.

In 1981, I joined one of Honolulu's larger firms. I and another lawyer who joined with me were the first Asian women at the firm, and the firm's first Native Hawaiian woman joined at the same time. This firm, like other Honolulu firms with more than fifty attorneys, had begun decades earlier and had not been open to hiring lawyers who were not White men when my father graduated from law school. By 1981, the firm was accustomed to having Asian men among its attorneys and was making a deliberate effort to further diversify its ranks to be more reflective of Hawaii's population. Although I joined the firm worried about whether I would feel comfortable there, it turned out that I enjoyed being there and loved being a civil litigator. I did not leave the firm until I became an Article III judge.

In April 1995, an Article III vacancy arose in the District of Hawaii with the sudden death of Harold Fong. When some attorneys asked me if I was planning to apply to fill the seat, I brushed them off, flattered that they saw me in that light while wondering why they thought I might apply when I had no political connections. But their inquiries made me think about something I probably would not have thought of myself. I concluded that I had little to lose by submitting an application. The vacancy was on a district court, which is a trial court, and I thought the job would be exciting and interesting.

I told few people that I was applying, and I soon came to learn that secrecy created its own problems. One of my law firm partners was asked by another applicant for a letter of endorsement and declined that request only upon learning of my application, which she supported instead. My husband, then the head of a state agency, was also asked for a letter by someone who did not know I was applying.

Because Senator Daniel K. Inouye and Senator Daniel Akaka of Hawaii were both Democrats, President Clinton sought their recommendation. At the time, they had not set up a formal merit selection committee, and they themselves and their chiefs of staff reviewed application materials and interviewed applicants. I put my application together without input from anyone on what to say or include. Somehow I learned that there were nearly fifty applicants, but generally I was in an information vacuum. In 1995, the internet was in its infancy. Cable television did not have today's plethora of news and opinion programs tracking the politics of judicial nominations. At most, one could watch Senate proceedings on C-SPAN without commentary. Social media did not exist, and email was something I used almost exclusively for communicating within my law firm. I tried my best to figure out who else might be applying and what my chances might be. Some people I knew told me they were applying. I tried to identify other likely competitors and talked to our mutual friends to see what I might learn of those likely competitors' plans.

When Senator Inouye and Senator Akaka interviewed me together, Senator Inouye asked whether I was related to Eichi Oki. I responded that he was my father. I knew that my father and Senator Inouye knew each other, although they were not close friends. Senator Inouye's service in the 442nd Infantry was legendary; he lost an arm in battle, and years later he was awarded the Medal of Honor. My father and Senator Inouye had both been undergraduates at the University of Hawaii, and both had become lawyers in Honolulu. Still, I assumed there were applicants with closer ties to Senator Inouye.

I did not expect anything to come of my application. Some time later, I picked up the telephone on my desk at the law firm and heard a deep voice telling me that my name was on a short list that would be sent to President Clinton. Thinking it was a prank call, I told the caller that the message was not at all funny. The voice assured me that the caller was indeed Senator Inouye and that he would not be joking about something so serious. Of course, I worried that my telephone response doomed my chances.

With the help of others, I learned who else was on the short list with me. Senators Inouye and Akaka thought they should send several names to President Clinton to avoid taking over the president's prerogative of selecting a nominee. I was one of four candidates on the list, with two former Hawaii State Bar Association presidents and one sitting state court judge. Three of the four were women, reflecting what I learned was President Clinton's hope to diversify the bench. Two of us were Asian women.

Various members of the legal profession, including judges, offered me encouragement and support, sometimes directly, sometimes through third parties. At one point, one of the individuals on the short list withdrew from consideration. Then, in September 1995, Senator Inouye's staff notified me that the senators were informing President Clinton that I was their preferred candidate.

A flurry of activity followed. I flew to Washington, DC, to meet with attorneys with the Department of Justice's Office of Policy Development (now the Office of Legal Policy). I asked them about Asian women who had already become Article III judges, and I recall that one of the attorneys was chagrined that no one had considered that I might be the first. I was rated "well qualified" by a substantial majority of the ABA committee, and "qualified" by a minority.[13]

I was nominated to Hawaii's federal district court on December 21, 1995. At the time of my nomination, internet searches for articles or remarks I had issued were not (as far as I knew) being performed, so the Clinton administration and the Senate Judiciary Committee had to rely on other sources (primarily materials I submitted or public records) to vet me. But this also meant that I did not have the benefit of easy online research.

In March 1996, I had a Senate Judiciary Committee hearing that attracted little attention. Republicans were in the majority in the Senate at the time. Only the most junior senators on the Senate Judiciary Committee (Spencer Abraham, a Republican from Michigan who presided over the hearing, and Russ Feingold, a Democrat from Wisconsin) attended. Both senators were cordial, going out of their way to note in off-the-record discussions in the hearing room that we had overlapped at Harvard Law School and joking about the joy of questioning their former law professors when they appeared in Senate Judiciary Committee hearings. Hearings for judicial nominees typically include several district court nominees and one court of appeals nominee. My hearing followed that pattern. We were all voted out of committee and sent to the full Senate for a confirmation vote. All the other nominees at my Senate Judiciary Committee hearing then proceeded to be confirmed by the full Senate, but a hold was placed on me by Senator Lauch Faircloth, a Republican from North Carolina. I became designated a controversial nominee, and the Republican majority in the Senate chose not to advance me further.

What made me controversial was my membership on the board of directors of the Hawaii chapter of the American Civil

Liberties Union (ACLU). This was a kind of continuation of my activities in law school, when I had served as the editor in chief of the *Harvard Civil Rights–Civil Liberties Law Review*. At the time I was a nominee, Hawaii was at the forefront of attempts to legalize same-sex marriage, with Hawaii's state courts ruling in favor of the right under the state constitution of same-sex couples to marry, and with the ACLU supporting the individuals seeking marriage licenses. My name on the Hawaii ACLU's letterhead was circled, and the letterhead was distributed in DC. This was the 1990s; same-sex marriage was a hot-button issue, years away from the developments of recent years. My nomination stalled. I joined a group of nominees who had been voted out of the Senate Judiciary Committee but could not get a vote on the floor of the Senate as the 1996 presidential election approached.

Under Senate Rule XXXI, a nomination lapses if confirmation does not occur within the same two-year congressional session during which the nomination was made. In January 1997, following the 1996 election, a new Congress was sworn in. President Clinton, who had been reelected, renominated me. The ABA repeated its rating from my initial nomination.[14] Then the Monica Lewinsky story broke, and there was nonstop news coverage about President Clinton's sexual behavior with the young intern. To my surprise, the Senate Judiciary Committee's initial reaction was to carry on with business as usual; having added new senators as members, the committee scheduled another hearing on my nomination.

At my second hearing, I expected more committee members and hostile questioning, and I got precisely that. While other district court nominees, along with a Ninth Circuit nominee, were questioned at the hearing, I came in for more searching questioning than the others. The others were not asked about controversial matters; I was asked about many issues that the ACLU had taken positions on, particularly by Senator John Ashcroft of Missouri and Senator Jefferson Sessions of Alabama, both Republicans. I was warned by Eleanor Acheson, head of the Office of Policy Development, that I should expect a host of written questions from senators after the hearing. I did get a large number of written questions, which I hastened to respond to so there would be no further reason to delay my confirmation.

After a time, I was once again voted out of the Senate Judiciary Committee. For this to happen, I had to have support from a majority of the committee members. With Republicans in the majority, that meant I needed some Republican votes. Senator Inouye's long-standing bipartisan relationships with colleagues were critical in that regard. But my confirmation process once again stalled.

I was grateful for the guidance I received in navigating through the process from the Office of Policy Development and from Senator Inouye's staff. My confirmation process took so long that I got to know those offices better than anticipated. Two of the attorneys assisting me learned they were expecting children, and the children were born while my nomination was pending. One attorney had two children while I was a nominee.

Several groups contacted me to offer help, but Senator Inouye's staff advised me that he was committed to getting me confirmed and that I should tell would-be advocates to lie low for now, for fear that they might undermine his behind-the-scenes efforts. I remember speaking with Karen Narasaki, who was then the executive director of the National Asian Pacific American Legal Consortium, and telling her that I was following Senator Inouye's advice. I did the same when the Alliance for Justice contacted me. I understood that I had turned out to present more difficulties than Senator Inouye had anticipated.

My slow progress on getting confirmed greatly affected my law practice. Initially, I refrained from appearing in federal court, restricting my court appearances to state court, and worked on federal court briefs for my partners without physically appearing in federal court. I was fortunate that my partners fed me work while I was forced to tell potential clients that I could not guarantee that I would still be at the law firm when their cases went to trial. Being a federal court nominee sounds like a good marketing point, but in reality, it meant that most clients had to worry about the expense of engaging me, and then having to pay a new lawyer if I got confirmed. The time from my initial nomination in December 1995 stretched to thirty months before my eventual confirmation in June 1998. There came a point when I resumed appearing in federal court, mostly because I could not keep up my end of my obligations to my law firm just being a kind of "super associate." There were long periods in which I had no news of any progress, and I resigned myself to the possibility that I would never be confirmed. In fact, I practiced how graciously I would respond if asked by President Clinton or Senator Inouye to withdraw from consideration.

As the months passed, Senator Inouye's office told me that I might as well bring in all the support I could. At that point, NAPABA mobilized. Margaret Fujioka (now a California Superior Court judge) was NAPABA's president, and she recruited Brian Sun and other NAPABA leaders to visit selected senators to seek support for me. At the 2019 NAPABA conference in Austin, Texas, Glenn Magpantay, now the executive director of the National Queer Asian Pacific Islander Alliance, told me that, as an attorney with the Asian Legal Defense Fund in the 1990s, he had lobbied senators on my behalf. The Office of Policy Development suggested I contact Senator Inouye's office to ask whether Senator Inouye would personally solicit support from Senator Strom Thurmond of South Carolina. Senator Inouye had already spoken with Senator Abraham to solicit his support. The office thought that the courtesy and long-standing personal relationship Senator Inouye shared with Senator Thurmond might ease their political differences. By the time I got this suggestion, it was late in the process. Senator Inouye was known for being circumspect in drawing on his political capital, and his staff told me that he had counted votes and was confident he had my confirmation assured without more personal outreach.

My vote by the full Senate was finally scheduled in June 1998. At the last minute, Senator Inouye considered postponing the vote because ten senators were going to be out of town, but he checked his vote count and decided to move ahead. As it turned out, three of the absent senators were Democrats, and seven were Republicans.[15] Mine was a roll call vote. Senator Inouye stood in the well of the Senate as his colleagues walked up to the clerk to cast their votes one by one.

Susan Oki Mollway, 1998. © 2021 Ed. Gross.

I was at home in Honolulu, keeping my own tally. When a vote is occurring, there is nothing a nominee can do to influence anything, so I did not have to be in DC. As I have already noted, this was before there was livestreaming on the internet, and C-SPAN was my only way of following the proceeding. I saw Senator Kay Bailey Hutchison, a Texas Republican, vote "nay" and then walk over to Senator Inouye and whisper something to him. I learned later that she had told him that if he needed one more vote, she would return and change her vote. I was watching for Senator Abraham to see whether the personal outreach from Senator Inouye might cause him to vote for me, even though I had been nominated by a president of the opposite party. Senator Abraham ran into the room at the very last moment, cast a "nay" vote, and then quickly left the room. I was confirmed 56 to 34. Of the 56 votes, 13 were cast by Republican senators,[16] even though I was considered a controversial nominee. This reflected what I now recognize as a less polarized time, although in 1998, I did not envision that the political landscape could get more polarized.

I have been repeatedly asked whether, had I known how things would play out, I would have declined to be on the Hawaii ACLU's board of directors. My answer has always been that I would make the same decision in a heartbeat. Politics is an uncertain game. One never knows what experiences might help or hurt one in the future, as once-unpopular positions become accepted and people in power change. For that reason, my recommendation to those interested in becoming judges is to engage in activities that interest them. This way, they will keep regrets to a minimum.

2

Kiyo A. Matsumoto

(E.D.N.Y.) (2008)

Born 1955 in Raleigh, North Carolina

Federal Judicial Service:
Judge, U.S. District Court for the Eastern District of New York
Nominated by George W. Bush on March 11, 2008, to a seat vacated
   by Edward R. Korman. Confirmed by the Senate on July 17, 2008,
   and received commission on July 22, 2008.

Other Federal Judicial Service:
U.S. Magistrate Judge, U.S. District Court for the Eastern District of
   New York, 2004–2008

Education:
University of California, Berkeley, BA, 1976
Georgetown University Law Center, JD, 1981

Professional Career:
Private practice, Seattle, Washington, 1981–1983
Assistant U.S. attorney, Eastern District of New York, 1983–2004
Adjunct professor of law, New York University School of Law,
   1998–2004[17]

Kiyo A. Matsumoto is the first Asian woman to become an Article III judge in the continental United States. This means she
is also the first Asian woman to become an Article III judge in
the Second Circuit, which covers New York, Connecticut, and

Vermont, and therefore also the Eastern District of New York. She was confirmed in 2008, a decade after I was.

When I interviewed her,[18] Matsumoto said that her grandparents came to the United States from Japan, and both her parents were born in San Francisco. Both of Matsumoto's parents were in college when they were forced to live in internment camps set up by the federal government during World War II to house people of Japanese ancestry. Matsumoto's father was sent to Poston, Arizona. Her mother was held in Tanforan, California, and then moved to Topaz, Utah. Although there are Asian men Article III judges who were themselves interned (A. Wallace Tashima of the Ninth Circuit and Robert Takasugi of the Central District of California), and an Asian man Article III judge (Anthony Ishii of the Eastern District of California) who is the son of people who were interned,[19] Matsumoto is the only daughter of internees to become an Article III judge.

Her parents' internment experience had a large influence on Matsumoto. She recalls that her mother said there were not enough attorneys challenging the internment. Matsumoto's mother's father was an art goods importer who had a friend, Wayne Collins, an attorney who objected to the internment and who offered to hold some of the family's belongings during World War II. Collins, as an ACLU attorney, went on to represent Fred Korematsu when he challenged his conviction for failing to obey the evacuation order directed at people of Japanese ancestry during World War II.

Allowed to take only what they could carry, Matsumoto's parents concentrated on clothes, pots, blankets, and other items they needed for daily life. Matsumoto's mother told her that the Japanese American Citizens' League encouraged the internees to show their loyalty to the United States by not resisting relocation.

After World War II, Matsumoto's parents returned to school. Her mother became a teacher, and her father became an architect. Matsumoto, the second of five children, was born in Raleigh, North Carolina, where her father was teaching architecture and designing homes. Although Matsumoto's family left North Carolina in 1961, the George Matsumoto Prize remains "North Carolina's highest honor exclusively for Modernist residential architecture."[20]

North Carolina was still largely segregated during the thirteen years Matsumoto was there. Her family had many friends in the academic community, but Matsumoto recalls that not everyone around her was as open-minded. Her younger sister was beaten at school and called the "N" word. She recalls a family outing at the beach that included the family's African American housekeeper and her daughter; they were all forced to leave the beach. When she gave the Eleventh Annual Korematsu Lecture at New York University in 2010, Matsumoto recalled that in North Carolina, "Nobody knew quite what to make of Asian Americans. They didn't know whether to categorize us as 'colored' or as 'white.' We grew up drinking out of 'colored' and 'white' water fountains."[21]

The family moved to the Bay Area in California in 1961. Housing discrimination was common, and it was difficult to move into a district with good schools because of racism. When her family found a home in a good neighborhood, a community meeting was convened to try to oust the family. Matsumoto says her father went to the meeting and asked the attendees directly why they feared his family. The neighbors backed down, and Matsumoto's family stayed. At the time, there were very few Asians in the neighborhood schools. Matsumoto said that besides being Asian, she and her siblings were noticeable because of the Southern accents they had acquired in North Carolina.

Matsumoto's father taught at the University of California, Berkeley, when free speech, migrant farm workers' rights, the Vietnam War, civil rights, and fair housing were the issues of the day, so she was "attuned to those issues" as she saw her parents throw their support behind them. She learned from that exposure that she should "never settle for being oppressed."

As early as junior high school, Matsumoto was interested in the law. She saw Asian lawyers ahead of her, like Dale Minami and Don Tamaki, being active on social issues in the Bay Area. In addition to knowing about her parents' internment experiences, she was influenced by having several uncles who had fought in the Japanese American 442nd Regimental Combat Team during World War II. She enrolled in law school, thinking it would lead to a career in which she could create change.

In 1981, Matsumoto began her legal practice in Seattle, Washington, at a law firm where she had had a summer job during law school. She was drawn to the firm because it focused on civil rights. What caused her to leave was hearing from a partner that he had just argued his first appeal before the Ninth Circuit. Thinking that she did not want to wait until partnership for such an experience, she looked for other opportunities. She applied for a position with the U.S. Attorney's Office in the Eastern District of New York, and in 1983 she was hired to work there. There were not many Asians in the community or in the office, and she recalls that, instead of being recognized by the public as an attorney, she was sometimes mistaken for the court reporter or the interpreter. Once, when she and a federal law enforcement agent were taking a flight together, the agent was asked whether Matsumoto was a prisoner he was transporting.

As an assistant U.S. attorney (AUSA), Matsumoto focused primarily on civil cases. She and her husband, a teacher and an artist, had children. As the children grew older, she thought about their college expenses and thus considered moving to private practice. But the chief district judge encouraged her to apply for a position as a magistrate judge. She did and was appointed in 2004.

In 2007, other judges suggested that she seek a district judgeship through Senator Chuck Schumer's merit selection committee. Matsumoto enjoyed being a magistrate judge and wondered whether she should refrain from applying out of deference to more seasoned magistrate judges who might also seek the district judgeship. Her colleague, Magistrate Judge Marilyn Go, encouraged her to apply. Matsumoto went to Denny Chin, then a district judge in the Southern District of New York and now on the U.S. Court of Appeals for the Second Circuit, for advice. He told her that applying was no guarantee that she would be selected, that there might not be future opportunities, and that if she had any interest in a district judgeship, she should apply if she was being encouraged to do so. Matsumoto applied.

She recalls being interviewed by members of Senator Schumer's committee, which sent a list of five candidates to Senator Schumer. Matsumoto had not met him until he interviewed her. As is typical for Article III applicants, at each step there were long periods of waiting. Then Senator Schumer, a Democrat, recommended her to President George W. Bush, a Republican, and Matsumoto was interviewed in Washington, DC. She received an ABA rating of "well qualified"[22] and was ultimately nominated for a position in the Eastern District of New York on March 11, 2008, as part of a bipartisan package that included nominees for the Southern District of New York and the Northern District of New York.

She received assistance throughout the process from Judge Denny Chin, John Yang of NAPABA, and Preet Bharara (then on Senator Schumer's staff and someone whom Matsumoto had met at a NAPABA conference). Matsumoto met Chris Kang, then working for Senator Richard Durbin of Illinois. She knew a former AUSA who was working with Senator Patrick Leahey of Vermont. The Asian American Bar Association of New York (AABANY) wrote a letter supporting her.

Matsumoto was aware that she was the only Asian woman being considered for an Article III judgeship in New York. Senator Schumer was undoubtedly aware of the significant Asian population in New York, and Matsumoto knew that he "paid attention" to diversifying the bench. At the time of her nomination, the Democrats controlled the Senate, so once she was nominated by President Bush, Senator Schumer, then on the Judiciary Committee, shepherded her nomination through the Senate.

Senator Schumer and Senator Sam Brownback of Kansas, a Republican, were very gracious to Matsumoto's father at her Senate Judiciary Committee hearing, an event that was emotional for her father. Senator Schumer remarked at her hearing,

I am not only pleased with Judge Matsumoto's nomination because of her integrity and qualifications, but I also believe

Judge Matsumoto will contribute to a diversity of perspectives to the Federal bench. Outside the Ninth Circuit, Judge Matsumoto will be only the third Asian American appointee to the Federal courts, and only the second in fourteen years.

Judge Matsumoto's father is here with us today. He and Judge Matsumoto's mother spent time in an internment camp during World War II, and I've always been hopeful that by ensuring that the Federal bench is filled with men and women of principle from a diverse range of backgrounds and experiences, we can avoid repeating such tragic mistakes of the past.[23]

Matsumoto was confirmed by a voice vote on July 17, 2008.[24] I was nearly as excited as she was by her confirmation, and I called

Kiyo A. Matsumoto, 2004

her that very day to congratulate her on being the second Asian woman to become an Article III judge.

Matsumoto advises attorneys interested in becoming federal judges to prepare to apply by getting experience in federal court. She also recommends being active in one's legal community through, for example, a local bar association like AABANY.

She notes, not by way of advice but just as an acknowledgment of her own situation, "I have been lucky to have a partner who is supportive and willing to share a lot of roles." She says her husband's teaching position allowed him to have a flexible schedule. He was an "involved" parent, something Matsumoto recognized as particularly valuable after she was appointed by U.S. Attorney Loretta Lynch to be the chief of the civil division of the Eastern District of New York's U.S. Attorney's Office. That position required her not only to litigate but also to supervise more than forty AUSAs in the civil division. Her husband saw no need to "adhere to traditional norms" in terms of marital roles.

In 2010, she noted that there was much more to be done to diversify the bench. She said, "That's evident in the labels that we continue to use—the first, or the second, or the only." Expressing hope that this would change "on the bench, in our government, in the arts, in the sciences, in commerce," she said that "the diversity of our society should be reflected in all of those places."[25]

3

Jacqueline Hong-Ngoc Nguyen

(C.D. Cal.) (2009) (9th Cir.) (2012)

Born 1965 in Dalat, Vietnam

Federal Judicial Service:
Judge, U.S. District Court for the Central District of California
Nominated by Barack Obama on July 31, 2009, to a seat vacated by
Nora Margaret Manella. Confirmed by the Senate on December 1, 2009, and received commission on December 4, 2009. Service terminated on May 15, 2012, due to appointment to another
judicial position.
Judge, U.S. Court of Appeals for the Ninth Circuit
Nominated by Barack Obama on September 22, 2011, to a new seat
authorized by 121 Stat. 2534. Confirmed by the Senate on May 7,
2012, and received commission on May 14, 2012.

Education:
Occidental College, AB, 1987
University of California, Los Angeles, School of Law, JD, 1991

Professional Career:
Private practice, Los Angeles, California, 1991–1994
Assistant U.S. attorney, Central District of California, 1995–2002;
deputy chief, General Crimes Division, 2000–2002
Judge, Superior Court of California, County of Los Angeles,
2002–2009

Miscellaneous Information:
Given name at birth: Hong-Ngoc Thi Nguyen[26]

Jacqueline Hong-Ngoc Nguyen is the first Asian woman to serve on a federal court of appeals (or circuit court). Before that, as a federal district judge, she was the first Asian woman Article III judge in California and the first Vietnamese Article III judge, male or female, at any court level in the country. She is also the first Asian woman who immigrated to the United States to become an Article III judge, and the first naturalized Asian woman to become an Article III judge. Even before she became a "first" in so many respects on the federal bench, she was the first Vietnamese American woman judge on the State of California's superior court.

In her interview,[27] Nguyen said she was born into Vietnam's civil war. A war-torn country was all she knew as a child, but she recalls her childhood as idyllic. She was surrounded by an extended family, and her family had domestic help. She describes herself as having been "quite spoiled." Her father was a major in South Vietnam's army, and her mother worked in the accounting department of the local mayoral office. But her carefree life changed in 1975. When she was nine, she and her family left Vietnam under harrowing circumstances.

Nguyen and her siblings were sent to Saigon (now Ho Chi Minh City) from their hometown of Dalat in anticipation of leaving Vietnam, possibly without their parents if that became necessary to save their lives. Nguyen's mother joined the children there later, and they stayed with Nguyen's aunt. Then, while the army was retreating from the fighting, Nguyen's father was able to travel to Saigon under cover of night in a fishing boat owned by the uncle of one of his military comrades. Nguyen says this was "very lucky because so many families got separated as they made their way to the capital to escape."

Nguyen's father and mother went out on a motorbike searching for ways for the family to leave Vietnam. They were painfully aware that although American military personnel and American civilians were being evacuated, many Vietnamese who had worked with the American military were being stranded. Nguyen's father was reaching out to all his contacts, including an American friend, William Minor, who was married to a Vietnamese woman. At some point shortly before Nguyen's parents' motorbike ride, Minor and his wife left for the airport without having a chance to let Nguyen's parents know. While on the motorbike, Nguyen's father had his wristwatch ripped off his hand by someone speeding past on another motorbike. Nguyen's parents gave chase on their motorbike through the streets of Saigon, but they could not catch the thief. (Nguyen says that her father has long joked that he was slowed down by the weight of Nguyen's mother on the back of the motorbike.) By the time they gave up, they were close to the home of Minor's mother-in-law and decided to go there to rest. They were drinking tea there when the mother-in-law got a phone call from her daughter, Minor's wife. This was a remarkable turn of fortune. Upon realizing that Nguyen's parents were there, the wife told them to rush to the airfield, where she and Minor could help them escape.

Nguyen's parents immediately returned to Nguyen's aunt's home, picked up the children in the middle of a meal, and hurried to the airfield, each child carrying his or her own small bag containing nothing but a change of clothes. An article about Nguyen reports that at the airfield, the children were "tossed over a fence" one by one and caught on the other side by her father's friend.[28] According to Nguyen, between shellings, planes were evacuating people. Nguyen's family boarded a plane as part of Minor's family, passing as related to him by marriage. It might thus be said that misfortune ended up being good fortune, with the snatching of Nguyen's father's wristwatch enabling the family's escape.

Nguyen was the second of six children. She recalls being air-lifted by a military transport plane to a refugee camp in the Philippines, where, having left Vietnam with only what they could carry, they had nearly nothing. The family transferred to Guam and later flew to Camp Pendleton in the San Diego area. At Pendleton, Nguyen and other refugees lived in tents, two to three families to a tent. She slept on a military cot.

Eventually, her family moved to Los Angeles. Her mother went to the University of California at Los Angeles to earn a dental assistant's certificate while also learning English. Even after getting a job as a dental assistant, Nguyen's mother took a second job cleaning dental offices at night. Nguyen's father considered becoming a security guard, thinking that his military background might make him suitable for such a position, but he ended up working at a bank and maintaining its mainframe computers. He also took a second job as a gas station attendant.

Nguyen's father later enrolled in training to manage a Winchell's Donut House. Eventually, he opened his own doughnut shop. According to Nguyen, this kind of business did not require a large capital outlay, so it was attractive to immigrants without access to significant funding. Her mother also helped run the shop, and Nguyen's parents counted on assistance from their children, who worked in the shop as well.

Nguyen spoke Vietnamese with her parents, but as she and her siblings became more comfortable with English and wanted to communicate with peers who grew up speaking English, family conversations came to include a mix of English and Vietnamese. Nguyen maintains her Vietnamese-language skills to this day, but she says that her language is "frozen at age nine." Her younger siblings are not as fluent in Vietnamese.

Nguyen became a naturalized U.S. citizen as a minor. Her entire family was naturalized at the same time except for one brother who, because of a paperwork glitch, could not be included and had to apply for naturalization as an adult.

At a young age, even while learning English herself, Nguyen translated material and wrote letters for her parents. She saw that a lack of understanding of how different systems worked in the United States left them powerless. Knowing that these authority figures in her life needed her help played a "really important" and "very impactful" role in her decision to become a lawyer.

In college, she majored in English literature and thought she might become a teacher. She knew that her parents, like many Asian immigrants, wanted her to study medicine or engineering, specialties that would ensure that she could get a good job. But she says she was "terrible at math" and not someone who enjoyed science. Her father worried that because she had not spoken English from birth, she might be at a disadvantage in the field of English literature, while she herself thought that, with a major in English, she would likely overcome any such disadvantage. Ultimately, she decided to go to law school. She does not recall having known any lawyers, but the seeds of her decision were planted while she was helping her parents as a child. She had absorbed the idea that the more she understood about how society functioned, the likelier it was that she could have a seat at the table when decisions had to be made.

She started her legal career in private practice, but after a few years, she became an AUSA, handling criminal cases in the Central District of California. She says she considered herself lucky to have wonderful colleagues and mentors, and she looked forward to being an AUSA for the rest of her career. Although she herself did not say this to me, as an AUSA, she was reportedly so effective that she became known as "the Smiling Assassin."[29] Nguyen married a lawyer who, like her, is an Asian immigrant. They have two children.

After she had been an AUSA for five or six years, people began telling her that she should consider applying for a state court judgeship. They noted that she had the temperament of a judge. Nguyen had not actually thought of herself as a judge, but she saw other women AUSAs moving into judgeships, and she saw Asian men sitting on the state and federal bench. She remembers feeling "incredibly proud to see Asian faces on the bench. . . . I looked up and said, 'Wow!'" They were few in number, but they were important role models for her. This combination of circumstances led her to explore the possibility of becoming a judge.

Nguyen applied for a position on California's superior court, hoping to be selected by Governor Gray Davis, a Democrat. The state court appointment process involved parallel evaluations by the county bar and the state Commission on Judicial Nominees Evaluation. If, having received the evaluations, a governor was interested in a candidate, the governor's appointments secretary scheduled an interview. In 2002, Nguyen was appointed to fill the remaining part of her predecessor's six-year term. Recognizing the historic nature of her appointment and the path she was blazing, especially among Vietnamese Americans, she said at the time,

"I'm very aware that there is an enormous responsibility with being the first anything. It has a lot of symbolic value."[30]

Nguyen faced a nonpartisan retention election a few years after she was appointed, when the partial term that she was originally filling expired. However, because no challenger emerged, she did not need to be listed as an unopposed candidate on any ballot; instead, she was automatically elected for a full six-year term. As it turned out, she did not complete that term.

As a state court judge, Nguyen had not actively considered seeking a federal position. Although her years as an AUSA caused her to think of herself as having grown up professionally as a federal practitioner, she was happy on the state bench. Her involvement with the filling of federal judgeships had been limited to recruiting other applicants to apply. The suggestion that she should apply came from the very person she assisted in that regard, Holly Fujie. Fujie, who served as the president of the California State Bar Association, was a member of the merit selection committee organized by Senator Dianne Feinstein, a Democrat, to review federal judicial applicants. Fujie later became a state court judge herself. She encouraged Nguyen to seek a federal district court judgeship. Others echoed Fujie. Nguyen knew that the federal district court in the Central District of California had an enormous caseload and no Asian or Pacific Islander woman was on the court. She recognized, as she had when she joined the state court, that the first such woman to join the court would have a great responsibility to represent her community. She decided to seek that responsibility.

Nguyen was rated "well qualified" by the ABA.[31] She remains uncertain of whether hers was one of several names sent to the White House or if hers was the only one. President Obama nominated her on July 31, 2009.

Nguyen recalls that John Yang and Vincent Eng of NAPABA were "great, answering questions and hand-holding" as she tried to navigate through the federal process. As she puts it, "Fortunately, there were no hitches." She was confirmed by the Senate, with the Democrats holding a majority, in December 2009. The roll call vote was 97–0, signifying strong bipartisan support.[32]

Jacqueline Hong-Ngoc Nguyen, 2020

Nguyen was a federal district judge for only about two and a half years. By May 2012, she had been confirmed as a Ninth Circuit judge, in what she says was among life's "unexpected opportunities." She recalls that she was "perfectly happy being a trial judge." She had not been thinking about herself as a possible appellate judge, but she was asked to apply for a circuit judgeship by people close to Senator Feinstein.

Vincent Eng of NAPABA recalls that Nguyen was viewed as not only qualified but also confirmable, having been recently confirmed to the district court. This was, Eng says, something that Senator Feinstein was concerned about because the Ninth Circuit seat Nguyen was nominated to fill had been open for some time. Goodwin Liu had been nominated for the seat by President Obama, but Liu withdrew his name after the Senate voted against cloture, meaning that the Senate did not agree to move forward with a vote on Liu's long-pending nomination.

Nguyen was hesitant about seeking a seat on the Ninth Circuit, but she ultimately concluded that this might be a once-in-a-lifetime opportunity. Nguyen applied, and Senator Feinstein recommended her to President Obama. This time, Nguyen was rated "qualified" by the ABA.[33] President Obama nominated her on September 22, 2011, describing her as "a trailblazer, displaying an outstanding commitment to public service throughout her career."[34]

Chris Kang, a NAPABA member, was a deputy White House counsel at the time. He was focused on increasing diversity on the federal bench, and he was active in updating Nguyen on the status of her nomination. He even reminded her that he had attended her Senate Judiciary Committee hearing when she was a nominee for the district court.

The Senate majority was Democratic, and Nguyen was confirmed on a 91–3 roll call vote.[35]

Nguyen has long been conscious that her appointments are seen as historic. She saw the Obama administration as seeking to diversify the bench, and although no one told her that being Asian or a woman influenced her progress, she knew she would attract attention as the first Asian woman to be nominated and confirmed to any federal court of appeals.

In 2016, Nguyen's name surfaced as a possible contender to fill the Supreme Court vacancy created by Justice Antonin Scalia's death.[36] Further, she was identified in the press as a possibility on the Supreme Court short list if Hillary Clinton won the 2016 election.[37] By this time, the Republicans held the majority in the Senate, and they famously kept the seat open until after President

Donald Trump was elected and nominated Judge Neil Gorsuch for the Court. In any event, the buzz around her did little to distract Nguyen; she simply continued her work in California.

Nguyen urges individuals interested in becoming judges to understand the process they must go through. She says, "Educate yourself about who the decision makers are and what they are looking for." She frequently speaks with prospective judicial applicants and sees a lack of such understanding. She says a candidate's "first step" is to be "thoughtful about how to put your best foot forward." The "second step" should be to seek help from mentors and advisers on which cases to list on application materials, who to list as references, and how to get through the entire process. She calls the process of applying "not easy," as it can leave one feeling "vulnerable." For this reason, applicants may appreciate the comfort of having the support of others who are knowledgeable about the process.

She notes that professional development is critical, saying, "Build up the right set of qualifications to make yourself as competitive as possible." But, she concedes, "a lot of it is luck." She says that she realizes and appreciates "that other people have paved the way."

On May 12, 2021, during a virtual brown bag forum sponsored by the Ninth Circuit to commemorate Asian American and Pacific Islander Heritage Month, Nguyen recalled the huge adjustment that faced her when she moved from a homogeneous country to one in which she was part of a minority subject to racial discrimination. Nguyen's sharing of her own experiences with others resonates in an environment of increased hate crimes against Asians during the coronavirus pandemic.

4

Dolly Maizie Gee

(C.D. Cal.) (2010)

Born 1959 in Hawthorne, California

Federal Judicial Service:
Judge, U.S. District Court for the Central District of California
Nominated by Barack Obama on August 6, 2009, to a seat vacated
    by George P. Schiavelli. Confirmed by the Senate on Decem-
    ber 24, 2009, and received commission on January 4, 2010.

Education:
University of California, Los Angeles, BA, 1981
University of California, Los Angeles, School of Law, JD, 1984

Professional Career:
Law clerk, Hon. Milton L. Schwartz, U.S. District Court, Eastern
    District of California, 1984–1986
Private practice, Los Angeles, California, 1986–2009

Other Nominations/Recess Appointments:
Nominated to U.S. District Court for the Central District of Cali-
    fornia, May 27, 1999; no Senate vote[38]

In 2010, Dolly Maizie Gee joined the federal bench in the Central District of California and became the country's first woman
of Chinese heritage to become an Article III judge. That it took
until 2010 for a Chinese American woman to be appointed is particularly distressing because California has such a large Chinese
population that one would have expected such an appointment

to have happened earlier in that state. Like several other judges in this book, Gee had a lapsed nomination and had to be nominated anew. She is the first Asian woman to have been nominated to a federal judgeship by two different presidents. She is also the first Asian woman to become an Article III judge after having served as a federal district court law clerk.

Standing only four feet eleven inches tall, Gee might seem easy to overlook or underestimate. But she has never allowed that to happen.

In her interview,[39] Gee described herself as the daughter of immigrants from Guangzhou in the Toisan area of China. Her father came to the United States in 1941, a time when, under the Chinese Exclusion Act, only one member of a family could come to the United States at a time. Gee's great-great-grandfather had worked on the transcontinental railroad in the United States and then returned to China after the enactment of the Chinese Exclusion Act. Her great-grandfather, an opium addict, remained in China, but her grandfather came to the United States on his own, later opening a small shop that produced and sold soy sauce, pickled cabbage, and monosodium glutamate in Brooklyn, New York. He sent funds back to his extended family in China. Gee's father helped out in the shop and then joined the U.S. Navy, fought during World War II, and went to college using his GI benefits. He became an aerospace engineer who worked on all the Apollo space missions and the space shuttle.

Gee's mother, from a small rural village in Guangzhou, was a teacher there. She married Gee's father in an arranged marriage when he returned to China for a while after World War II. By around 1950, both of them were in the United States. They settled in Brooklyn, where Gee's grandfather lived and worked. Gee's mother, limited by her lack of English, became a garment worker. Gee's mother's father operated a laundry, and Gee thought of her family as having the quintessential Chinese immigrant experience.

Gee has a brother who is seven years older than she is. She and her brother spoke Toisan at home. English was a language they learned at school. Gee recalls that her parents thought it was important for the children to speak English but also wanted their children to preserve their Chinese-language ability.

Gee grew up serving as a translator for her mother, helping her apply for jobs, make medical appointments, and navigate through the difficult conditions that garment workers in the United States faced. This experience inspired Gee to pursue a career in law and civil rights. In her mind, being Chinese was inextricably intertwined with that decision. She notes that she and her brother were always conscious of the hard lives their parents had had as children in China. Her parents had lived in a rural area during a depression, and they survived the Japanese invasion and occupation of China, when her mother's family home was burned. Hungry, afraid, and away from the villages they had known, her parents had survived on money sent by relatives who had left China to work in the United States. Once in the United States, Gee's parents continued to struggle with limited funds. When they moved to Los Angeles so her father could complete his studies, they confronted rampant discrimination against the Chinese, including in the form of discriminatory housing covenants. She says that, consciously and unconsciously, she and her brother were driven by their understanding of their parents' privations "to honor our parents' and ancestors' sacrifices and struggles in some meaningful way."

After law school, Gee served as a law clerk to Judge Milton L. Schwartz of the Eastern District of California. Then, as a lawyer in private practice in Los Angeles, she specialized in labor law, representing unions and employees. She loved private practice. President Clinton appointed her to a five-year term on the Federal Service Impasse Panel, which conducted mediation and arbitration proceedings when federal employee unions, which are barred from striking, had disputes with management that needed to be resolved. She was asked to apply for other nonjudicial positions but declined because they would have required relocation to Washington, DC, and she wanted to remain in Los Angeles.

Gee had not thought of becoming a judge herself, but she readily agreed to help a friend recruit minority candidates for Article III judgeships in California. The friend, who was a member of Senator Barbara Boxer's merit selection committee, lamented to Gee that the applicant pool lacked diversity, and Gee pitched in by encouraging diverse people to apply. Active in the bar, Gee had contacts with state court judges whom she urged to apply for federal judgeships. When she failed to persuade them to do so, her friend suggested that Gee herself apply.

Gee told her friend, "I can't get confirmed because I am a union labor lawyer." Her friend told her "to put my money where my mouth was." After all, Gee was an outspoken advocate for diversity. She continued to demur, and her friend's term on Senator Boxer's committee ended. But this friend was indefatigable. Even after leaving the committee, this friend sent Gee an application form, threatened to fill it out for Gee, and noted that if Gee wanted an accurate application, Gee should indeed apply herself. In 1999, she submitted her application to Senator Boxer's committee to placate her relentless friend, and also to help diversify the applicant pool. She was so certain that nothing would come of her application that she did not mention her application to her law firm partners, even after she had separate interviews with Senator Boxer's committee and Senator Dianne Feinstein's committee, and even after she learned that she was on a list of three names that had been sent to President Clinton. She knew the other two candidates, who were Asian men, and she wished them luck. When Gee learned that Senator Boxer, a Democrat, planned to recommend that President Clinton nominate her, she was "horrified." She said that her law firm partners were taken by surprise. Gee received a "qualified" rating from the ABA.[40] With Senator Boxer's recommendation, President Clinton nominated Gee for a position on the U.S. District Court for the Central District of California on May 27, 1999.

Gee recalls that "people came out of the woodwork to try to help me." She met a very pregnant Nancy Choy, then the executive director of NAPABA, and John Yang, a NAPABA member who was among those leading the effort to increase Asians in the federal judiciary. Gee recalls meeting briefly with Vincent Eng in 1999. Eng became the chief shepherd guiding numerous

NAPABA-supported judicial nominees, but at that time he was not yet the power he would become. Gee saw him as collaborating with Karen Narasaki at the National Asian Pacific Legal Consortium. NAPABA was still learning how best to influence federal judicial appointments. The Los Angeles bar weighed in on Gee's behalf, and labor unions and community groups lent their support. I remember having a prominent Honolulu official ask me to contact Gee to offer whatever information I could, and I did so.

Much focus was placed on Gee's Chinese background and her potential to be the first Chinese American woman in the entire nation, let alone California, to become an Article III judge. Gee's supporters thought that the race angle was a nonpartisan factor that could help her. Gee flew to Washington, DC, to meet with Eleanor Acheson, head of the Office of Policy Development, and other attorneys in the office. Despite all the activity surrounding her process, her nomination appeared frozen. She had been nominated by a Democratic president at a time when Republicans controlled the Senate, and the 2000 presidential election was looming. She waited to be scheduled for a Senate Judiciary Committee hearing.

Asian Pacific Islander groups decided to be proactive to get movement for Gee. May was Asian Pacific American Heritage Month, and a ceremony marking the month was scheduled in the Rose Garden. The National Council for Asian/Pacific Islanders decided to give President Clinton an award during the ceremony, which they hoped would also be an opportunity to push for Gee's confirmation. Gee was told that she should attend the ceremony. Joined by others, Bill Lann Lee, then the acting assistant attorney general heading the Civil Rights Division of the Department of Justice (and later a recess appointee to that position), was working on getting Senator Orrin Hatch of Utah, the chair of the Senate Judiciary Committee, to support Gee. Every bit of leverage counted. Gee needed to fly to DC and stand in the Rose Garden.

There was just one small hitch in the Rose Garden plans—a matter that might seem insignificant to others but was monumental for Gee. The ceremony coincided with her planned honeymoon in Europe. But Gee knew that Article III judgeships were not available every day, so she contacted a friend for help with getting her plane ticket changed without a penalty and then went to the Rose Garden, while her husband, a banker, flew alone to London, fully expecting that Gee would shortly follow.

Gee did follow, but not as shortly as anticipated. The Rose Garden ceremony was postponed a day, requiring Gee to call her friend to change her plane ticket yet again. Eventually, the ceremony took place, and President Clinton noted Gee's sacrifice:

> Today I want to thank the Senate for the progress made yesterday in confirming 16 judges. But we still have too many nominees who have waited too long.
>
> One of them is a woman named Dolly Gee. I met with her yesterday; I'm going to embarrass her a little bit now. I nominated her for the U.S. District Court for the Central District of California. She has some good news in her life: She got married last weekend. The bad news is she's supposed to be on her honeymoon. [Laughter] The worst news is her husband is on her honeymoon—[laughter]—in London. But because she wanted to be here with you, she sent him there without her. [Laughter] And I think every one of you should take it as a personal responsibility to try to persuade the Senate to confirm her.
>
> Dolly, stand up there. [Applause]
>
> Before I took office, it had been 14 years since the last Asian-Pacific American had been appointed to the bench. I've had the honor to appoint five, and Dolly would be six. Six is a nice round number, and she ought to be part of it.
>
> I thank her for her service in Los Angeles, serving with great distinction on the Federal Service Impasse Board helping to mediate labor disputes. And again I say, in addition to that, in her distinguished career as a civil litigator, she has, nonetheless, languished with her nomination for more than a year in the Senate. The quality of justice suffers when people like Dolly are denied a hearing and a vote. So I hope we will get it.[41]

At a dinner that followed the ceremony, President Clinton continued to recognize Gee: "I had a lot of fun today with Dolly Gee. I think she's still here; she's not on her honeymoon yet."[42] Still, no movement occurred in the Senate. The process of rushing around in a panic, then having to wait for things to occur, will sound familiar to all but the most fortunate nominees.

Gee's nomination lapsed. As noted earlier, a nomination lapses if a confirmation does not occur before the end of the two-year congressional session in which the nomination occurs. Gee, nominated in late May of 1999, was not confirmed before a new Congress convened in January 2001, following the elections in 2000. She did not know of any express opposition to her; she saw herself as simply being ignored as the 2000 election neared. Gee continued in her private practice during the years that George W. Bush, a Republican, was the president.

After Obama was elected president in 2008, Gee's relentless friends encouraged her to submit her name for a new judicial vacancy in the Central District of California. Gee was young enough to apply again, even in an era when politicians wanted judicial nominees to be likely to have many years ahead of them on the bench. But Gee's response was "been there, done that." Her friends assured her that the second time around, things would be easier, especially because President Obama's political party held the Senate majority. They told her that she should submit her name for the good of the community. Gee gave in.

This time, she interviewed with Senator Boxer's committee, but not Senator Feinstein's separate committee. If there was a short list, Gee had no idea who else was on this list with her.

On August 6, 2009, President Obama nominated Gee to fill a seat in the Central District of California. Things moved quickly, largely because the White House and the Senate were both controlled by the same political party. Gee received a "qualified" rating from the ABA (as she had with her 1999 nomination),[43] having been warned by her ABA interviewer that the nature of her practice, which left her with little trial experience, was a concern. This approach favored attorneys handling criminal cases, who were likelier to have extensive trial experience, over labor lawyers, who focused mainly on arbitration. Gee nevertheless sailed through.

Gee appeared before the Senate Judiciary Committee on September 23, 2009, less than two months after President Obama nominated her. Senator Boxer introduced her to the committee members at the hearing, acknowledging the presence of Gee's mother and saying that "she was a garment worker who never taught Dolly to sew because she did not want her daughter to have to stitch clothes for a living."[44]

Gee says the hearing was "surreal." Senator Al Franken of Minnesota chaired the hearing, at which three of the four district court nominees being questioned were Asian (Gee; Jacqueline Nguyen, nominated to the Central District of California; and Edward Chen, nominated to the Northern District of California). The fourth nominee, Richard Seeborg, nominated to the Northern District of California, was White. Seeborg has been the subject ever since of a joke told by NAPABA's Vincent Eng, who by 2009 was one of the leaders in the association's efforts to place more Asians on the federal bench. I have heard Eng say that he tells applicants that they should strive to be like Richard Seeborg. When asked who Seeborg is, Eng responds, "Exactly," meaning that the way to get confirmed is not to attract attention as a nominee.

On December 24, 2009, Gee was confirmed by a voice vote. Eng recalls that Gee never overcame her worry that she might not be confirmed because of her background as a lawyer who represented labor unions. He told her on the day of her confirmation vote that she would be confirmed, but she did not believe him.

Eng believes that one reason Gee's background as a union lawyer was not raised as an issue was that she was being considered at the same time that some Republicans were voicing objections to Edward Chen, nominated for the Northern District of California. Goodwin Liu had not yet been nominated for the Ninth Circuit, but there was already considerable discussion about his potential to become a federal judge, maybe eventually a Supreme Court justice, with Republican opposition anticipated. Senator Jefferson Sessions of Alabama was particularly conscious of complaints

Dolly Maizie Gee, 2018. Barnet Photography.

about targeting Asian candidates. Eng says that opposition to Gee would have heightened that perception, and that Gee may have escaped opposition as a result.

A few years later, Gee was encouraged to seek the Ninth Circuit seat that Goodwin Liu had been nominated for but had not been confirmed to. Eng remembers hearing that Gee's labor union background, which she had thought might be an impediment to her district court confirmation, was actually attractive to the Obama administration. However, the White House deferred to

California's senators for recommendations, and Gee opted not to apply with her senators. Jacqueline Nguyen encouraged Gee to apply for the Ninth Circuit seat that Nguyen ultimately ended up filling. Gee says, "I decided, contrary to popular opinion, that I would have more impact where I was." Now, years later, she confirms, "I think I made the right decision for me in that regard," even though she recognizes that a circuit judgeship would have given her more flexibility in terms of time and allowed her to focus more on her mother's health (not to mention that her commute to the nearest Ninth Circuit courthouse would have been shorter than her commute to the district court). She also says that the district court is "more fun." A district court is where trials occur and involves much closer contact with attorneys and litigants than a circuit court, where appeals are handled without any witness testimony and where attorneys appear to present legal arguments within strict time limits, often without their clients.

Looking back, Gee advises prospective applicants to "be more open to it than I was." She recalls how strongly she resisted applying and cautions applicants against concluding that they lack the requisite experience and qualifications. She says that if you have the qualifications and a good temperament, "do not step in your own way." Gee is quick to recognize that, especially for Asian women who grew up when she did, it is unnatural and indeed "extremely uncomfortable" to sell themselves. Yet this is precisely what successful applicants must do, all the while avoiding veering into what Gee describes as being "off-putting" by being "overly desirous" of appointment.

Gee's two nominations by different presidents were a decade apart, so the road to a federal district judgeship was unusually long for her, but it took her to a position she enjoys.

5

Lucy Haeran Koh

(N.D. Cal.) (2010)

Born 1968 in Washington, DC

Federal Judicial Service:
Judge, U.S. District Court for the Northern District of California
Nominated by Barack Obama on January 20, 2010, to a seat vacated
by Ronald M. Whyte. Confirmed by the Senate on June 7, 2010,
and received commission on June 9, 2010.

Education:
Harvard University, BA, 1990
Harvard Law School, JD, 1993

Professional Career:
Fellow, U.S. Senate Committee on the Judiciary, 1993–1994
U.S. Department of Justice, 1994–1997; special counsel, Office of
Legislative Affairs, 1994–1996; special assistant to the deputy
attorney general, 1996–1997
Assistant U.S. attorney, Central District of California, 1997–2000
Private practice, Palo Alto, California, 2000–2008
Judge, Superior Court of California, County of Santa Clara,
2008–2010

Other Nominations/Recess Appointments:
Nominated to U.S. Court of Appeals for the Ninth Circuit, February 25, 2016; no Senate vote[45]

Lucy Haeran Koh is the first woman of Korean heritage to become an Article III judge. She is also the first Asian, male or female, to become an Article III judge in the Northern District of California, and the first person of Korean ancestry, male or female, to become a federal district judge.[46]

Koh is the first in her family to be born in the United States. When interviewed,[47] she noted that her mother as a child had walked from North Korea to South Korea, and her father fought Communist forces during the Korean War. After Koh's parents immigrated to the United States, her mother became a nutrition professor and her father became a small businessman. Koh, who was born in Washington, DC, is the youngest of three children. Her grandmother on her mother's side played a large role in raising her. Koh spoke Korean with her parents and grandmother and English with her siblings.

Koh's childhood spanned several states. She lived in Maryland until she was four and then lived in Mississippi from kindergarten through seventh grade. She recalls being the only non–African American student in her class from kindergarten through second grade in Mississippi. In the third grade, she transferred to an integrated school, which (after she had moved away) fell under an integration consent decree.

Koh's husband, Mariano-Florentino Cuellar, now a justice on the California Supreme Court, noted the effect Mississippi had on Koh during her time there: "The civil rights dramas affecting the era were just getting worked out, and that probably had some impact on her long-term interest in law and on how the law affects people's lives."[48]

After Koh completed the seventh grade, her family moved to Oklahoma, where she completed high school. When she was in the tenth grade, she was inspired by a world history teacher who was involved in local Democratic Party politics to volunteer for the Democratic Party, campaigning for candidates at agricultural youth events, sheep shows, and other places. At the time, the Democratic Party was in what Koh calls its "waning days" in

Oklahoma. She recalls, "Every candidate I worked for lost." But this high school experience started her down a path she followed later. Her schooling in Mississippi and Oklahoma left an impression that affected the rest of her life.

As an undergraduate at Harvard University, Koh majored in social studies and stayed politically involved, campaigning for Michael Dukakis when he ran for governor of Massachusetts for the second time, and again when he was the Democratic presidential nominee in 1988. She ran the effort to start "Dukakis for President" chapters on college campuses and canvassed in New Hampshire.

Koh stayed at Harvard for law school. As a student, she did legal research and prepared legal memoranda for the National Association for the Advancement of Colored People. Her student activities fostered her interest in public interest law.[49] Koh was also active in student efforts to increase diversity in the law school faculty.

Koh was a member of a group of students that came to be known as "the Griswold 9," who occupied the hallway outside Dean Robert Clark's office in Griswold Hall for about twenty-four hours in April 1992 to protest the lack of faculty diversity. The sit-in was peaceful, but the law school administration decided to discipline the students. Koh recalls that Harvard Law School initially sought a yearlong suspension for the students but then reduced its proposal to a semester-long suspension. A hearing was held before an administrative board of three law professors. Members of the law school faculty prosecuted and defended the students, and the defense was also assisted by a law student. Philip Lee wrote an extensive academic paper about the Griswold 9.[50]

Koh says that while the law school was pursuing discipline, the Rodney King riots erupted in Los Angeles. Focusing on racial tensions, national news outlets began following what was happening with the Griswold 9. Harvard Law School's handling of the matter thus came under national scrutiny. Ultimately, the discipline meted out to Koh was the placement of a "warning" in her file. Koh says that the decision makers determined that there was no clear policy forbidding anyone from sitting for long periods outside an administrative office, so there was a question as to whether the students had received fair notice that they would be disciplined. According to Philip Lee, any "warning" was to be removed at graduation if the student did not commit an additional violation of rules,[51] but Koh still reported this removed warning on her bar applications.

After law school, Koh had a Women's Law and Public Policy fellowship, which provided her with a stipend while she worked at an organization of her choice. She chose to work with Senator Edward Kennedy of Massachusetts. He was on the Senate Judiciary Committee, and Koh had heard from a friend who had worked for him how effective he was at getting things done. She knew that, as the chair of a subcommittee, Senator Kennedy could place staff on issues he deemed important to the Judiciary Committee. Koh worked on women's rights.

After her fellowship, Koh took various positions in the U.S. Department of Justice working on legislation and policy. A few years later, she wanted to move into litigating. Her friends encouraged her to join a U.S. Attorney's Office to get litigation experience. They described being an AUSA as a "great job." While many of her friends joined the U.S. Attorney's Office in the Eastern District of Virginia, Koh wanted to be with her grandparents in California. Her first choice was to be in the San Jose division of the U.S. Attorney's Office in the Northern District of California, which would have put her close to her grandparents. However, she was offered a position in the Central District of California, so she went there instead. Her practice there was exclusively criminal, focusing on major fraud crimes. As an AUSA, she also received training in intellectual property crimes and became interested in that area of law. Three and a half years into being an AUSA, she moved to the Bay Area and went into private practice. The move also brought her closer to her grandparents.

Koh's transfer out of the U.S. Attorney's Office in the Central District of California was partially influenced by her student loan obligations. As an attorney at the U.S. Department of Justice and as an AUSA, she was no longer eligible for the low-income protections available for student loans that she had had during her fellowship with Senator Kennedy. Her timing was excellent. Law firms in the Bay Area were seeing an exodus of young associates who were joining start-up technology companies. This was before the tech bubble burst, and Koh was in the right place at the right time and filled a need.

Koh took an active role in the Asian Pacific American Bar Association of Silicon Valley (APABA SV). Members of the group urged her to apply for a state court judgeship. She knew she would need help to get appointed. Her practice was mainly federal, and much of her work had been outside of California. She had done very little work in California's state courts, so she was grateful to APABA SV for connecting her with state court judges. They advised Koh about matters such as what kind of letters of recommendation to include with her application. Koh submitted as many letters of support as she could. She even did some mock interviews. It also helped that she had some familiarity with the application process from having previously served on the county bar committee that vetted judicial candidates.

In June 2007, Koh applied for an opening on the California superior court. Judge Ronald Lew (now a senior federal district judge in the Central District of California) suggested that she think about the state court application as akin to a baseball game, with different stages in the process representing different bases. She ran the bases and was appointed in January 2008 to the superior court by Governor Arnold Schwarzenegger, a Republican who, according to Koh, appointed numerous Democrats and independents, including LGBTQ individuals.

In March 2009, Koh applied to fill an opening on the federal district court in the San Jose division of the Northern District of California. That division, with three district judges, had not had an opening for eleven years. It was the only division that she wanted to be in so she could be close to her family.

California's senators alternated responsibility for making federal judicial recommendations, and the San Jose opening fell to Senator Barbara Boxer. Koh did not have much information on the federal process. She found the application form online and reused materials from her state court application. Thinking that she should once again submit as many supporting letters as possible, she gathered letters from community organizations, bar associations, and elected officials. When she finished her application, she had included forty-one letters. After she became an Article III judge, she learned that some elected officials did not like applications stuffed with supporting letters.

For further support, Koh looked to her husband. At the time, Cuellar, on leave from the Stanford Law School faculty, was the special assistant to the president for justice and regulatory policy in the Obama administration. In 2008, he had led President Obama's transition team on immigration issues. In February 2009, he moved to Washington, DC, but flew home every weekend to be with Koh and their two children. Koh hoped that he would be able to help her navigate the confirmation process.

Koh expected that there would be numerous other qualified applicants, many of whom she knew, some very well. She also knew that some of her state court colleagues would not apply. After all, at the time a federal district judge earned less than his or her state counterpart and had a bruising caseload. She was very conscious that the San Jose division of the federal district court had never had a woman Article III judge. And the Northern District of California as a whole, which had a male Asian magistrate judge (Edward Chen) and, the year Koh was nominated, appointed an Asian woman magistrate judge (Donna Ryu), had no Asian Article III judge at the time Koh was applying.

Koh counted herself lucky that she was not in private practice when she went through this process. She had a wonderful state court position that she could stay in if she did not get a federal position. She knew that she would be less seasoned as a judge than some of her competitors. Nevertheless, Senator Boxer eventually submitted Koh's name to President Obama. Koh believes that Boxer sent only a single name to the president.

Koh received a "qualified" rating from the ABA.[52] After she was nominated by President Obama on January 20, 2010, lengthy periods of silence followed. She recalls that Susan Davies in the White House Counsel's Office assisted her, and that NAPABA, particularly John Yang and Vincent Eng, provided information about the process. Koh says that without the information she received from them, she would have been in the dark much of the time. With Democrats in control of the Senate, Koh was confirmed on June 7, 2010, on a roll call vote of 90–0.[53]

As a sitting federal district court judge, Koh was naturally aware when openings arose, either on her own court or on the Ninth Circuit, to which appeals from her court were taken. She decided to seek a Ninth Circuit position and applied to Senator Feinstein. By that time, Koh had been identified as the most frequently cited of the federal district judges appointed between 2010 and 2015.[54] Koh says that NAPABA was very helpful to her when she sought a Ninth Circuit seat. President Obama nominated her on February 25, 2016. Koh's ABA rating this time indicated that a substantial majority of the ABA committee rated her "well qualified," with a minority rating her "qualified."[55] However, she did not receive a Senate vote, and her nomination lapsed. She had been nominated close to the end of President Obama's second term. A presidential election was coming up, and she was caught in a slowdown in judicial confirmations.[56] While such a slowdown was not unusual, in Koh's case it was complicated by the unexpected death of Justice Antonin Scalia of the Supreme Court. That occurred shortly before Koh was nominated. As it turns out, Koh may have a chance to test whether other issues derailed her confirmation. She is young enough that, with a Democrat having been elected president in 2020, she might be considered to fill a Ninth Circuit vacancy.

Even while a court of appeals nominee, Koh was identified in the press as a possible Supreme Court contender if Hillary Clinton won the 2016 election.[57] In fact, Koh's husband, Cuellar, was similarly identified at the time.[58] A few years later, Cuellar was again on a Supreme Court short list,[59] this time a list created by Demand Justice, a self-described "progressive movement" founded by Brian Fallon and Chris Kang, the latter, as noted earlier, a former deputy

Lucy Haeran Koh, 2015. Photo by Asa Mathat.

White House counsel in the Obama administration.[60] Demand Justice's 2021 short list of recommended Supreme Court contenders did not include Koh.[61]

Koh says that those interested in becoming judges should become informed about the selection process, which can change over time even within the same administration. She recounts Judge Ronald Lew's recommendation to her that an applicant space out his or her support rather than having everyone weigh in at once, with the thought of saving some support for key points at which the applicant might need a push. She thinks having had a prior judgeship in California helped her become a federal judge. She counsels applicants to be "the best you can be" but also to recognize that there will be things you cannot control and that you should not take personally.

6

Leslie Emi Kobayashi

(D. Haw.) (2010)

Born 1957 in Mount Holly, New Jersey

Federal Judicial Service:
Judge, U.S. District Court for the District of Hawaii
Nominated by Barack Obama on April 21, 2010, to a seat vacated by
    Helen W. Gillmor. Confirmed by the Senate on December 18,
    2010, and received commission on December 22, 2010.

Other Federal Judicial Service:
U.S. Magistrate Judge, U.S. District Court for the District of Hawaii,
    1999–2010

Education:
Wellesley College, BA, 1979
Boston College Law School, JD, 1983

Professional Career:
Deputy prosecutor, City and County of Honolulu, Hawaii, 1983–1984
Private practice, Honolulu, Hawaii, 1984–1999
Adjunct professor, William S. Richardson School of Law, University
    of Hawaii at Manoa, 2000, 2001[62]

Leslie Emi Kobayashi is the first (and, to date, only) former magistrate judge, male or female, in the District of Hawaii to become an Article III judge. When she became a magistrate judge in 1999, she was the first woman to become a magistrate judge in her district. The District of Hawaii has yet to have another woman magistrate judge. Kobayashi is also the only Japanese American appointed to an Article III position by President Obama.

When interviewed,[63] Kobayashi told me that she is the oldest of three daughters born to a father whose parents came to Hawaii from Japan and a mother whose grandparents had come to Hawaii from Japan. Kobayashi's father, who spoke Japanese to his parents, was the first in his family to go to college. He ended up becoming a dentist. Kobayashi's mother, who spoke some Japanese but mainly English growing up, was a music teacher.

As a senior in college, Kobayashi contemplated her options, which included joining the Peace Corps, going to graduate school in international relations, joining the foreign service, and going to law school. Her mother discouraged her from joining the Peace Corps, warning her that her temperament would ensure that the experience would traumatize rather than inspire her. Ultimately, Kobayashi went to law school, opting to study on the East Coast because she wanted the experience of being as far from Hawaii as possible. However, she returned to Hawaii after she obtained her degree.

Kobayashi spent some time as a local prosecutor, but for most of her years practicing law, she was a civil litigator in a small law firm in Honolulu. Two of the name partners in the firm served as her mentors.[64] They were both highly regarded litigators, with personal styles that differed greatly. One was known in the local legal community for being effective in a way that was always outspoken, sometimes profane, and occasionally arguably offensive. Kobayashi recalls that he would yell about avoiding being theoretical and about focusing on the real impact of cases on clients.[65] Her other mentor, who had a Ninth Circuit nomination but was never confirmed, became a Hawaii Supreme Court justice. He was known for his unfailing courtesy and kindness, attributes so notable that I and others thought they gave him a nearly religious (although never sanctimonious) air. Kobayashi says that he counseled her to treat people in a way that allowed them to retain their dignity.[66]

Kobayashi rose to be the managing partner of her firm. Eventually, the stress of the position caused her to seriously consider changing careers. When she saw an advertisement for a vacant magistrate judgeship in the District of Hawaii, she decided to apply. She was pregnant at the time and not optimistic about being selected. A member of the committee screening magistrate judge applicants for the district judges told her that the vacancy would be filled right away and was unlikely to fit her pregnancy schedule. It was therefore a surprise for her to receive a letter from the chief district judge assigning her an interview date with the district judges (including me).

Kobayashi remembers how distracted she was by the sofa she was sitting on during the interview for the magistrate judge position. The seat was so low and deep that she worried about whether, in her second trimester, she would be able to extricate herself when the interview was over. Her older son was born shortly before her investiture.

Enjoying her position as a magistrate judge, Kobayashi counted herself lucky not to have to handle the felony sentencings that she saw her district judge colleagues work on. In 2007, she was retained for a second eight-year term as a magistrate judge. By that time, her husband, Clarence Pacarro, had become a state trial judge, making Kobayashi part of a two-judge couple as they raised their two children, the second of whom had been adopted as an infant while Kobayashi was a magistrate judge.

Two years into her second term as a magistrate judge, Kobayashi saw no downside to putting her name in to fill the district judge vacancy created when Helen Gillmor assumed senior status. If Kobayashi failed to get a district judgeship, she still had years left on her existing magistrate judge term.

She was contacted by John Yang and Vincent Eng, who were instrumental in NAPABA's efforts to increase the number of Asian Article III judges. They encouraged her to apply and offered to help her complete written materials to submit to the merit selection committee that Senator Daniel Inouye and Senator Daniel Akaka, both Democrats, had set up. This newly created committee was modeled on a proposal by the American Judicature Society and was intended to reduce political influences in judicial selection.

The NAPABA early outreach and offer of assistance was an approach that NAPABA hoped would be effective. Yang and Eng knew that NAPABA members worked in influential positions within the Obama administration and could help NAPABA applicants. In particular, they were looking to Chris Kang.

Kobayashi was conscious that other magistrate judges in her district might apply. However, not only were they both men (one was Asian), but they were older than she was, so it was natural for them to consider whether they wanted to work the extra years they would be committing to if they wanted to qualify for Article III senior status. They ultimately opted not to apply to fill the vacant district judgeship.

The day after Kobayashi was interviewed by the senators' committee, the senators and their chiefs of staff informed her that she was on a short list of three being sent to President Obama. Kobayashi knew and respected the other candidates, but she was happy to learn that the senators had indicated to President Obama that she was their preferred applicant.

Kobayashi was aware that President Obama wanted the federal judiciary to better represent what the United States looked like. He wanted to increase the number of minority and women judges. In this endeavor, he was aided by Kang.

Kobayashi received a "well qualified" rating from a substantial majority of the ABA committee, with a minority rating her "qualified."[67] She was nominated on April 21, 2010. Vincent Eng then went into high gear. He lobbied to move Kobayashi up in the queue of nominees-in-waiting, advising her from afar on what to expect and how to position herself.

Kobayashi drew on various contacts. Her younger sister had a friend whose husband worked with Senator Maria Cantwell of Washington, a Democrat, and who was close to Kang's wife through Kang's prior work with Senator Richard Durbin of Illinois, also a Democrat. Kang began emailing Kobayashi's sister for help with the nomination. Kobayashi took advantage of NAPABA's growing influence and followed Eng's advice that she gather support from law enforcement officials. Kobayashi contacted

Honolulu's elected city prosecutor for help. She reached out to a lawyer who had earlier served as Hawaii's attorney general, who said he knew Vice President Joseph Biden and would contact him to urge that he support Kobayashi. She received support from the Hawaii State Bar Association and also had lunch with a prominent state official with Republican connections who said he would speak to Republicans on her behalf.

While Kobayashi waited to be confirmed, she saw that there were Asian nominees who were facing opposition. Goodwin Liu was making his way through what would end up being an unsuccessful attempt to join the Ninth Circuit, and Edward Chen was facing opposition (which he eventually overcame) as a former ACLU lawyer who had become a magistrate judge and was then seeking a district judgeship in the Northern District of California. Still, as a nominee of a Democratic president who had to be confirmed by a Senate with a Democratic majority, she remained hopeful.

In July 2010, while at a magistrate judges' workshop in Santa Fe, New Mexico, Kobayashi learned that her hearing before the Senate Judiciary Committee was about to be scheduled. She returned home to pick up what she needed for the hearing and, only four hours after landing back in Honolulu, got on a flight to Washington, DC.

Kobayashi faced two problems before arriving in DC because of the short notice. First, there were no available hotel rooms because of a Microsoft convention. Uncertain where she could stay, she called her husband, and he mentioned Kobayashi's plight to a mutual friend, who in turn offered her daughter's apartment, which was vacant at the time. Kobayashi was grateful. Second, she had an eye infection and would need to get medication in DC. She frantically called a friend who was married to a doctor for help.

Kobayashi met with Eng for guidance once she arrived in DC. Her Senate Judiciary Committee hearing turned out to be a marvel of diversity. Three other district court nominees shared the hearing with her, an Asian man and two African Americans. They were joined by a Latina circuit judge nominee. One of the nominees, Judge Carlton Reeves of the Southern District of Mississippi, described the hearing as follows:

> For a brief moment, there were so many "firsts"—each one
> making our judiciary better reflect the best of America. I know,
> because I was there. On the day of my confirmation hearing, five
> of us—all people of color—appeared before the Senate Judi-
> ciary Committee. There was Mary Murguia, a first-generation
> Mexican-American headed to the Ninth Circuit Court of
> Appeals. Denise Casper, the first African-American female
> federal judge in Massachusetts. Edmond Chang, the first
> Asian-American judge in Illinois. And Leslie Kobayashi, the
> first Japanese-American confirmed during the Obama Admin-
> istration. Finally, there I was, the *second* black federal judge in
> Mississippi's history, ready to claim the seat once held by Harold
> Cox. The only white men in the room were the two Senators.[68]

Partway through the hearing, Senator Inouye entered the room.
At the time, as the most senior member of the Senate's majority
party, he was the Senate president pro tempore, third in the line
of succession to the presidency (following the vice president and
the speaker of the House). Kobayashi became acutely conscious
of the respect and deference accorded him. As she put it, "Everyone
froze." When he spoke in support of her, all eyes were on him and
everyone listened. Then he asked for leave to return to a meeting of
the Senate Appropriations Committee, which he chaired.

Kobayashi was asked a single question at the hearing. It was
about following the guidance of the U.S. Sentencing Commission.
After the hearing, she had to respond to standard written questions. Only Judge Reeves had to answer more customized questions,
probably because, in his capacity as the head of the Magnolia Bar
Association (Mississippi's minority bar association), he had written to oppose a circuit judge nominee. She, by contrast, was not
considered controversial in any respect, particularly because she
had been a sitting magistrate judge for so many years by then.

She returned home and resumed her regular duties. She did not receive advance notice as to when the full Senate would vote on her. As it turned out, she was confirmed by voice vote on December 18, 2010.[69] She learned about her confirmation through a congratulatory email that she received while at a party.

Another Asian judge, Edmond Chang of the Northern District of Illinois, was confirmed the same day. As president and executive director of the Asian American Justice Center, Karen Narasaki remarked that that day was "the first time that two Asian Pacific Americans have been confirmed as federal judges on the same day."[70]

The process of stepping down from her position as a magistrate judge and assuming her new position as a district judge required her to submit a letter of resignation from her magistrate judgeship. This was slightly nerve-wracking because this resulted in a gap before her commission as a district judge was signed by President Obama. Like all judges, she imagined complications, but luckily none arose. I swore her in as a district judge on December 22, 2010. This was the first time that an Asian Article III judge swore in another Asian Article III judge.[71]

Kobayashi reminded me during her interview that I urged her to make the switch from magistrate judge to district judge as soon as possible so that her time as an Article III judge could begin to run, a matter that affected not only her salary but also the date on which she would later become eligible to take senior status. My own recollection is that the district judges were about to select the magistrate judge who would fill her old position, and Kobayashi could vote only if she were a district judge. Right before Christmas, Kobayashi joined the Article III ranks.

Kobayashi earned the distinction of being one of the ten most cited new district judges.[72] Although performance as an Article III judge is beyond the scope of this book, I mention this matter here because it appears likely that the decision that caused Kobayashi to be cited so frequently in the years after she became a district judge might have been a decision that she issued as a magistrate judge.[73]

Leslie Emi Kobayashi, 2020

Kobayashi considered applying to fill the vacancy in the Ninth Circuit that would be created when Judge Richard Clifton, residing in Hawaii, took senior status on November 13, 2016. Kobayashi says that Vincent Eng and John Yang of NAPABA, as well as some Ninth Circuit judges, encouraged her to apply. However, she learned that Senator Mazie Hirono of Hawaii, a Democrat and the first Asian woman elected to the U.S. Senate, was hesitant to recommend an active district judge in Hawaii for the Ninth Circuit, out of concern that doing so might cause the District of Hawaii to lose a district court judgeship. The District of Hawaii is among the district courts with a "temporary judgeship."[74]

Temporary Article III judgeships have not been created in recent years, but anyone who serves as the chief district judge in a federal district that still has such a judgeship is likely to become an expert on the topic. Temporary judgeships are strange positions, devised as a kind of political compromise when districts with heavy caseloads needed new judgeships but various members of Congress were concerned either about whether a district's caseload would drop in the future or about the uncertainty of which political party would be in control of the White House and thus able to fill any new judgeship. The latter concern could relate either to when the judgeship was created or to when the temporary judgeship expired. The "temporary" status belongs to the district, not to any individual judge, so the "temporary" appellation ends up applying to whichever judge's position becomes vacant after the expiration date. The judge who initially fills a temporary judgeship has lifetime tenure and faces no issue during that tenure. However, a problem arises if any vacancy is created after the temporary judgeship expires, as that position cannot be filled by a new judge.[75]

At the time Kobayashi was contemplating applying for a Ninth Circuit position, Hawaii's temporary judgeship had expired. Any new vacancy created by the elevation of a district judge while the temporary judgeship was in a lapsed state could not have been filled. (The temporary judgeship was later retroactively extended by Congress.[76]) Senator Hirono recognized that she could avoid creating a vacancy during the lapse in the temporary judgeship by looking at candidates who were not active district judges. (The existing active district judges may continue in their positions given their lifetime tenure, and the hope is that future extensions or a conversion to a permanent judgeship will be enacted before any of the now-active judges creates a vacancy.) As it turned out, President Donald Trump was elected in 2016, and even without the "temporary judgeship" issue, Kobayashi might not have been his choice for the Ninth Circuit, given her prior appointment by a Democratic president.

Continuing as a district judge, Kobayashi thinks that "there is no one path" to what she calls "the best job in the world." To get the job she describes as "awesome" and "interesting," she counsels aspirants, "Don't be a specialist. Try to touch as many areas of the law as possible. Learn to be a problem solver." Her advice to would-be judges goes beyond lawyerly counsel. While she says that "obviously you have to be competent," she notes that other people can throw roadblocks in one's way. One can reduce that possibility if one does what one should do even without career advancement in mind: "Be nice to people in a sincere way." She sums it up by saying, "Be kind."

7
Cathy Bissoon
(W.D. Pa.) (2011)

Born 1968 in Brooklyn, New York

Federal Judicial Service:
Judge, U.S. District Court for the Western District of Pennsylvania
Nominated by Barack Obama on January 5, 2011, to a seat vacated by
   Thomas M. Hardiman. Confirmed by the Senate on October 17,
   2011, and received commission on October 19, 2011.

Other Federal Judicial Service:
U.S. Magistrate Judge, U.S. District Court for the Western District
   of Pennsylvania, 2008–2011

Education:
Alfred University, BA, 1990
Harvard Law School, JD, 1993

Professional Career:
Law clerk, Hon. Gary L. Lancaster, U.S. District Court, Western
   District of Pennsylvania, 1994–1995
Private practice, Pittsburgh, Pennsylvania, 1995–2008

Other Nominations/Recess Appointments:
Nominated to U.S. District Court for the Western District of Pennsylvania, November 17, 2010; no Senate vote[77]

Cathy Bissoon is the first South Asian woman to become an Article III judge. She is the first Asian woman to become an Article III

judge in the Third Circuit, which includes Pennsylvania, New Jersey, Delaware, and the Virgin Islands. With a father from Puerto Rico, she is the first Latina to become an Article III judge in Pennsylvania.

Bissoon's mother came to the United States from Trinidad. In her interview,[78] Bissoon described her mother as descended from people who left India as part of the Indian diaspora and ended up in the Caribbean as indentured laborers working in sugarcane fields. One of sixteen children, Bissoon's mother lived in crowded conditions where multiple people slept together on a bed. Leaving Trinidad to seek better opportunities, Bissoon's mother joined relatives who had moved to New York City. Bissoon's father, a Latino born in Puerto Rico, also moved to New York City, where he ultimately joined a union and did electrical work. Then, when Bissoon was only four years old, he was stabbed to death.

As a widow, Bissoon's mother worked as a seamstress making sweaters for dogs, a job she left after marrying an auto glass installer who was originally from Trinidad, where he had gone to school with Bissoon's mother. Bissoon took his last name as a child, formalizing that name change as an adult. She was the oldest child in her family; she grew up in New York City with two younger half-siblings. Television had a big influence on her. She first entertained the idea of becoming a lawyer after seeing actors playing lawyers on soap operas she watched with her mother. She knew not a single lawyer as a child. She describes herself as having come from a blue-collar background, not the highly educated, well-to-do background that many may associate with recent South Asian immigrants coming to the United States directly from India for an American education. Something about the way lawyers were depicted in soap operas appealed to Bissoon, even though they did not match her own demographic profile.

Bissoon grew up speaking English and more immersed in the Indian side of her family than in her deceased father's Latino side. In the summer after she graduated from high school, she worked at an accessories store at a local mall until she left to begin college. When her manager asked if she knew anyone who might take her spot, Bissoon checked with her mother, who had been a homemaker for years. Her mother got the job and remained there until she was in her sixties, when the store let her go, telling her that she "didn't fit the image they wanted for the store."

Bissoon was the first person in her family to go to college. She says this was a "new thing in my home" that was "not necessarily an expectation." From college in New York, where she majored in political science, Bissoon went to law school, but unlike some of her classmates, she gave no thought to becoming a law clerk to a judge. The judiciary was not a world she knew anything about at the time, and she did not consider that she might become a judge someday. But after joining a private law firm in Pittsburgh, she understood the value of a judicial clerkship. Just a few months later, she left the firm and became a law clerk to Gary Lancaster, a federal district judge in Pittsburgh. This gave Bissoon her first opportunity to see a judge at work, and she remembers thinking, "Boy, if a job like this ever opens up, I would love to do it." At the time, this "seemed a bit like a pipe dream" to her.

Bissoon returned to private practice after her clerkship. She focused on labor and employment law, so her practice took her to federal court. When a vacancy arose for a magistrate judge, she decided to apply. This decision was born out of her experience as a law clerk. In applying, she thought to herself that district judges would be the ones selecting the magistrate judge, and the district judges knew her and her work.

Bissoon was not selected to fill the position, but she applied for the next magistrate judge vacancy. Once again, she was not selected. When another opening was available, she applied. On this third try in 2008, she was finally selected.

Magistrate judges in the Western District of Pennsylvania are on the civil case wheel and have what Bissoon describes as a "very robust consent system." Under this system, parties in civil cases regularly consent to having magistrate judges, rather than district judges, preside over their cases, including at trial. Absent the consent of all parties, a magistrate judge may not preside over a civil trial.[79]

Bissoon, married to Gregory Bradley, an in-house general counsel, and with two children, had an eight-year term as a magistrate judge but served for only a few years before considering seeking a district judgeship. Judge Thomas Hardiman had been elevated from the district court to the Third Circuit in 2007, and his district court seat had been vacant for some time. Bissoon sought the advice of Judge Lancaster, for whom she had clerked. He encouraged her to apply, although he was not optimistic about her chances of getting nominated. In fact, he warned her that she certainly would not be selected, given her lack of political connections. He nevertheless thought that applying would make her name known to decision makers, which could eventually be helpful.

Bissoon did apply, even though she saw herself as being at a disadvantage because she did not know influential people. Going from being a magistrate judge to becoming a district judge was not common in the Western District of Pennsylvania. She knew that if she succeeded, she would be only the second person in her district to go down that path.

Her application consisted of a written submission to a merit selection committee established by Senator Bob Casey and Senator Arlen Specter. Senator Specter had by this time switched his political affiliation from Republican to Democrat, making both of Pennsylvania's senators Democrats. The committee interviewed all the applicants rather than only a selected handful. Bissoon knew that she was likely competing with very well-connected applicants and assumed that one of them would be selected instead. She was therefore surprised when Senator Casey called her to say that he was sending her name to President Obama. Having been interviewed only by the committee, and not having met either Senator Casey or Senator Specter, Bissoon asked Senator Casey if he planned to interview her. He responded that he knew enough about Bissoon to proceed. He told her that he was sending the president a single name—hers—not a short list. Bissoon had been active in a local Asian group, but she was uncertain whether Senator Casey knew her ethnicity at the time he called her.

Bissoon says that being picked seemed "crazy" to her. It was certainly "unexpected." The ABA gave her a "qualified" rating,[80] and President Obama nominated her on November 17, 2010. Bissoon was part of a group of Pennsylvania nominees. The other nominees were all White men, and Bissoon knew that diversifying the federal bench was important to President Obama. Her status as a woman of color was not, however, widely publicized.

Bissoon's nomination came right after the 2010 congressional elections. The Senate was controlled by the Democrats at the time, but the 111th Congress was getting very close to adjourning. Bissoon did not get a hearing before the Senate Judiciary Committee in the lame-duck session. Her nomination lapsed. President Obama renominated her on January 5, 2011, and the ABA repeated its rating.[81]

The 2010 election slowed things down for Bissoon in another respect. Senator Specter had been defeated in the Democratic primary in Pennsylvania by Joe Sestak. Sestak then lost the general election to Senator Pat Toomey, a Republican. Bissoon says that the Pennsylvania senators have a long-standing agreement that, if the senators are from different parties, the senator from the party in charge of the White House gets to pick three nominees for every one that the senator from the other party chooses. Senator Casey and Senator Toomey developed a good working relationship with respect to judicial nominations, especially for the district courts, and Senator Toomey returned a blue slip for Bissoon, meaning that he approved of proceeding to confirmation. This took some time, and Bissoon had to wait for her hearing before the Senate Judiciary Committee. After that, on October 17, 2011, the Senate, with Democrats having retained a majority, confirmed Bissoon on a roll call vote, 82–3.[82]

Bissoon jokes that, for a while, she was a "secret Asian." People who had not met her had no idea about her ethnic background. NAPABA had not come forward to support her nomination, perhaps because it had not realized her South Asian heritage. She recalls that after she became a district judge, she received a call from Denny Chin, then a judge on the Second Circuit and the

Cathy Bissoon, 2008. Photo by Roy Engelbrecht.

president of NAPABA's Judicial Council. Chin told her that people were just learning that she was an addition to the ranks of
Asian federal judges. He asked her whether she recognized that
she was the first South Asian woman to become an Article III
judge. She had not known that before getting the call. In fact, she
had not realized that she was the first South Asian woman to be

a federal judge at any level when she became a magistrate judge in 2008. Echoing my experience on learning that I was the first Asian woman to become an Article III judge, Bissoon had simply assumed that, so far into the history of the United States, some South Asian woman must certainly have preceded her to the federal bench somewhere in the country.

Bissoon says that people thinking about seeking judgeships should not fall victim to second-guessing. She notes, "Given my experience and how unlikely it would have seemed to me to be selected, I say, 'Go for it!'" Having heard that one needed political connections to get an Article III spot, Bissoon says that all she had was legal work: "Someone saw I did my work well." Although an appointment based only on the merits of one's work sounds like what Bissoon calls "an unlikely scenario," that can happen. After all, "nothing went as I understood it should go."

Perhaps drawing on the experience of having applied three times to be a magistrate judge, she sees little downside to seeking a judgeship: "If you don't make it, you can make it some other time." She also advises that being a magistrate judge can create "a great pathway" to an Article III judgeship.

8

Miranda Mai Du

(D. Nev.) (2012)

Born 1969 in Ca Mau, Vietnam

Federal Judicial Service:
Judge, U.S. District Court for the District of Nevada
Nominated by Barack Obama on August 2, 2011, to a seat vacated by
    Roger L. Hunt. Confirmed by the Senate on March 28, 2012, and
    received commission on March 30, 2012. Served as chief judge,
    2019–present.

Education:
University of California, Davis, BA, 1991
University of California, Berkeley, School of Law, JD, 1994

Professional Career:
Private practice, Reno, Nevada, 1994–2012
Member, Kori LLC, Reno, Nevada, 2005–2012[83]

Miranda Mai Du is the first Asian woman to become an Article III judge in the District of Nevada. She is the second woman
of Vietnamese descent to become an Article III judge. In 2019, she
became the chief judge of her court—the second Asian woman to
become a chief district judge.

  Du was born in Vietnam. Her father, who was in South Vietnam's army, was of Chinese heritage. Her mother, who ran small
businesses, was of Vietnamese heritage. When Saigon fell to Communist forces in 1975, Du's family was acutely conscious of being in
a vulnerable position, having been on the losing side of Vietnam's

civil war. In our interview,[84] Du recounted her family's journey to the United States, relying not only on her childhood memories but also on family accounts that she has been taping and collecting in anticipation of writing a book about her experiences.

Du's family did not immediately flee Vietnam. While former members of South Vietnam's army were being forced into reeducation centers, Du's father evaded that fate by keeping a low profile in densely populated Saigon, now known as Ho Chi Minh City. The rest of Du's immediate family stayed in a small town at the southern end of Vietnam. Du, the middle of three children, remembers living with her father's parents during this period.

Du's paternal grandfather organized the extended family, assigning each of his children a task to aid the family in an eventual escape from Vietnam. People who wanted to leave were doing so illegally. The family knew that success would require a great deal of planning. One uncle's task was to acquire a boat that the family could use to escape; Du's father's assignment was to learn to navigate the boat. While the family's plans were proceeding, the Vietnamese government devised a program that allowed those of Chinese descent to leave legally. Du's family qualified, given her father's heritage. Still, this legal avenue required the payment of fees, and with corruption rampant in Vietnam at the time, Du's family continued to keep plans secret.

One night in 1978, when Du was nine years old, her family boarded one of several boats leaving together. Du was in a small fishing boat that carried more than one hundred passengers, including members of Du's immediate family and extended family. Part of a huge exodus, the passengers (among those who came to be known as "boat people") were starting out on an extremely dangerous journey. As the escaping boats set out from Vietnam, the Vietnamese navy opened fire on them, and Du's boat was separated from the others. Du was at sea, sitting in the boat, for days. Eventually, her boat made it to Malaysia, but the Malaysian authorities, overwhelmed by the stream of refugees from Vietnam, turned the boat away, saying the refugee camp there was already overcrowded and the boat should head to a camp in Singapore.

Du's father, the assigned navigator, knew that a storm was on its way and feared the boat would not make it to Singapore. People on shore began yelling at the people on Du's boat, telling them to sink their boat and swim to shore because the authorities would not turn away individual swimmers who came ashore. The people on Du's boat made a hole in the boat so it would sink, and the passengers then all jumped into the ocean. Du did not know how to swim, so her uncle carried her as he swam to shore, where the authorities took them in.

Malaysia had set up a refugee camp on Bidong Island, and Du's family lived there for a while before moving to Kuala Lumpur. The United Nations was processing the refugees and accorded Du's family priority because Du's father had been in South Vietnam's army. Somehow, Du's father was able to add his father's family unit to his own, so Du's grandparents and Du's minor uncles and a minor aunt were deemed part of the family unit. (The uncles and aunt were considerably younger than Du's parents; they were Du's father's half-siblings, the children of Du's grandfather and his second wife.) The family consisted of ten individuals, all of whom were sponsored by a single American family when they sought entry into the United States. When Du and her family left Malaysia after spending a year there, Du's grandmother, who was ill, stayed behind in Kuala Lumpur with other relatives. She would join Du later.

Du traveled to Alabama, where an American family had offered to sponsor Du's family. The sponsor ran a dairy farm outside the town of Winfield, which was considered ideal for Vietnamese refugees, who were expected to have farming backgrounds. Du's father had never farmed, however, so working on a dairy farm was a considerable adjustment for him.

Another Vietnamese family with an American sponsor moved to the same area as Du's family. The children from Du's family and that other Vietnamese family were the only Asians at Du's school in Winfield. Du speaks gratefully about her treatment at school as a third-grader. Du spoke Vietnamese at home, as well as the Chinese dialect Hakka. The school created a program for the Vietnamese children to learn English. In addition to English,

Du learned to speak Mandarin and Cantonese from after-school classes. Residents in the area also sponsored members of Du's extended family. At some point, Du's family moved from the Winfield area to Tuscaloosa. Du's father worked as a dishwasher in a Chinese restaurant and learned to cook. Du says that even today, "he makes the best bao." Her mother enrolled in classes to learn English and sewing and became a seamstress. In 1980, the family moved to Seattle to join one of Du's aunts and her family. After a year there, Du's family moved to California. In California, Du's parents held a variety of jobs. For a time, Du's father worked as a security guard and supplemented that income by gathering discarded cardboard boxes around Chinatown in Oakland to sell to a recycling center. Du recalls helping him with the cardboard boxes after school and on weekends. Later, Du's parents owned and operated a manicure salon and subsequently ran their own gas station in Berkeley, California. To this day, Du's aunt and two uncles own gas stations in northern California's Bay Area.

While Du was in high school, her parents became eligible to apply for American citizenship. They studied for the naturalization test and became citizens. Du then received derivative citizenship, which is available to minors whose parents are naturalized. Du tells the story of her path to citizenship whenever she presides over naturalization ceremonies.

Between her junior and senior years in high school, Du was part of the federal government's Upward Bound program, open to low-income students and students whose parents did not have college educations. The program took Du to the University of California's Berkeley campus, where she was encouraged to think about what she might study in college. Du expressed an interest in history, which her mother thought was an impractical major. However, Du's counselor encouraged Du, noting that she could go from a history major to law school. This was the first time Du began to think about becoming a lawyer. She ultimately had a double major in history and economics, the latter to appease her mother, who thought that Du should consider medical school or a degree in engineering.

Du's parents were "adamant that education was a priority" but also were concerned that Du should concentrate on a field in which having English as a second language would not disadvantage her. They were very distrustful of government, given their experiences in Vietnam. When Du mentioned studying law, her parents were not supportive. Du recalls realizing that "the legal profession was very empowering, especially for people like me." She saw law as "giving voice" to people, especially immigrants. She also says that she "was rebellious" in disregarding her parents' concerns and deciding to attend law school.

After law school, Du went into private practice, concentrating in employment law, representing employers. Hired by a law firm to work in Las Vegas, she found that she did not like living there and moved to Reno.

As a practitioner, Du gave no thought to becoming a judge. She says, "I have often wondered if it was because of the limitations of my imagination that I never thought of it." She had thought that she might one day have a public interest job, but she liked her law firm, and "the years went by."

In 2011, Du got an unexpected call from the head of Senator Harry Reid's Nevada office asking Du to meet with Senator Reid at the airport. Du was mystified, but of course she went to the airport. At the time, the Democrats controlled the Senate, and Reid was the majority leader. Du had a pleasant conversation with Reid and his wife, after which Reid remarked that Du probably knew why he wanted to meet her. She replied that she had no idea. Reid then explained that Du had a compelling personal story, that there was a judicial vacancy in Las Vegas, and that he wanted her to fill it. Reid said that he was his own committee; whatever choice he made was what would be submitted to President Obama. (Nevada's other senator, John Ensign, a Republican, was the subject of a lengthy investigation by the Senate Ethics Committee and ended up resigning in May 2011. Dean Heller, a Republican, filled the resulting vacancy and was later elected to the seat.) Du was so surprised that she expressed concern about whether she was qualified. Reid said that he had heard other people express that about themselves, but Du was his pick. Du asked for time to talk to her husband.

Du's husband, William Charles Martin, was enthusiastic about the offer and urged Du to agree. Du says Martin was always supportive of her. She had met him through their mutual running activities (he owned Eclipse Running, a running supplies store). When they got married, Du became a stepmother to Martin's sons. Although Martin lived to enjoy Du's first few years as a judge, he passed away in 2018 after a relapse of leukemia.

Du had one specific concern about agreeing to Reid's offer. The judicial vacancy was in Las Vegas, and Du wanted to live in Reno. This issue was resolved when Du learned that the federal district court had a tradition of accommodating judges who wanted to move back to Reno and that, given the preferences of the other Nevada federal district judges, Du would be able to move back to Reno after spending a year working in the Las Vegas courthouse. Du agreed.

Du flew to Washington, DC, to meet with attorneys at the Department of Justice. Almost immediately, she was contacted by John Yang and Vincent Eng of NAPABA. In fact, Du says that was when she first learned about NAPABA. Yang and Eng "were wonderful," offering assistance to her when she "had no idea what the process was." Reid's staff kept Du advised, and Governor Brian Sandoval, an acquaintance of Du's, was supportive as well. Du received information from sitting federal judges about what to expect. She went to a NAPABA conference in Atlanta and met other Asian judges. She spoke with Dolly Gee. She also attended the investiture ceremony for District Judge Edward Chen of the Northern District of California, where she met me and Leslie Kobayashi.

A substantial majority of the ABA committee rated Du "qualified," with a minority rating her "not qualified."[85] The ABA provided no reason for the "not qualified" minority rating, which Du found "disappointing," especially for someone who had been a high achiever all her life.[86] Chris Kang, who served as deputy White House counsel while Du's nomination was pending, told me that,

Miranda Mai Du, 2019

in general, a minority "not qualified" rating (unlike a majority or unanimous rating) did not have much impact on him.

Reid was steadfast in his support of Du, assuring her that getting her confirmed was a priority for him. With Reid as the Senate majority leader, Du had a powerful ally. She was confirmed on March 28, 2012, by a roll call vote of 59–39.[87]

Asked what advice she had for individuals interested in joining the bench, Du says, "No matter what their goal, focus on being true to who they are and maintaining integrity." She notes that "opportunities will come," and would-be applicants should look for them while being diligent and enjoying what they do.

Du says that she would like to think that her reputation as a lawyer contributed to her becoming a judge. She had no political connections before being contacted by Senator Reid, and she had assumed that she lacked the necessary "pedigree" to be a judge. She says that "people like me" did not fit the expected model. She felt "like an imposter" because she saw the profession "elevate people with a certain pedigree." She thought that one needed something "more" than just good lawyering to be elevated, and she "was not born into 'more.'" She concludes that she might not have become a judge "but for the fact that some forces advocated for" and intended to increase diversity on the bench. She praises Senator Reid for thinking about the makeup of the judiciary and the importance to his legacy of increasing diversity, and for recognizing how his interests meshed with President Obama's focus on diversifying the federal courts.

9

Lorna Gail Schofield

(S.D.N.Y.) (2012)

Born 1956 in Fort Wayne, Indiana

Federal Judicial Service:
Judge, U.S. District Court for the Southern District of New York
Nominated by Barack Obama on April 25, 2012, to a seat vacated by
    Shira A. Scheindlin. Confirmed by the Senate on December 13,
    2012, and received commission on December 13, 2012.

Education:
Indiana University, BA, 1977
New York University School of Law, JD, 1981

Professional Career:
Private practice, New York City, 1981–1984, 1988–2012
Assistant U.S. attorney, Southern District of New York, 1984–1988[88]

Lorna Gail Schofield is the first judge of Filipino ancestry to
become an Article III judge in the nation, and the first Asian
woman to become an Article III judge in the Southern District
of New York.

In her interview,[89] Schofield said her father (the source of her
surname) was mainly Western European, with a "smidgen" of
Native American heritage. Her mother was a Filipina who grew
up speaking Tagalog. Her mother immigrated to the United States
from the Philippines in the aftermath of World War II, having
met Schofield's father while he was serving in the U.S. Air Force
in the Philippines. The family settled in Indiana, where Schofield

was born. When she was three, her father left the family. She was raised in Indiana as an only child by her mother, who was a pharmacist. Although her mother had Filipino friends that Schofield socialized with and spent holidays with, she had few Asian classmates in the blue-collar neighborhood she grew up in. She spoke English at home with her mother and did not identify as Asian or Filipina. She was simply American. Schofield says that, as she was growing up in Indiana, ethnic studies had not yet become an academic staple, and except for her mother's friends, there was no Filipino or Asian community where she lived that she could feel a part of. However, her Asian heritage caused her to be cast in city holiday festivals as one of the "three Marys"—the Asian Mary, accompanied by a White Mary and a Black Mary.[90]

Growing up, Schofield knew that her mother wanted her "to excel." Beginning in elementary school and continuing through high school, she liked public speaking. She participated in community theater and was active in high school debate and extemporaneous speaking. From an early age, Schofield began thinking about a job that involved speaking in front of people. Her mother wanted her "to be Barbara Walters."

Schofield had double majors in German and English in college. She thinks her mother might have suggested law as a possible career for her, but Schofield had a mind of her own and started graduate school in comparative literature. In that setting, she saw that students who were native speakers in more than one language had an advantage. She concluded that, with English her sole native language and French and German only studied in school, she was "not at the top of the heap." Her mother died when Schofield was twenty. No longer feeling rebellious in response to any maternal suggestion and facing the need to support herself, Schofield decided that she "needed to be practical." Seeing many of her old debate friends going into law, Schofield entered law school at New York University.

After graduating, Schofield stayed in New York, working in a private law firm for a few years, then in the criminal division of the U.S. Attorney's Office in the Southern District of New York for about four years. From there she returned to private practice, where she was a civil litigator for more than two decades. After a legal career of more than thirty years, she began thinking about changing her life. Her firm had an early retirement program that she qualified for, and she thought about possibly seeking a judgeship. She was encouraged by a close friend who worked in government at the time who told her, "You really should do that." Schofield also had former colleagues who had moved to the bench. She decided, "What the heck! I should apply."

Between 2010 and 2011, there were several vacancies in New York's federal courts, and Schofield submitted an application to the committee that Senator Chuck Schumer, a Democrat, had established to screen federal judicial applicants. While Senator Kirsten Gillibrand, also a Democrat, was responsible for recommending individuals to fill certain positions, Schofield's understanding was that Schumer was in charge of the position that she was looking at. When Schumer's committee interviewed Schofield on August 30, 2010, she found that one of the committee members was particularly excited that she had applied. That member was Herbert Rubin, who sponsored the Judge Rose L. and Herbert Rubin Law Review Prize at New York University School of Law for the most outstanding law student in international, commercial, or public law. Rubin saw from Schofield's application that she had won that prize as a law student in 1981.

A few weeks later, Schumer himself interviewed Schofield. What followed was a period during which Schofield saw no progress on her application. She knew other people who were interviewing for federal judgeships with Schumer's committee, and some of them were recommended to President Obama, while her application appeared to be in limbo. She came to think that her chances of being chosen were "slim." She realized that being chosen to be a federal judge was "like being hit by lightning, not something you can count on, not something you can prepare for." She knew that one had to be in the right place at the right time, and as she saw successive openings filled by others, she thought she was not going to be chosen.

For about a year, nothing happened, although Schumer's staff told her she was on a short list of potential nominees. An attorney leading Schumer's selection committee advised her that it would help her to have support from the Filipino community. Schofield was uncertain how to get such support, not having grown up in New York and not having any ties to the New York Filipino community. Fortunately, someone put her in touch with NAPABA.

As part of its effort to increase Asian judges on the federal bench, NAPABA connected Schofield with Filipino community organizations. Getting connected was, of course, just the start of what had to be an awkward outreach. Schofield was met by questions she described as "difficult" but justified. The organizations asked why they should help her when she had had no interaction at all with them and was unknown to them. Her response was that she was being considered for a possible federal judgeship, was of Filipino ancestry, and knew of no other Filipinos being similarly considered. She pledged that if she did become a judge, she would, within the boundaries of what a judge could ethically do, work to support the Filipino community. Her effort was rewarded, and the organizations wrote supporting letters.

Schumer interviewed Schofield for a second time in September 2011, about a year after her earlier interview with him. But the months continued to pass. By the end of 2011, Schofield concluded that "it was not going to happen." She retired from the practice of law, but then something unexpected happened. She became seriously ill.

In early 2012, while Schofield was undergoing chemotherapy, Schumer's staff called and said that Schumer intended to recommend that President Obama nominate her to a federal district court seat in the Southern District of New York. Schofield reacted by saying, "Wait. I have retired and am in chemotherapy. I am not in a position to pursue anything." She asked for a week to consider what to do.

During that week, Schofield examined her situation, which obviously was not what it had been when she had originally submitted her application to Schumer's committee in the summer of

2010. She concluded that she was being offered an opportunity that was "not going to come again." She called to say that she was "pleased, delighted, and honored" that her name was being put forward. Schumer sent her name to President Obama.

Schofield received a "well qualified" rating from the ABA committee, with two members abstaining.[91] She was very familiar with ABA ratings, having served for three years as the Second Circuit's representative on the ABA Standing Committee that rated nominees. Her experience was that the ABA looked at professional competence, judicial temperament, and ethical behavior without examining political affiliation.

President Obama nominated Schofield on April 25, 2012. Schofield's nomination was supported by NAPABA, the Filipino American Lawyers Association of New York, and the Asian American Bar Association of New York. In a press release, NAPABA described Schofield's "life story" as "a testament to the American story of hard work and perseverance that beats the odds." Support also came from the Asian American Justice Center, the National Federation of Filipino American Associations, and KAYA: Filipino Americans for Progress.[92] Asian American law enforcement officers also lent their support.

Even though Schofield had waited a while for Senator Schumer to submit her name to President Obama, she was in no rush to appear at a hearing before the Senate Judiciary Committee. She had lost her hair during chemotherapy. It was growing back, but it was still very short and was gray and curly, unlike her usual hairstyle. She hoped and requested that her hearing would be "later rather than sooner." With the 2012 election nearing, however, it could not be delayed very much, even though the Democrats controlled the Senate. Schofield's hearing occurred on June 6, 2012. Shortly after that, activity on judicial nominees stopped as the Senate waited for the election.

The Senate moved quickly once the election was over. Obama had been reelected, and the Democrats had held onto their majority in the Senate. On December 13, 2012, Schofield was confirmed by a roll call vote of 91–0.[93]

Lorna Gail Schofield, 2009. Photo by David Lindner.

Judges do not need to assume their judicial offices immediately upon being confirmed. In fact, because a nominee does not always have a great deal of notice as to when confirmation will occur, a judge may have professional or personal obligations to address before going on the bench and may delay taking the judicial oath of office. In Schofield's case, she had planned a vacation for early 2013. In addition, the judges who occupied the courthouse that she was about to move into were in a state of transition following a lengthy renovation, so she was told that she could wait until March to move in if she wanted to avoid having to move twice, once into temporary chambers and then later into her permanent chambers. She nevertheless took her oath in the same month she was confirmed, having been urged by a friend (in what Schofield says was not entirely in jest) to do so because then, "If you're hit by a bus, you'll die a federal judge." However, she did not have to cancel her vacation.

Schofield, who is divorced and has one child, regularly takes time out from her caseload to counsel would-be judges. She advises getting an early start on keeping records of speeches, articles, and press releases that one prepares because such information must be included in the Senate Judiciary Committee's questionnaire and can be very burdensome to compile retroactively. She also advises keeping track of the dates and purposes of international trips, which must be listed on the Federal Bureau of Investigation background check form.

She recommends trying to do both civil and criminal work, representing both plaintiffs and defendants, and handling legal matters over a broad range of areas. While recognizing that clients often seek attorneys steeped in specialty fields, Schofield says that the ABA values breadth of experience as well as trial experience, values that she says are "not misplaced" in evaluating judicial applicants. She stresses that attorneys should never sacrifice their reputations in the area of ethical behavior and should treat adversaries with respect even while zealously representing clients.

Although recognizing that it is hard for most women to self-promote, Schofield urges women to do exactly that. Litigators need to do that anyway to market themselves to clients, she says, and lawyers have to get used to advocating for themselves to be successful anywhere in the profession.

Schofield recommends embracing what makes you different from others. She says, "If you look different from everyone in the room, embrace that. If everyone wears a blue suit, I will wear a red suit. You can't be shy about who you are." She urges confidence in your own being and not passing yourself off as something you are not.

10

Pamela Ki Mai Chen

(E.D.N.Y.) (2013)

Born 1961 in Chicago, Illinois

Federal Judicial Service:
Judge, U.S. District Court for the Eastern District of New York
Nominated by Barack Obama on January 4, 2013, to a seat vacated by
    Raymond Joseph Dearie. Confirmed by the Senate on March 4,
    2013, and received commission on March 5, 2013.

Education:
University of Michigan, BA, 1983
Georgetown University Law Center, JD, 1986

Professional Career:
Private practice, Washington, DC, 1986–1991
Trial attorney, Special Litigation Section, Civil Rights Division, U.S.
    Department of Justice, 1991–1998; senior trial attorney, 1992–1998
Assistant U.S. attorney, Eastern District of New York, 1998–2007,
    2008–2013; chief, Civil Rights Litigation Unit, 2003–2006; dep-
    uty chief, Public Integrity Section, 2006–2007; chief, Civil Rights
    Section, 2006–2007, 2008–2013
Deputy commissioner for enforcement, New York State Division of
    Human Rights, 2008

Other Nominations/Recess Appointments:
Nominated to U.S. District Court for the Eastern District of New
    York, August 2, 2012; no Senate vote[94]

Pamela Ki Mai Chen is the first openly gay Asian woman to become an Article III judge. She is also the first woman of Chinese descent to become an Article III judge outside of California. She is the second Asian woman Article III judge in the Eastern District of New York, joining Kiyo Matsumoto.

Chen started our interview[95] by discussing her parents' paths. They came separately to the United States from China during World War II and met while in graduate school at the University of Chicago. Their intent was to return to China to join the Nationalist movement there, but that changed when Chiang Kai-shek was defeated by the Communists. Chen's mother's family was being persecuted by the Communists in China, and Chen's parents were stranded in the United States. Ultimately, her father, who earned a graduate degree in economics, became an auditor with the Internal Revenue Service. Her mother became a college professor in English literature.

Chen, the youngest child in her family, has two brothers. All three of the children were born in the United States. Chen says her parents became U.S. citizens based on the citizenship of Chen's oldest brother, a derivative path she says is no longer available following changes in the law.

Chen grew up in Chicago. Her parents spoke English at home, and she learned some Mandarin from hearing them and from attending Sunday classes at a Chinese-language school that her mother started, but she says her Mandarin is extremely limited.

Chen says that her family background was a "great motivator" in her decision to become a lawyer. One of her brothers went into medicine, and the other became a lawyer, now in-house with a private entity and very much involved in the business aspects of that company. Chen began her legal career in private practice and later moved to the Department of Justice. She spent much of her career as an AUSA in the Eastern District of New York. Her partner is a lawyer with a federal agency.

As an AUSA, Chen did not initially have in mind the possibility of becoming a federal judge. She had the vague notion that judges were "plucked out" of practice by decision makers, or that they had political connections that brought them to the attention of influential people. Her first exposure to the process of becoming a federal judge came when another AUSA, Margo Brodie, was encouraged by a district judge in the Eastern District of New York to apply for a position as a magistrate judge. Brodie did not become a magistrate judge, but then she was encouraged to apply for a district judgeship. Chen followed Brodie's progress as she was recommended by Senator Schumer's merit selection committee, had her name sent by Senator Schumer to President Obama, and then was nominated in 2011 and confirmed in February 2012. Still, Chen thought that Brodie's situation was unique. Even when a friend told Chen that she should apply because Senator Schumer was looking for a gay candidate, Chen did not spring into action, instead thinking that it would be better to be selected as a matter of merit. But the seed had been planted, and Chen began exploring the possibility of applying.

She decided to submit an application to Senator Schumer's committee. She received advice from Judge Denny Chin of the Second Circuit and Judge Kiyo Matsumoto of the Eastern District of New York. Chin had a list of questions that Senator Schumer or his committee might ask, which helped Chen prepare for her interview. In fact, Chen got an interview with the committee almost immediately. She credits the support of the Asian American Bar Association of New York (AABANY) as having been "hugely helpful" in making her appear to be a viable candidate.

Chen knew that she would have stiff competition for the vacancy. At one point, AABANY notified Chen that another Asian was likely going to be selected; it was not her turn. However, that person was never nominated.

Nothing happened for a while. For months, Chen waited with no idea of how her application was faring. She sought help from AABANY, which wrote a supporting letter to Senator Schumer's committee. But ultimately, it was Robert Raben, the head of the Raben Group, a lobbying and consulting group, who got the process moving.

At the time, Vincent Eng was working at Raben's company. Eng was front and center with other Asian judicial candidates on behalf of NAPABA, and he offered to help Chen. Eng told Raben about Chen's situation. Raben was particularly interested in helping LGBTQ candidates. He also had a lengthy working relationship with Senator Schumer, so he had access that Chen lacked. Raben discovered through his contacts that members of Schumer's committee were concerned about a case that Chen had handled, in which District Judge John Gleeson had raised concerns about possibly perjured trial testimony.

Gleeson had issued a ruling that appeared to suggest that Chen and a colleague might have suborned perjury. An investigation by the Office of Professional Responsibility in the Department of Justice cleared Chen, concluding that she and her colleague had not been at fault but had instead simply relied on the cooperating witness's pretrial statement. The witness had not been truthful with Chen and her colleague, but they had not known that at the time they called him to the witness stand. In considering Raben's discovery, Chen says, "I owe my life to that guy. I don't know that I would have figured out the problem without his intercession."

The knowledge that committee members were focused on Judge Gleeson's ruling put Chen in a quandary. She was at a loss as to how to address the problem. A friend suggested that she go to Judge Gleeson for help. The prospect appeared daunting, but Chen decided to try it. Judge Gleeson "could not have been better." He immediately disclaimed any intent to accuse her of having suborned perjury and enthusiastically endorsed her application. Chen believes that he may have contacted Senator Schumer and the merit selection committee on her behalf. She calls the incident "a good lesson about having to advocate for yourself." Even though she was successful in her self-advocacy and in having to "beat the bushes," she did not come to like doing that. In fact, she says, "I hate that!"

Chen had been warned by Raben that Schumer's committee had a reputation for being tough on women of color when evaluating them.[96] The committee nevertheless recommended Chen to

Senator Schumer, who interviewed her. He asked her about her taxes to determine whether she had hired domestic help without complying with tax laws. Senator Gillibrand interviewed her separately. The senators had an agreement to divide responsibility for candidates, and Schumer took over Chen's candidacy. Chen understood Schumer to be focused on whether a candidate was qualified, had an appropriate temperament, and would add diversity to the bench. Like President Obama, Schumer hoped to increase diversity, and Chen knew she checked off three boxes: being a woman, being Asian, and being gay. From her standpoint, in terms of adding diversity, decision makers appeared more focused on her sexual orientation than on her being an Asian woman. Schumer forwarded Chen's name to President Obama.

Most judicial applicants present backgrounds that reflect a concentration in either civil or criminal matters. Chen was unusual in that, at the time she was applying for a district judgeship, her experience was in what she terms "equipoise"; she had spent about half of her career handling criminal matters, and the rest handling civil matters.

Chen received a "qualified" rating from the ABA.[97] She believes that the rating was a reflection of the absence of any civil trial from her résumé. This absence is not unusual even for experienced civil litigators, who find that the expense and uncertainty of trial often leads parties to settle disputes before trial occurs, notwithstanding the time that a litigator may have spent in preparation.

President Obama nominated Chen on August 2, 2012. Chen found the time before her nomination more stressful than the time afterward. As a nominee, she continued to appear in federal court without noticing any impact on her cases or on her personal life.

The Democrats controlled the Senate, and they scheduled a hearing on President Obama's nomination of Chen the next month. Chen got a hearing more quickly than most of the other judges in this book. This may have been a reflection of a number of factors, including Senator Schumer's influence (among other things, he was a member of the Senate Judiciary Committee), and the majority's interest in getting as many of President

Obama's nominees confirmed as possible. At her hearing before the Senate Judiciary Committee, Chen was asked about her political activities with the Democratic Party and on some campaigns. No one asked Chen about the case that had been the subject of her discussion with Judge Gleeson. Nor was she asked about her sexual orientation. Chen says that "nobody thought being gay would be a problem." Still, she was "a little worried." Even though other openly gay judges had been confirmed ahead of her, some had run into obstacles. Chen remembers that Schumer introduced her partner at her hearing.

The speed with which Chen got a hearing before the Senate Judiciary Committee did not end up being followed by a speedy confirmation vote in the full Senate. Chen's nomination and hearing were very close to the presidential election. The Senate adjourned without voting on her.

As noted earlier, under Senate Rule XXXI, a nomination lapses if confirmation does not occur in the two-year congressional session in which the nomination occurs. President Obama renominated Chen on January 4, 2013, after the new Congress was sworn in, and the ABA carried over the "qualified" rating it had given her earlier.[98]

The Democrats kept their majority in the Senate in the 2012 election. Chen was not called back for a second hearing before the Senate Judiciary Committee, although she was sent some new written questions to answer. She did not have to wait long to be confirmed. The full Senate confirmed her by voice vote on March 5, 2013.[99]

Chen says she now speaks on panels and at events where she encourages Asians in particular to consider applying for judgeships. She says she works with AABANY in trying to identify Asian candidates. She urges attorneys to realize that "you're worthy if you do a good job." She advises, "Don't plot through and censor yourself." She credits Goodwin Liu, who failed to be confirmed to the Ninth Circuit and became a California Supreme Court justice instead, with having written things he cared about, and she counsels applicants to be like him and "do what you love."

Pamela Ki Mai Chen. Photo by Michael Keel.

A judicial appointment is never guaranteed, so she says that if you limit yourself in the hopes of becoming a judge, "you will be unhappy and miss out on a career." At the same time, she says, "When you are ready to apply, make sure your house is in order. Don't post on social media or let others post about you. Be decent to everybody." She says applicants should "ask for help" and then "hope the stars align."

11

Indira Talwani

(D. Mass.) (2014)

Born 1960 in Englewood, New Jersey

Federal Judicial Service:
Judge, U.S. District Court for the District of Massachusetts
Nominated by Barack Obama on January 6, 2014, to a seat vacated
    by Mark Lawrence Wolf. Confirmed by the Senate on May 8,
    2014, and received commission on May 12, 2014.

Education:
Radcliffe College, BA, 1982
University of California, Berkeley, School of Law, JD, 1988

Professional Career:
Law clerk, Hon. Stanley A. Weigel, U.S. District Court, Northern
    District of California, 1988–1989
Private practice, San Francisco, California, 1989–1999
Private practice, Boston, Massachusetts, 1999–2014

Other Nominations/Recess Appointments:
Nominated to U.S. District Court for the District of Massachusetts,
    September 24, 2013; no Senate vote[100]

Indira Talwani is the first Asian woman to become an Article III
judge in any federal court in the First Circuit, which covers Massachusetts, Rhode Island, New Hampshire, Maine, and Puerto Rico.
She is the second South Asian woman in the country to become
an Article III judge.

During our interview,[101] Talwani said that both her parents came to the United States as immigrants, her father from India and her mother from Germany. Her father came to the United States to attend graduate school following a period when he lived in Norway. He attended Columbia University, became a marine geophysicist, taught at Columbia while Talwani was growing up, and later taught at Rice University in Texas. Talwani's mother left post–World War II Germany to come to the United States as a teenager. Initially sponsored by a family friend, Talwani's mother later made her way to New York City. She got a job in the German Department at Columbia, where she met Talwani's father.

Talwani is the second of three children. She grew up in the state of New York, and English was the language spoken in her home. The family structure she grew up in is mirrored in her present family, as she and her husband, a lawyer in private practice, have three children.

As an undergraduate, Talwani had an interdisciplinary major in social studies. After college, she and her boyfriend (now her husband) moved to California, mainly because he wanted to be independent of his East Coast family. Talwani wanted public interest work and identified labor unions as entities that were bettering communities. She got a job as a labor union organizer but came to think that she would benefit from expanding her skills to include those of a lawyer. She went to law school, after which she clerked for a federal district judge, Stanley A. Weigel of the Northern District of California, then joined a San Francisco law firm that specialized in representing unions.

The lawyers at her firm had all been law clerks for federal judges, many for U.S. Supreme Court justices. At the law firm, Talwani had a chance to watch one of her partners, Marsha Berzon, become a Ninth Circuit judge.[102]

As Talwani and her husband raised their children, they decided to move back to the East Coast to be near family members who could help them with their children. Talwani joined a small Massachusetts firm with a labor law focus. She says that she became well known nationally through her legal activities, which included being the editor for the ABA treatise on family medical leave. Although she participated in local bar activities, she did not consider herself among those regularly viewed by Massachusetts decision makers as judicial prospects. But when Senator Elizabeth Warren invited applications, Talwani put her name in.

Talwani had a number of reasons for applying. First, she had clerked for a federal district judge, so she had some concept of what being a judge involved. Second, her experience at her San Francisco firm, with its many former clerks, had given her what she called a "fair sense" of the judiciary and the process by which people became judges. That included watching Berzon make her way through the process to become a Ninth Circuit judge, as well as watching a colleague at her Massachusetts firm become a state court of appeals judge. Third, Senator Warren had made it clear that the selection process would be open and that people from a variety of backgrounds were welcome to apply. Talwani saw that Warren was not exclusively focused on diversity in terms of race and gender; she was also looking for diversity in applicants' professional and life experiences. To Talwani, it "felt like an appropriate time" to apply.

One of the first people Talwani went to for help after she decided to apply was an attorney from her old San Francisco law firm, Stephen Berzon, Marsha Berzon's husband. He put her in touch with Vincent Eng of NAPABA, whom Talwani found "very helpful."

Just a few days after she had submitted her application to Senator Warren, Talwani learned that her mother had suffered a ruptured brain aneurysm. She jumped on a plane to Los Angeles to be with her mother. It was then that Eng, not knowing about Talwani's personal crisis, reached out to her to offer assistance. Talwani thanked him for his kindness but said she had to focus on her mother. Talwani spent the next two weeks at her mother's bedside and was there when she received a call from Senator Warren's committee inviting her to be interviewed. Eng tried to help without being intrusive. He sent her some material he thought would be helpful, including a list of questions that might come up in the interview. Talwani was grateful for this unemotional approach at a time of high emotion in her life. The last thing she wanted was to have pep talks and other telephone conversations about her application. Her mother passed away without ever regaining consciousness.

Talwani returned to Massachusetts and was interviewed by Warren's committee, having had only Eng's materials as preparation. Afterward, she was interviewed by NAPABA's board of directors, which wanted to get to know her before providing formal support. Talwani felt awkward receiving such support, as she had not been active with NAPABA, but Eng assured her that NAPABA wanted to help. Local unions and local bar groups, as well as groups in Washington, DC, also provided support.

At the time, Senator Warren controlled which recommendations would be sent to President Obama for federal positions in Massachusetts. John Kerry had just left his position as the other Massachusetts senator to become President Obama's secretary of state. Mo Cowan was appointed to fill the vacant senatorial seat for less than half a year, until Senator Edward Markey won a special election to Kerry's old seat in July 2013. In the meantime, as noted in her Senate Judiciary Committee questionnaire,[103] Talwani communicated with Warren: "On May 8, 2013, I was interviewed by the Committee in Boston, Massachusetts. I was informed by the Chair of the Committee that the Committee recommended my nomination to Senator Warren. On June 17, 2013, I was interviewed by Senator Warren in Boston, Massachusetts, and she informed me that my name would be forwarded to the President."

Talwani says that even before Warren submitted her name to the White House, the White House had heard about her. Possibly Eng had mentioned her to Chris Kang in the White House Counsel's Office. The White House apparently was eager to move forward with her. Talwani went to DC for an interview, then received a "qualified" rating from the ABA on September 24, 2013.[104] She was nominated the same day, along with another district judge nominee for the District of Massachusetts and a First Circuit nominee.

Although she cannot recall how, Talwani came to understand that President Obama was making it a priority to diversify the federal bench in terms of race and gender. She knew that various advocacy groups were pressing the White House to diversify the bench, and she was also aware that as nominations of diverse candidates occurred, they were celebrated.

Talwani did not get an immediate hearing before the Senate Judiciary Committee. She was in what she called a "logjam" that held up judicial nominees, and the Senate changed its rules in late 2013 to address this. This was the famous "nuclear option," under which the Democratic majority in the Senate retained the filibuster for Supreme Court justices and for most legislation, but eliminated it for nominations for lower court nominees and executive branch nominees, allowing them to be confirmed based on simple majority votes rather than requiring sixty senators' votes.[105]

A large number of judicial nominations that were pending in late 2013 were returned by the Senate to President Obama under a provision in Senate Rule XXXI providing for such a return, even without the ending of a congressional session, whenever a nomination had not been acted on by the Senate at the time when the Senate adjourned or took a recess for more than thirty days. Obama renominated Talwani on January 6, 2014, and the ABA maintained her "qualified" rating.[106] She appeared before the Senate Judiciary Committee on January 8, 2014, while one of the cases she was working on was making its way through the Supreme Court. She had to supplement her earlier submissions to the Senate Judiciary Committee with copies of the Supreme Court briefs as they were filed.

Talwani was voted out of committee on a split vote, with Republican opposition. However, she was confirmed without opposition by the full Senate. The vote was 94–0 by roll call vote on May 8, 2014.[107]

Talwani notes that becoming an Article III judge involves what she calls a "turn of fortune." She says that the open process that Senator Warren employed helped her become a judge. She could put her name in and be considered fairly rather than having to depend on knowing influential people. She notes that had she waited to have someone urge her to apply or to fill a kind of "casting call," she would likely not have her present position. She advises would-be applicants to put their names in "because you can do it."

At the same time, Talwani says that decision makers would do well to look beyond the "usual channels." She points to her experience on a committee that screened bankruptcy judge applicants for the First Circuit. The committee saw that the initial group of attorneys was noticeably nondiverse, and she suggested that the committee reach out to affinity bar associations for additional applicants. "Sure enough," she says, a different applicant pool resulted.

Talwani made an interesting observation about the increasing presence of Asians on the federal bench. She sees South Asians making up a large percentage of the increase, while other Asian groups perhaps are not as well represented. Noting that South Asians are relatively new to the United States and most South Asian lawyers are well under the age of sixty, she wonders why they have seen such growth on the bench, as opposed to Asian groups that have been in the United States for many more generations.

12

Jennifer Choe-Groves

(Ct. Int'l Trade) (2016)

Born 1969 in Chicago, Illinois

Federal Judicial Service:
Judge, U.S. Court of International Trade
Nominated by Barack Obama on July 30, 2015, to a seat vacated by
    Gregory Wright Carman. Confirmed by the Senate on June 6,
    2016, and received commission on June 8, 2016.

Education:
Princeton University, AB, 1991
Rutgers School of Law–Newark, JD, 1994
Columbia Law School, LLM, 1998

Professional Career:
Assistant district attorney, New York County, New York, 1994–1997
Private practice, New York City, 1998–2002
Private practice, Washington, DC, 2002–2005, 2010–2013
Senior director of intellectual property and innovation and chair of
    the Special 301 Committee, Office of the U.S. Trade Representa-
    tive, Executive Office of the President, 2005–2010
Chief executive officer, Choe Groves Consulting LLC, Burke, Vir-
    ginia, 2013–2016
Chief executive officer, Titanium Law Group PLLC, Washington,
    DC, 2014–2016

Miscellaneous Information:
Given name at birth: Jennifer Domee Choe[108]

Jennifer Choe-Groves is the first Asian (regardless of sex) to serve on the Court of International Trade. She is also the second woman of Korean heritage to become an Article III judge, following Lucy Koh.

During her interview,[109] Choe-Groves explained that she decided to use a hyphenated last name as a judge, although previously she had used her given last name as her middle name and had adopted "Groves" as her surname upon getting married.

Both her parents were born in Korea. They came separately with their families to the United States to get away from the Korean War. They were high schoolers at the time and did not know each other. Choe-Groves's mother went on to become a dietitian and open a number of gourmet-related businesses. Her father became a chemist at a private company and was also a professor. Choe-Groves and her younger brother grew up speaking only English at home. Her parents wanted to ensure that their children did not speak English with a foreign accent. As a result, although Choe-Groves can understand some Korean, she never learned to speak the language.

She thought about law at an early age. A family friend who was a judge encouraged her to take that path. When she was twelve, she recognized that she was a good writer and that law might be a natural path for her. At the time, her father, an avid inventor, was drafting patent applications for his many inventions. Lacking confidence in his own English-language ability, he had Choe-Groves review his writing before he submitted anything to the in-house patent attorney who would ultimately see the applications. Thus, even as a child, Choe-Groves understood the value of protecting intellectual property.

There was another reason that Choe-Groves was interested in protecting intellectual property. She was musically talented, playing the piano and composing pieces. She quickly grasped the importance of copyright protection.

Born in Chicago, Choe-Groves grew up on the East Coast and enrolled in Juilliard's precollege program. Asked about the difficulty of abandoning a possible career in music, Choe-Groves says that it was not very hard to opt out of a music career. First, her parents did not want her to become a musician. They wanted her to go into a more stable profession. She says, "It was always understood that I would go to medical school or law school." Second, Choe-Groves was part of a rarefied musical community, where she had classmates who, from a very young age, had been on the international stage. Some of them were in great demand, playing solos nearly every weekend in concerts accompanied by major orchestras throughout the United States and abroad. Choe-Groves compared herself to them and concluded that she would not achieve that level of success. She primarily performed on the East Coast, and, as she put it, "I won every competition I entered in New Jersey," where she went to school before and during college. Although clearly an accomplished musician, she did not envision herself having the national and international recognition that some of her more illustrious classmates had.

Choe-Groves and her husband, a lawyer, have two children, both of whom are musically talented. Both her children have already indicated that an artistic career is definitely in the cards for them. She is careful to encourage her children to do as they want in that regard.

Having opted out of a musical career, Choe-Groves went to Princeton University, where she majored in English and women's studies. As an undergraduate, she also taught piano to so many students that she has been described as having run "a de facto music school."[110]

Choe-Groves was interested in public service even as an undergraduate. While volunteering as a rape crisis counselor and assisting battered women,[111] Choe-Groves met Linda Fairstein, an attorney whose work with rape, child abuse, and domestic violence greatly impressed her. This led directly to Choe-Groves's decision to join the Manhattan District Attorney's Office under the leadership of District Attorney Robert Morgenthau (where Fairstein had worked) after she completed law school. There, Choe-Groves worked on domestic violence prosecutions. But she maintained her interest in intellectual property issues. Seeing no overlap between those issues and her prosecutorial work, she knew that she would eventually leave her prosecutorial job to practice in intellectual property. To keep abreast of intellectual property law, Choe-Groves, at the same time that she was at the District Attorney's Office, worked at night and on the weekends on articles about intellectual property issues, which she published.

A few years into her practice at the District Attorney's Office, Choe-Groves considered her career options and knew that she could "pivot" into private practice. The logical move would have been to become a criminal defense attorney. Instead, she went back to school to get an LLM, partially in anticipation of specializing in intellectual property law.

Choe-Groves went into private practice and developed an interest in international matters, partly as an outgrowth of her family background and partly because intellectual property is a field that crosses borders. She spent several years in the Office of the U.S. Trade Representative working on intellectual property and innovation issues, and she later opened her own consulting firm and law office.

As was the case for many of the judges in this book, Choe-Groves's idea of becoming a judge was planted in her mind by someone else. In her case, that someone was her mother. Not in the legal profession herself, Choe-Groves's mother watched her daughter juggle work and family responsibilities, and she suggested to Choe-Groves that as a judge she could have more control over her schedule. Choe-Groves's mother told her, "You'd make a good judge. It's a good profession for a woman." Choe-Groves then got the opportunity to take her mother's advice.

Choe-Groves's path to an Article III judgeship was not the typical one. Although she had begun to think about becoming a judge, she had not actually told anyone about this. As it happened, she did not need to take the initiative in applying. Instead, she had the good fortune of being invited to apply. President Obama's administration was looking for people involved with international law to fill a vacancy on the Court of International Trade, a federal trial court that has exclusive jurisdiction over international trade disputes across the country. Choe-Groves knew politically connected people, but she had not been vying for a judgeship. In fact, she had never represented any party in any proceeding in the Court of International Trade and had "no idea there was even an opening."

People that Choe-Groves describes as "connected to the White House" reached out to her. Vincent Eng of the National Asian Pacific American Bar Association (NAPABA) recalled that when the Obama administration was looking to fill the spot, NAPABA members involved with promoting an Asian presence in the federal judiciary identified Choe-Groves as a promising candidate. James Ho, now a Fifth Circuit judge but at the time in private practice, and Wan Kim, who had served in President George W. Bush's Department of Justice as the assistant attorney general in charge of the Office of Civil Rights, knew that Choe-Groves had a background that might put her in line for a nomination and suggested that she be considered.

Based in New York City, the Court of International Trade sometimes sits in Washington, DC, but its judges can sit anywhere in the United States, or even abroad. Because the court handles international trade disputes for the entire country, it has no senators who control recommendations to the White House. Choe-Groves, having no senators she could identify as being in charge, says, "I basically was on my own." She got information on what to expect from Eng, who notes that she also received support from Arizona Republican Jon Kyl, a former senator who lived near Choe-Groves's summer home and became what Eng calls her "adopted senator." She says, "I'd never spoken to anybody who'd gone through this before." Eng introduced her to people who could provide background. Among those from whom Choe-Groves learned were judges on the Court of International Trade, who spoke with her both before and after she was nominated.

The Court of International Trade consists of nine judges. By statute, "not more than five of such judges shall be from the same political party."[112] Choe-Groves was seeking an Obama nomination to a Republican seat on the court.

Jennifer Choe-Groves

NAPABA wrote a letter on Choe-Groves's behalf to the White House, and community and nonprofit organizations that Choe-Groves had been active in similarly lent their support. She had the impression that she was the only candidate being considered. No one from the administration ever mentioned to her that being an Asian woman was an advantage in the selection process. She worked her own connections, but she was very conscious that she lacked an actual member of the Senate to push for her confirmation.

A substantial majority of the ABA committee ranked Choe-Groves "qualified," with a minority ranking her "not qualified."[113] She received no explanation for that minority rating.[114]

President Obama nominated Choe-Groves on July 30, 2015. She then went before the Senate Judiciary Committee. The Senate majority had flipped as a result of the 2014 elections, so the Republicans were now in control. But this did not lead to immediate confirmation of a nominee to fill a Republican seat on the Court of International Trade.

Shortly after her Senate Judiciary Committee hearing, Justice Antonin Scalia died. The committee had not yet voted Choe-Groves out of committee, and she worried about whether she might get stuck in committee. As the 2016 presidential election neared, her worry grew, but Choe-Groves was ultimately voted out of committee and then confirmed by the full Senate by voice vote on June 6, 2016. She says, "I was very lucky."

Choe-Groves calls her position a "fantastic job" and highly recommends that anyone interested apply. She advises those interested in federal judgeships to prepare by acquiring experience that will be helpful on the bench. She says that getting on her court, with its specialized class of cases, may involve a lesser need for political connections and a greater focus on substantive preparation. Most of the judges on the Court of International Trade tend to have practiced in New York or Washington, DC. She notes that, of course, lawyers in other cities who focus on international disputes could be equally qualified, but the court has traditionally been made up of lawyers who practiced on the East Coast.

Choe-Groves considers herself "very fortunate to have the chance to be a federal judge" and is "honored to serve." She says now is a particularly interesting time to be on the Court of International Trade, given the issues coming before the court.

13

Karen Gren Scholer

(N.D. Tex.) (2018)

Born 1957 in Tokyo, Japan

Federal Judicial Service:
Judge, U.S. District Court for the Northern District of Texas
Nominated by Donald J. Trump on September 7, 2017, to a seat
    vacated by Jorge Antonio Solis. Confirmed by the Senate on
    March 5, 2018, and received commission on March 6, 2018.

Education:
Rice University, BA, 1979
Cornell Law School, JD, 1982

Professional Career:
Private practice, Dallas, Texas, 1982–2000, 2009–2013, 2014–2018
Judge, Texas District Court, Ninety-Fifth Judicial District,
    2001–2008; presiding judge, Dallas County civil district judges,
    2007
Arbitrator and mediator, American Arbitration Association,
    2014–2018

Other Nominations/Recess Appointments:
Nominated to U.S. District Court for the Eastern District of Texas,
    March 15, 2016; no Senate vote

Miscellaneous Information:
Former names: Karen Gren Johnson; Karen Anne Gren[115]

Karen Gren Scholer is the first Asian woman to become an Article III judge in any court within the Fifth Circuit, which covers Texas, Louisiana, and Mississippi.[116] She is the first Asian woman Article III judge to have been nominated by presidents of different political parties.[117] To top that off, she was nominated by presidents of different parties for different district courts.

During her interview,[118] Scholer said that her mother was born in Japan, where she met Scholer's father, an American who was the son of Polish immigrants.[119] Scholer's parents met while Scholer's mother was working in the office of a doctor who had many American patients, one of whom was Scholer's father, previously in the 82nd Airborne but at the time a civilian traveling salesperson. Scholer said that her mother's dogs were taken by American servicemen occupying Japan after World War II. One of the ways that her father wooed her mother was by buying her a dog.

Scholer and her younger brother spent their first few years in Japan. When Scholer was four, the family moved to the United States. The family lived in Cleveland, moved to Denver, and then, right before Scholer entered the seventh grade, to Dallas. Scholer's father continued to work in sales, and her mother was a homemaker.

Scholer told a newspaper reporter, "Growing up, I wanted to fit in desperately. . . . And kids can be cruel, and some of them did say cruel things."[120] As a result, "when my mother spoke Japanese to my brother and me, we covered our ears because we didn't want to hear Japanese."[121] She identified her "biggest regret" as being "that I lost my ability to speak Japanese."[122]

Scholer's mother had a college degree, but Scholer's father was the first in his family to enter college. He did not complete requirements for a bachelor's degree, so when Scholer graduated from college, she was the first on her father's side of the family to get a college degree.

Scholer had a triple undergraduate major, concentrating in legal studies (an interdisciplinary program), political science, and sociology. In college, she was not committed to a legal career. She ultimately entered law school because it was a "good place to go" with her undergraduate background and a "respectable place to be on hold." She says that she was not encouraged in that regard by her parents or close friends. She chose to attend Cornell Law School because it offered the most attractive financial aid package.

The summer after her first year in law school, she worked at a private law firm and "loved it." She says that the opportunity changed her way of thinking and motivated her to become a lawyer. Her view was only heightened by her experience at another law firm after her second year of law school. She began her third year determined to become a trial lawyer, which she said made sense to her because she is "a people person." She says that she "buckled down" and took trial-related classes, including trial advocacy and evidence. After completing law school, she went into private practice in Dallas.

Scholer became Karen Gren Johnson when she married Mark Johnson, a law school classmate who had been a year ahead of her in high school. They have three sons.

Scholer was active in nonprofit and bar organizations, as well as in the Asian community. She says that she embraced her Asian roots and spent hours with a group of women who exchanged accounts of growing up with Asian mothers. She notes that there are "common cultural things that keep Asian American women from seeking public office" and cause them to find it "repugnant to talk about yourself, ask for money, ask for help," and rely on anything "beyond being high quality at what you do."

When people encouraged her to seek a state judgeship, she says they were telling her "what was already in [her] heart." She decided to run for a state trial judgeship because she "wanted to serve." Her mother, however, thought Scholer was taking a foolish risk in leaving her law firm partnership to run against an incumbent judge. Scholer says that her mother was "completely unsupportive" and considered it "shameful" for her to have her name on billboards.

In Texas judicial elections, judges are required to list a political party affiliation. Scholer ran as a Republican. A month or two before the Republican primary election in which Scholer was running, her mother, who was taking care of Scholer's young sons at the time, realized, "God is not answering my prayers" that Scholer not run. Scholer's mother decided it was time to face reality; she put up one of Scholer's yard signs. Scholer's mother then wanted everyone around her to do the same. Scholer ended up easily defeating the incumbent, becoming the first Asian elected to a judgeship in Dallas County, which has a population of about two million. Four years later, she ran unopposed for another four-year term. She says that her constituents included Asians, women, and Democrats.

In 2007, while a state court judge, Scholer began what became an eleven-year journey to an Article III judgeship. That she was seeking a federal judgeship was not a surprise. Even in 2002, while Scholer was fairly new on the state court bench, a reporter had written, "Lawyers' only concern about her: Because she is relatively young, a staunch Republican and a minority, she would be considered a prime candidate for appointment to a federal bench."[123]

Scholer's 2007 application for an Article III position was for a seat in the Northern District of Texas. Applications were reviewed by the Federal Judicial Evaluation Committee, a committee of more than thirty-five Texas lawyers selected by Senator Kay Bailey Hutchison and Senator John Cornyn, both Republicans, to screen applicants.[124] Scholer says that the committee winnowed the field down to a dozen applicants, and the senators then interviewed their top four candidates. Scholer was among the four who were interviewed, but it was Reed O'Connor whose name was ultimately forwarded to President George W. Bush and who was confirmed to the Northern District of Texas seat in November 2007.

After eight years on the state trial bench, Scholer decided not to run again. Her decision coincided with "a blue wave in Dallas County in which every trial bench was won by a Democrat."[125] Scholer says, however, that her reasons for not running were personal. First, she still wanted to advocate, which required her to return to practicing law. Second, she was preparing to get divorced and thought that it would be difficult for her to take on what she said would have been a "full-time job" to run in what she knew would be a contested election. She says that she was also conscious of the impact on her children. She joined a firm as an equity partner, keeping her married name of Johnson even after the divorce until she remarried. Her second husband, Gunnar Scholer, is a businessman.

The 2008 election changed the political landscape for Scholer. Not only was she facing President Barack Obama, a Democrat, but she had a new senator in Ted Cruz, the Republican who was elected after Senator Hutchison retired.

In July 2014, Scholer once again applied to fill an existing vacancy in the Northern District of Texas. Once again, she was interviewed, this time by Senators Cornyn and Cruz. But before the senators informed her about whether they were going forward with her, an opening arose in the Eastern District of Texas. This was in the Sherman Division of the Eastern District of Texas, a single-judge division based in Plano, not very far from North Dallas. Scholer applied for that position in April 2015. In July 2015, two things happened. First, the Texas senators sent Scholer's name to President Obama with their recommendation that he nominate her for a seat in the Northern District of Texas. Second, a little later in the same month, Scholer was interviewed by the senators' Federal Judicial Evaluation Committee for a seat in the Eastern District of Texas. She also had interviews with two House members from Texas in September 2015.

Scholer recalls that in early 2016, the Obama administration had before it a package of five potential nominees to fill vacancies in Texas. She was in that package. She says that she was asked whether she preferred the Northern District of Texas or the Eastern District of Texas. At the time, Plano was a fast-growing location, with numerous businesses moving there and a large Asian population. It was seen as the "Dallas of the future." Scholer said that she was fine with either district, but after being pressed further, she said that she had a slight preference for the Eastern District of Texas.

A substantial majority of the ABA committee rated her "qualified," and a minority rated her "well qualified."[126] President Obama nominated her for a district judgeship in the Eastern District of Texas on March 15, 2016.

In his remarks at Scholer's investiture, Judge Amos Mazzant III of the Eastern District of Texas notes that during the time in 2016 that Scholer was waiting for a hearing before the Senate Judiciary Committee, she took a trip to Japan, which she had not visited since she was four. During her trip, Senator Cornyn's office called her to say that her hearing was being scheduled in Washington, DC. Scholer flew home in a rush, and then flew to Washington, DC, met with Department of Justice attorneys to prepare for her hearing, and had her hearing on September 7, 2016. Unfortunately, notwithstanding all this flying around in a rush, she did not get voted out of committee given the upcoming 2016 presidential election, which put a halt to proceedings involving judicial candidates. Her nomination lapsed.

In early 2017, after President Donald Trump won the 2016 election, Scholer applied again for a district judgeship, submitting applications for positions in both the Northern District of Texas and the Eastern District of Texas. According to Judge Mazzant, drama ensued once again. She flew to Florida right before the wedding of one of her sons, only to have to turn around and return home for yet another interview with the Texas senators' Federal Judicial Evaluation Committee, after which she flew back to Florida for the wedding rehearsal dinner.

Senators Cornyn and Cruz interviewed Scholer again. Cornyn was the majority whip, and both Cornyn and Cruz were on the Senate Judiciary Committee, so Scholer had reason to be hopeful that this attempt would be successful. This time around, she declined to state a preference between the Northern District of Texas and the Eastern District of Texas. She knew that her prior nomination by Obama might put her at a disadvantage with the Trump administration. She was not the only candidate being considered for the position in Plano in the Eastern District, while at the same time, the Northern District was eager to fill any vacancy it had. Scholer's sons had begun urging her not to move to Plano and asking that they remain in their existing home. Senator Cornyn made it clear that he was willing to accommodate Scholer's district preference. Ultimately, Scholer's name was forwarded to Trump for the Northern District, and she was nominated for that district on September 7, 2017.

The ABA provided a new evaluation of Scholer for her 2017 nomination. This time, a substantial majority rated her "well qualified," and a minority rated her "qualified."[127]

Scholer did not have a second Senate Judiciary Committee hearing. She was confirmed by the Senate on a 95–0 roll call vote on March 5, 2018.[128]

Scholer had her official swearing in right after Trump signed her commission as a district judge. A judge is typically sworn in officially with little ceremony. Family and close friends, colleagues, and court staff may attend, but the number of attendees is usually small. A judge may later have an investiture, which is usually a much larger and more formal event, attended by lawyers, members of the community, and dignitaries and involving considerable pomp and circumstance. In Scholer's case, her official swearing in occurred in a packed courtroom, as lawyers, members of the local Asian American Bar Association, friends, family, and other judges quickly gathered to celebrate.[129]

After her larger-than-usual swearing in, Scholer thought about skipping an investiture. She says that her husband insisted that she had to have one. When Scholer asked why, he said, "You're the Susan Lucci of federal judges."[130] Having been told to do it for her fans, Scholer held an investiture.

Scholer was conscious that being an Asian woman was a point in her favor when she was nominated by Obama, who could see that her record included considerable Republican credentials. She says, "I'm not an ideologue," and "nobody knows my views on hot-button issues." She thinks that being an Asian woman was probably less of a factor when she was nominated by Trump.

With both her nominations, Scholer says that NAPABA was very helpful behind the scenes and "heartily endorsed [her] very quickly" without seeming to care about political affiliation. She describes NAPABA as putting total strangers together to help

Karen Gren Scholer, 2018

each other; she herself was helped by judges ahead of her who contacted her through NAPABA. She recalls, for example, that Jennifer Choe-Groves spent more than an hour on the phone with her helping her prepare during the nomination process. Scholer says that she herself has "paid it forward" by spending many hours counseling those thinking about applying for federal judgeships or going through the nomination or confirmation process, including Jill Otake, who is discussed later in this book. Scholer notes that people in the process are understandably anxious and are grateful for the support of the "network of nervous people across the country" that NAPABA supports.

Scholer says, "I don't think I could have gotten here without caring about the community and working with the community." She says that someone seeking an Article III position needs to have the community "lifting you up and wanting you to be there," and that happens if you have "rolled up your sleeves" and worked to make your community better.

She likens the chance of becoming an Article III judge to the chance of being struck by lightning, an analogy that Lorna Schofield also uses. She says that you cannot really plan to get an Article III judgeship, and that if you structure your life around that dream, you will be disappointed. At the same time, one can avoid doing disqualifying things. In particular, she says to be careful about what appears in print about you. Although seeking an Article III judgeship can be discouraging, she says applicants should not give up!

14

Jill Aiko Otake

(D. Haw.) (2019)

Born 1973 in Honolulu, Hawaii

Federal Judicial Service:
Judge, U.S. District Court for the District of Hawaii
Nominated by Donald J. Trump on December 21, 2017, to a seat
    vacated by Susan Oki Mollway. Confirmed by the Senate on
    August 1, 2018, and received commission on August 3, 2018.

Education:
Georgetown University, BS, 1995
University of Washington School of Law, JD, 1998

Professional Career:
Deputy prosecuting attorney, King County, Washington, 1998–2001,
    2002–2005
Law clerk, Hon. Simeon R. Acoba Jr., Supreme Court of Hawaii,
    2001–2002
Assistant U.S. attorney, Western District of Washington, 2005–2014;
    deputy supervisor, Terrorism and Violent Crimes Unit, 2011–2013;
    co-supervisor, General Crimes Unit, 2013–2014
Adjunct professor, Seattle University School of Law, 2007
Instructor, Oregon Sexual Assault Task Force, 2012
Assistant U.S. attorney, District of Hawaii, 2014–2018; deputy chief,
    Special Crimes Section, 2016–2017; acting chief, Special Crimes
    Section, 2017–2018[131]

Jill Aiko Otake is the first biracial Asian woman to join the federal bench in the District of Hawaii. She is the third Asian woman Article III judge in her district, all three of whom are of Japanese ancestry. Otake is the second Asian woman in the nation to be named to an Article III position by President Trump. She is the first Asian woman to fill an Article III seat vacated by another Asian woman (me) and the first Asian woman to become an Article III judge after a state appellate court clerkship. She is also the first woman of any racial background to come directly from a prosecutorial practice to the federal bench in the District of Hawaii. This is true with respect to Article III and non–Article III judgeships in her district, even though at one time the District of Hawaii had an Asian woman (Florence Nakakuni) as its U.S. attorney.

During her interview,[132] Otake said that one set of her great-grandparents on her father's side came to Hawaii from Japan to work on sugarcane plantations on Kauai. Her grandparents were born in Hawaii and spoke English. Her father, born in Hawaii, became a dentist. Otake's mother was a fourth-generation American of Danish extraction. She was a licensed practical nurse and then became the office manager for Otake's father's dental office.

In Hawaii, Otake is considered *hapa haole*, or half-White, *hapa* being the Hawaiian word for "half." Often shortened to just *hapa*, the term is by no means derogatory.

Otake is the oldest of three children. She says that her birth order "had a significant impact" on her and was a big reason that she was "so driven." She has two brothers, one of whom is a criminal defense attorney in Honolulu.

Her father died when she was twelve. At the time, she and her brothers were in a prestigious private school in Honolulu that included elementary school through high school. The school sought to help her and her brothers stay in the school after her father died. That help included hiring her mother to work in health care and after-school care, not just for the salary, but also for the accompanying tuition waiver benefits that school employees had at the time. Later, Otake's mother returned to school herself to get bachelor's and master's degrees, and then to become a social worker.

As early as the sixth grade, it occurred to Otake that she might want to become a lawyer. She recognized that she had a knack for public speaking, so she began to think of herself in jobs that involved that skill. Law fit the bill. In a comment reminiscent of Lorna Schofield's mother's desire that Schofield emulate Barbara Walters, Otake says that she recognized that there were, of course, other professions she could have considered, like television reporting, but they did not appeal to her.

Otake says that through high school and college, she focused on subjects that interested her the most, which tended to be in humanities-oriented areas. Her undergraduate major was Russian. Knowing that law schools accepted students with all manner of academic majors, she viewed her undergraduate years as offering her what was likely her only opportunity to become proficient in Russian. She spent time in Russia and even toyed with the idea of getting a PhD in Russian. What stopped her was the realization that she wanted to end up living in Hawaii, where job opportunities using that degree might be scarce. She returned to the idea of going into law and committed to it.

Otake attended law school in Washington's Seattle area and spent most of her legal career there as well. She began as a local prosecutor and later became an AUSA.

While practicing in Seattle, Otake learned that four federal district judgeships would likely open up in the area around the same time. Around 2012, a federal district judge there encouraged her to apply, noting that even if she was not selected to fill one of the anticipated openings, she might be selected for a later vacancy and then would become the first Asian Article III judge in the Western District of Washington. She recalls how thrilling the suggestion was, but by then she and her husband had already decided to return to Hawaii.

Otake had children and helped raise stepchildren who are now adults. She had her children in mind when she made what she says was "a conscious decision to come back" to Hawaii. Referring to "intangible things about Hawaii," she says, "I really wanted my kids to grow up in the culture I did." That culture includes maintaining relationships with extended family members. Before the coronavirus pandemic began in 2020, Otake had been taking her family for Sunday dinners at the home of the daughter of the extended family's matriarch, who is in her nineties. These dinners, which included up to a dozen adults and between five and seven children, were potluck affairs that Otake valued.

In Honolulu, Otake quickly made her mark as an AUSA. Her husband, who had retired from law enforcement in Seattle, got a job with the State of Hawaii working on analyzing traffic fatalities, gathering traffic data, and training people in detecting when drivers were impaired.

A federal district judge in Honolulu heard about the high regard that the Seattle federal judge had for Otake and formed a similar opinion. On Christmas Eve 2014, that judge invited Otake to discuss the matter in chambers. The judge told her that she should apply to fill the position that I was about to create by taking senior status. A few weeks earlier, I had given notice that I would be taking senior status in November 2015.

Although this conversation echoed the one in Seattle, Otake says, "I honestly did not think it was at all realistic." The Honolulu judge agreed that it was a long shot. Otake did what she could to improve her chances. Leslie Kobayashi, by then a district judge in the District of Hawaii, encouraged and advised her. Even though an AUSA does not need to pass the bar examination in the jurisdiction the AUSA appears in, Otake took the Hawaii bar examination in the summer of 2015, as advised by Kobayashi and NAPABA's Vincent Eng, to whom Kobayashi had introduced Otake. Otake thought that because she planned to stay in Hawaii, taking the Hawaii bar was a good idea no matter what happened.

Eng provided a wealth of information and assistance to Otake. Otake says, "I wouldn't be here if it weren't for Vincent and NAPABA." Eng was the source of what she calls "wise advice on everything," including which cases to focus on when answering the questionnaire that Hawaii's senators' merit selection committee required her to complete. Otake thinks Eng may have offered similar advice to other Asian candidates in the District of

Hawaii. He not only provided substantive and emotional support, but he took on the task of gathering letters endorsing Otake. Eng also introduced Otake to Karen Scholer, with whom she spoke frequently and from whom she sought advice. In considering where she might find support, Otake hoped that favorable comments would come from Simeon R. Acoba Jr., the retired Hawaii Supreme Court associate justice for whom she had clerked, and from former colleagues in Seattle (including Jenny Durkan, the U.S. attorney there, who became Seattle's mayor). She had been active in the Asian bar in Seattle, and she also thought the defense bar in Seattle would support her.

While eager to gather support, she was also cautious about letting people know she was seeking a judgeship. She says that her father's death had made her "more Type A" and she "was worried people would think, 'Who does she think she is?'" She had not been practicing law in Hawaii very long, and she imagined that people would label her a "carpetbagger." Although during her interview with me, Otake did not mention the Hawaii federal district judge who had been appointed just a few years before she was nominated, some local bar members had noted that Otake would be the second nominee in a row who, although born and raised in Hawaii, had practiced law for many years away from Hawaii and then had returned for only a few years before being nominated.

Senator Mazie Hirono and Senator Brian Schatz, both Democrats, had appointed a merit selection committee that interviewed applicants. Otake says, "I had such low expectations about the outcome that I was relaxed" during the merit selection committee interview. She recalls being prepared but "comfortable." She was "completely shocked" to be included on a short list of three candidates that the senators sent to President Obama. When she learned who else was on the list, she concluded that she was "a longer shot than before" because the other two candidates were both extremely well qualified, had more years of practice in Hawaii, and likely had more connections to the community and to the White House.

President Obama did not nominate Otake. Instead, he nominated Clare Connors, a former AUSA who had moved into private practice with a Honolulu firm that focused on representing plaintiffs in civil cases. The other person on the short list was David Louie, who had a long history as a civil litigator in Honolulu and had recently completed serving as Hawaii's attorney general (an appointed position) under a Democratic governor.

Connors was not ultimately confirmed. She was caught in the general slowdown on judicial confirmations as the 2016 presidential election neared.

Following President Trump's election in 2016, Hawaii's senators negotiated a deal with the Trump administration in which the Hawaii district judgeship would be filled by someone from the list that had been sent to President Obama, and in return, the senators would not object to Trump's choice of Mark Bennett, a Republican, for Hawaii's seat on the Ninth Circuit.[133]

Eng recalls hearing that Senator Hirono, a member of the Senate Judiciary Committee, thought the agreed-upon process was that the district judge short list of three candidates would be submitted to the Trump White House, and that anyone from the list could be selected, while Senator Schatz may have thought that Connors would be renominated in the same manner that Trump had renominated a number of other Obama nominees whose nominations had lapsed. According to Eng, the senators' different approaches may have contributed to the White House's decision to take a fresh look at everyone on the short list and to invite Otake to an interview in Washington, DC, with members of the White House Counsel's Office.

Within two weeks of being interviewed in DC, Otake received a call telling her that she was the nominee. She says she was "flabbergasted" to be nominated, and also "very, very excited." She recalls having a raft of questions.

Otake, nominated on December 21, 2017, by President Trump, was described as an "unusual nominee," not only because she came from a list of candidates initially recommended by Democratic senators to a Democratic president, but also because, as noted earlier, "while Otake [was] a native of Hawaii, she ha[d] spent almost all of her legal career practicing, not in her home state, but

Jill Aiko Otake, 2020

in Washington."[134] Still, the expectation was that she "would sail to confirmation."[135] Referring to the months of negotiations with White House Counsel Don McGahn and his staff, Senator Hirono said that the deal showed that meaningful consultation between Congress and the White House could yield agreement on qualified, nonideological nominees.[136]

Otake received a "well qualified" rating from the ABA.[137] She recalls that the ABA evaluator commented that the District of

Hawaii's active district judges were primarily AUSAs. She adds that she learned that someone had accused her of having had a "screaming match" with opposing counsel, which confused her because she had never done such a thing. A friend who was involved in vetting Otake for the ABA thought that the commenter might have mistaken Otake for another Asian woman.

Because Trump had been criticized for the lack of diversity in his judicial nominees, Otake surmises that being an Asian woman may have helped her to be nominated and confirmed. She says, "I always viewed being from a community of color as something that would help me." With Republicans in control of the Senate, Otake was confirmed by voice vote on August 1, 2018, about seven months after Trump nominated her.[138]

Thinking about others who might be considering seeking judgeships, Otake sees "no singular path" to a federal judgeship. "So much of it is timing and luck," she notes. Given the uncertain effect of politics on any particular nomination, she counsels, "Try to be a trial attorney if you want to be a federal district judge."

15
Neomi Jehangir Rao
(DC Cir.) (2019)

Born 1973 in Detroit, Michigan

Federal Judicial Service:
Judge, U.S. Court of Appeals for the District of Columbia Circuit
Nominated by Donald J. Trump on January 23, 2019, to a seat vacated
   by Brett M. Kavanaugh. Confirmed by the Senate on March 13,
   2019, and received commission on March 18, 2019.

Education:
Yale University, BA, 1995
University of Chicago Law School, JD, 1999

Professional Career:
Law clerk, Hon. J. Harvie Wilkinson III, U.S. Court of Appeals for
   the Fourth Circuit, 1999–2000
Counsel for nominations and constitutional law, U.S. Senate Com-
   mittee on the Judiciary, 2000–2001
Law clerk, Hon. Clarence Thomas, Supreme Court of the United
   States, 2001–2002
Private practice, London, United Kingdom, 2002–2005
Associate counsel and special assistant to President George W. Bush,
   2005–2006
Professor, Antonin Scalia Law School, George Mason University,
   2006–2019; director and founder, Center for the Study of the
   Administrative State, 2015–2017
Administrator, Office of Information and Regulatory Affairs, Office
   of Management and Budget, 2017–2019

Other Nominations/Recess Appointments:
Nominated to U.S. Court of Appeals for the District of Columbia
    Circuit, November 14, 2018; no Senate vote[139]

Neomi Jehangir Rao is the first South Asian woman to become a federal court of appeals judge. She is also the first Asian woman who was a Supreme Court law clerk to become an Article III judge. In addition, she is the first Asian woman to become an Article III judge after having been a law clerk at the federal court of appeals level. To date, she is the only Asian woman to become an Article III judge after having a legal career primarily in academia.

During her interview,[140] Rao said that her parents came to the United States from India for what she called the "typical" reason of seeking better opportunities. In 2017, during a hearing before the Senate Homeland Security and Government Affairs Committee in connection with her nomination to be the administrator of the Office of Information and Regulatory Affairs (OIRA), which is part of the Office of Management and Budget, Rao described her parents' experience: "Leaving India in 1972, my parents arrived in Detroit in the middle of a snowstorm without winter jackets, but with their medical degrees, $16, and the optimism of the recently married. They always imparted by example the importance of integrity, perseverance, kindness, and a commitment to service."[141] Rao's parents, who both ended up practicing medicine in the United States, were Zoroastrians. Noting that the term *Parsi* is used for Zoroastrians living in India, Rao said that her parents were descended from people who had moved from Persia to India over a thousand years ago. Rao, the oldest of two children, was born and raised in Michigan.

Rao is Jewish, having converted to Judaism decades ago. She says that she and her husband, a lawyer who is also Jewish, are raising their two children in their religion.

Law was a field that Rao began thinking about as an undergraduate at Yale University. At Yale, she wrote extensively for the *Yale Herald* and the *Yale Free Press*. These college writings, particularly those relating to rape, turned out to figure prominently during her judicial confirmation process.

In a column Rao wrote as editor in chief of the *Yale Free Press* in November 1993, she decried college student groups focusing on perceived "sexual and racial oppression": "The recent hysteria, activism, and coalition-forming that occur[r]ed in relation to the Chicano Dean is just one example of this phenomenon. Myths of sexual and racial oppression prop[a]gate themselves, create hysteria and finally lead to the formation of some whining new group. One can only hope to scream, 'Perspective, just a little perspective, dahling!'"[142] Rao was questioned about this particular piece during her Senate Judiciary Committee hearing in 2019.[143] She explained that there was "a very narrow set of issues on the Yale campus in a specific type of activism and multiculturalism that existed at Yale at that time. And you know, I guess I—you know, I always thought it would be best to have more tolerance and understanding rather than dividing people up into groups."[144]

The context of Rao's piece is made clearer by a separate article that did not figure at all in the hearing—an article she coauthored that outlined concerns about Yale's system of "ethnic deans" for undergraduates.[145] Rao told me that she did not recall that specific article. I was nevertheless interested in it for two reasons. First, I was writing about a group of individuals with three things in common: their jobs, their sex, and their identification as Asian. Rao's article on "ethnic deans" discussed race. Second, Rao's comments about Yale's faculty form a kind of counterpoint to Lucy Koh's advocacy for greater diversity in Harvard Law School's faculty.

Rao's article described Yale's "ethnic deans" as having been appointed to serve as "a more sympathetic and understanding ear for grievances like suspected racism, which students may feel uncomfortable explaining to their dean or master."[146] According to the article, opponents of the deanships were arguing that "the need of a separate voice in the administration for selected ethnic groups hardly seems justified."[147] It goes on to say, "If non-minority students at Yale have no particular voice except, perhaps, for their [Yale College Council] representative, why should each collective of ethnic students receive a professional, faculty representative? Concern about quality teaching, student life and college housing are, after all, shared by every undergraduate, the critics say."[148]

An article that was the subject of discussion after Rao was nominated[149] was one that she wrote for the *Washington Times* as an undergraduate:

> Welcome to the multicultural college campus.
>
> Here you will be defined by your race, gender, ethnicity and sexual orientation even before you enroll in classes. The labels come quickly and stick hard.
>
> Arriving at Yale three years ago, I thought diversity on campus would mean that racial and gender differences would be taken in stride. I thought wrong.
>
> Though the bean counters consider me a minority (Asian Indian, if you're curious), I find myself in the awkward position of not considering my race and gender very important. To the "multicultural police" this means I'm a "traitor." According to them, I'm supposed to be out there marching to "take back the night," demonstrating for more Asian-American deans or throwing myself on the ground, covered with ketchup, to protest the mistreatment of Haitian refugees. Unfortunately, these preachers of tolerance apparently cannot tolerate a minority woman who claims an identity independent of race and gender.
>
> . . .
>
> Instead of marching to "take back the night," reading "My Tongue" or fasting in a cage for Haitians, those truly concerned with tolerance should be fighting for individuals who want to escape the multicultural nightmare.[150]

While explaining during her Senate Judiciary Committee hearing the context of her writings from decades ago, Rao said that "to be honest, you know, looking back at some of those writings and rereading them I cringe at some of the language that I used, and you know, I was young."[151] She added that "in the intervening two decades I like to think that I have matured as a thinker and writer and indeed, as a person."[152] This was not an explanation that she tied directly to the writings quoted previously; rather, it was a general statement about her Yale-related writings.

Between completing her undergraduate studies and entering law school, Rao wrote for the *Weekly Standard*, a conservative political magazine. She told me during her interview, "I've always been interested in government. I studied political philosophy and political theory as an undergraduate, so law school seemed like a natural extension of that."

After law school, Rao clerked for J. Harvie Wilkinson III on the Fourth Circuit, worked with the Senate Judiciary Committee (including on judicial nominations), and then clerked for Clarence Thomas on the U.S. Supreme Court. She spent a few years in private practice in London, worked in the White House Counsel's Office in President George W. Bush's administration, and then joined the faculty at what became the Antonin Scalia Law School of George Mason University. Her longest employment was at George Mason, where she stayed for more than a decade. Her most recent employment before becoming a judge was as the administrator of the OIRA under President Trump. Her position at OIRA brought her into contact with Donald McGahn while he was Trump's White House counsel.

Having previously worked on judicial nominations and confirmations, Rao says that she "knew enough about the process" not to automatically think that she would become a judge. She attributes her own judgeship to "timing, circumstances, and luck." She says that she had a good relationship with McGahn and recalls that when Brett Kavanaugh was elevated from the DC Circuit to the Supreme Court, she and McGahn discussed "the possibility of my being nominated." She did not know of other individuals being considered, although she assumed that others expressed interest. Rao shared her discussions about a possible nomination with only her family and most trusted friends.

One commentator noted, "Unlike other lower court nominees, Rao had a personal interview with President Trump on October 12, 2018."[153] Vincent Eng of NAPABA thought the unusual interview occurred because Rao might have been identified as a possible Supreme Court nominee.[154] She was clearly on a fast track, although it turned out that President Trump named Amy Coney Barrett rather than Rao to fill the next Supreme Court vacancy, which opened up in 2020.

Rao was nominated to the DC Circuit on November 14, 2018, before the ABA had given her a rating. Her nomination was announced by President Trump the day before, at the White House celebration of Diwali, the Hindu Festival of Lights.[155] With her nomination came advice, support, and assistance from a host of individuals and various organizations. She recalls that NAPABA reached out to her and was helpful, and the North American South Asian Bar Association also provided support.

NAPABA issued a press release applauding Rao's nomination.[156] Vincent Eng recalls that the Trump administration indicated that supporting op-eds by NAPABA would also be helpful to Rao. Eng tried to organize op-eds for placement in publications, but he says that he ran into questions within NAPABA about which members' names belonged on the pieces. Eng said it was unfortunate that, because this was never resolved, op-eds ended up not being submitted at all.

A nominee for an Article III position in the District of Columbia has no home-state senator to rely on to champion her candidacy. Of course, at the same time, the nominee does not need to worry about whether a home-state senator will return a blue slip, the Senate Judiciary Committee's document signifying a senator's support for a nomination (the absence of which can kill a nomination). Rao met with a number of senators, including Majority Leader Mitch McConnell of Kentucky, Senate Judiciary Committee chair Lindsey Graham of South Carolina, Mike Lee of Utah (whom Rao knew from prenomination interactions), and Marsha Blackburn of Tennessee. These meetings were arranged through the Department of Justice. To Rao's understanding, the choice of senators was not always linked to a senator's position in the Senate hierarchy. Instead, she says, the selection of whom she should meet with was "largely driven by the interest of the senators."

Although Rao never heard that her gender or race played a role in her nomination or confirmation, she notes that in every administration, there is "always an effort to find qualified candidates who share a president's judicial philosophy who are not White men."

Rao says that there had been some hope that, with her nomination coming in November, she might get a hearing before the Senate Judiciary Committee in December, but that did not occur. Her nomination lapsed, and Trump renominated her on January 23, 2019. A majority of the ABA committee gave her a "well qualified" rating, with a minority giving her a "qualified" rating.[157] Rao then waited less than two weeks for a hearing before the Senate Judiciary Committee. She recognized that in getting a hearing on February 5, 2019, she was leaping ahead of other nominees who had been waiting longer. She attributed this rapid timing to the priority that Senator Mitch McConnell, the Senate majority leader, had placed on filling the DC Circuit vacancy. Courts of appeals are just one step below the Supreme Court, and the DC Circuit is often viewed as a particularly important court of appeals because of the nature of the cases that are filed in that court.

Rao had a lengthy paper trail for members of the Senate Judiciary Committee to examine, not only in the form of her college writings, but also in later pieces, some written before or after law school but many written during her career as an academic. Academics nominated for judgeships invariably face scrutiny of what some view as controversial positions taken in their writings. In this regard, Rao was hardly alone. Such scrutiny occurred by Republicans opposed to Obama's nomination of Goodwin Liu to the Ninth Circuit, for example. That Democrats scrutinized Rao's writings was to be expected.

Particular attention was paid to Rao's college writings on sexual assault. She had written that a male student who forced a woman to have sex against her will should be held responsible, but "at the same time, a good way to avoid a potential date rape is to stay reasonably sober."[158] Questioned about whether she was victim-blaming, Rao told Senator Kamala Harris, a Democrat from California, "Senator, I was only trying to make the common sense observation about the relationship between drinking and becoming a victim."[159] Senator Joni Ernst, a Republican from Iowa, asked Rao about an April 1993 article she had written about feminism. That article began, "I am a feminist. But what does that mean? As a movement, feminism has failed to provide women with a coherent set of beliefs."[160] The article, which goes on for more than thirty paragraphs, went on to note, "Camille Paglia's view on date rape has often been criticized for its insensitivity because she seems to 'blame the victim.' Paglia, however, accurately describes the dangerous feminist idealism which teaches women that they are equal. Women falsely believe that they should be able to go anywhere with anyone."[161] Having earlier emphasized that the rapist is "of course at fault," Rao responded to a question about her reference to "the dangerous feminist idealism" by saying, "I very much regret that statement and I've always believed strongly in the equality of women and men, and for equal rights and opportunities for women. I'm honestly not sure why I wrote that in college."[162]

After her hearing before the Senate Judiciary Committee, Rao sent a letter to the committee saying that in college, "I failed to recognize the hurt that my words could cause a survivor of such crimes. I recognize now the arguments I made might discourage a victim from coming forward or seeking help. . . . If I were to address these issues now, I would have more empathy and perspective."[163]

Rao was also questioned about more recent writings in which she posited that laws banning dwarf tossing infringed on the dignity of individuals who wanted to determine for themselves whether to earn a living by agreeing to be tossed.[164] Noting that an individual had objected to the ban on the ground that he was prepared and willing to be tossed, she had written that such a choice was analogous to a choice by a woman to earn a living through prostitution.[165] The other topics that senators questioned Rao about included her views on deregulation and specific matters that OIRA, which she headed, worked on.

Rao says that, to respond to the many questions she faced, she worked with attorneys in the Department of Justice and White House Counsel's Office. Concerns were raised not only by Democratic senators. Some Republican senators also raised concerns about Rao on various grounds. For example, Senator Josh Hawley, a Republican from Missouri, and Senator Tom Cotton, a Republican from Arkansas, worried that Rao might not be on the same page with them in opposing abortion. An attempt to help Rao came from a powerful source: the Supreme Court's Clarence Thomas, for whom Rao had spent a year as a law clerk. Justice Thomas reportedly spoke to Senator Hawley and Senator Tim Scott from South Carolina to support Rao.[166]

Justice Thomas is known for lending his support to selected embattled nominees. I recall hearing from a judge nominated by President William Clinton that Justice Thomas had been helpful. Indeed, the *Washington Post* noted, "Thomas, famously taciturn during oral arguments at the high court, has previously worked in private in support of other judicial nominees. In the 1990s, he intervened or offered to help several stalled African American judicial candidates, including those nominated by Democrats, according to several black judges interviewed by *The Washington Post* in 2004."[167] Besides having to respond to senators' questions, Rao faced criticism in the press and on legal blogs,[168] while various commentators came to her defense.[169]

Rao notes that what helped her get through the process was her familiarity with it, the result of her prior work with the Senate Judiciary Committee and the White House Counsel's Office, and the support of her family and friends. She thinks that her earlier work experience with nominees might have made her "maybe better prepared for it than other nominees," but she says, "Still, it is different when you're the nominee." She says that she recognized that "you need a thick skin," and she concludes, "My skin got a bit thicker."

With Republicans holding a Senate majority, Rao was confirmed on a roll call vote of 53–46 just a little over a month after her Senate Judiciary Committee hearing.[170] All the Republican senators voted "yea," and all the Democratic senators (except one senator listed as "not voting") voted "nay."[171] Rao was sworn in by Justice Thomas, an event reported by the media in India.[172]

Neomi Jehangir Rao. Photo by Robin Reid.

Rao advises anyone interested in a federal judgeship to learn as much as possible about what the position entails. She identifies clerking for a judge as the best way to do that, especially clerking at the level of court on which you are interested in serving. She notes that her own experience as an academic also helped prepare her for being an appellate judge because academia involves the substantive work of research and writing that appeals also require. She noted that an appellate court involves a more sequestered setting than other legal jobs, and not everyone is "dispositionally suited to being a judge."

She says that an applicant needs to be "ready for your life to be opened up and scrutinized." An applicant also needs to realize that becoming a judge involves "a fair amount of serendipity." While becoming a judge is "not just luck," there are many deserving candidates who never become judges. She therefore advises against spending one's entire life trying to become a judge.

Continuing Growth

This book by no means reflects the end of Asian women's addition to Article III ranks. I discuss only the first fifteen Asian women to become Article III judges, and while I was writing this book, more Asian women became Article III judges. Unfortunately, as explained in the Introduction, I could not interview the sixteenth judge, Martha Maria Pacold of the Northern District of Illinois. Pacold was included in President Donald Trump's 2020 additions to his list of potential U.S. Supreme Court nominees.[173]

Nor did the timing allow me to interview the seventeenth and eighteenth judges—Trump nominee Diane Gujarati, confirmed in September 2020 to the Eastern District of New York, and Joe Biden nominee Regina Marie Rodriguez, confirmed in June 2021 to the District of Colorado. With Gujarati's appointment, the Eastern District of New York joined the District of Hawaii in having three Asian woman district judges. I include here the Federal Judicial Center biographies for Pacold and Gujarati (but not for Rodriguez, whose biography came out on the eve of this book's publication).

Martha Maria Pacold

Born 1979 in Richmond, Virginia

Federal Judicial Service:
Judge, U.S. District Court for the Northern District of Illinois

Nominated by Donald J. Trump on May 21, 2019, to a seat vacated by John W. Darrah. Confirmed by the Senate on July 31, 2019, and received commission on August 16, 2019.

Education:
Indiana University, BA, 1999
University of Chicago Law School, JD, 2002

Professional Career:
Law clerk, Hon. A. Raymond Randolph, U.S. Court of Appeals for the District of Columbia Circuit, 2002–2003
Law clerk, Hon. Jay S. Bybee, U.S. Court of Appeals for the Ninth Circuit, 2003–2004
Law clerk, Hon. Clarence Thomas, Supreme Court of the United States, 2004–2005
Counsel to the attorney general, U.S. Department of Justice, 2005–2006
Special assistant U.S. attorney, Eastern District of Virginia, 2006–2007
Private practice, Chicago, Illinois, 2007–2017
U.S. Department of the Treasury, 2017–2019; executive secretary, 2017; deputy general counsel, 2017–2019

Other Nominations/Recess Appointments:
Nominated to U.S. District Court for the Northern District of Illinois, June 11, 2018; no Senate vote[174]

Diane Gujarati

Born 1969 in New York, New York

Federal Judicial Service:
Judge, U.S. District Court for the Eastern District of New York
Nominated by Donald J. Trump on May 21, 2019, to a seat vacated by John Gleeson. Confirmed by the Senate on September 10, 2020, and received commission on September 18, 2020.

Education:
Barnard College, BA, 1990
Yale Law School, JD, 1995

Professional Career:
Law clerk, Hon. John M. Walker Jr., U.S. Court of Appeals for the
    Second Circuit, 1995–1996
Private practice, New York City, 1996–1999
Assistant U.S. attorney, Southern District of New York, 1999–2020
Deputy chief, Appeals Unit, Criminal Division, 2006–2008
Deputy chief, White Plains Division, 2008–2010
Chief, White Plains Division, 2010–2012
Deputy chief, Criminal Division, 2012–2020
Adjunct professor of clinical law, New York University School of
    Law, 2015–2018

Other Nominations/Recess Appointments:
Nominated to U.S. District Court for the Eastern District of New York,
    September 13, 2016; no Senate vote
Nominated to U.S. District Court for the Eastern District of New York,
    May 15, 2018; no Senate vote[175]

As I was working on this book, R. Shireen Matthews, nominated by President Trump to the Southern District of California on
October 17, 2019,[176] was awaiting confirmation, but the congressional session ended without her being confirmed. As this book nears
publication, other Asian women have been nominated by President
Biden. Florence Y. Pan has been nominated to a district judgeship
in the District of Columbia. Tana Lin has been nominated to the
Western District of Washington. Angel Kelley has been nominated
to the District of Massachusetts, and Sarala Vidya Nagala has been
nominated to the District of Connecticut. Doubtless there are Asian
women even now seeking nomination to Article III positions. Their
stories may become the stuff of someone else's future project.

PART III

Analyzing the Data

Certain features about the fifteen judges I have profiled leap off the page. Other similarities and contrasts have to be teased out. In this part, in addition to comparing the judges' experiences, I look at the impact of being Asian women on those experiences.

I have broken this analysis into four sections.

First, I examine the timing of the increase in the number of Asian women who have become Article III judges.

Second, I examine a number of demographic factors. Some can be measured entirely by numbers (e.g., particular ethnic backgrounds, the locations of the judges, ages), while others require something more than statistics.

Third, I single out some factors I describe as "attitudinal." This discussion looks at some recurring personality traits I identified among the fifteen judges I profiled.

Fourth, I compare the fifteen judges to a small group of Asian women who appear very much like them but who are not Article III judges, in order to see whether I can identify specific factors that appear to have contributed to who became a judge.

Timing of Growth

Women in general were not admitted to law school in significant numbers until the 1970s, after the passage of civil rights laws. The number of women law students increased greatly in the 1980s.[1] By 2018, as I have noted in part 1, women made up more than half the lawyers in the United States. I went to law school from 1978 to 1981 and was part of the growth in women law students. Although there were certainly Asian women lawyers practicing years before I passed the bar, I was part of a significant increase in their numbers. It took until the 1990s for the increased number of Asian women who went to law school in the late 1970s and in the 1980s to have practiced long enough to be considered for federal judgeships. In the last dozen years, when most of the fifteen judges profiled here were appointed, Asian women were numerous enough to be part of the applicant pool in many federal districts.

The timing of recent Asian immigration trends may also have affected when Asian women joined the pool of judicial applicants. Around the time that Barack Obama was elected president in 2008, the children of the immigrants who fled Vietnam in the 1970s had been lawyers long enough to think about seeking judgeships. Similarly, the daughters of recent Korean, Filipino, and South Asian immigrants were reaching a good age to apply.

Also significant is the role the National Asian Pacific American Bar Association (NAPABA) played. With the exception of Cathy Bissoon (the "secret Asian"), all the judges I profile here had support from NAPABA as they made their way through confirmation. NAPABA existed before I was nominated, of course,

163

and even before I came on the scene, the association was working to increase the number of Asian Article III judges. Those efforts became more focused around the time President Obama was elected. By then, the number of Asian candidates for federal judgeships was growing, and NAPABA was savvy enough to see how to capitalize on having a president who was interested in diversifying the judiciary, while also having NAPABA members in the administration eager to help in that regard. Following in the footsteps of Susan Davies, Chris Kang, working with Vincent Eng and John Yang, was focused on increasing diversity in Article III ranks, as was his successor, Margaret Whitney. It is, in short, no accident that the growth occurred when it did. The growth spiked under President Obama, as I detail later.

It is probably true that some of the fifteen judges might have been confirmed even without NAPABA's help. But some of them might not have been. Pamela Chen, for example, attributes her nomination to insights she got from Robert Raben about a case involving Judge John Gleeson, and Chen and Raben connected through the efforts of Vincent Eng. Jennifer Choe-Groves was identified as a potential candidate for the Court of International Trade by members of NAPABA, who reached out to her. While it is not always possible to point to NAPABA as having been essential to a particular candidate's success, the association has clearly become, over the past dozen years or so, an influential participant in the process of getting individuals through nomination and confirmation.

Demographic Factors

Particular Asian Ethnicities

The most obvious distinction among the fifteen judges is their Asian heritage. The Pan-Asian category includes a large number of ethnicities, and the judges' Asian backgrounds clearly differ. Women of Japanese ancestry (Susan Mollway, Kiyo Matsumoto, Leslie Kobayashi, Karen Scholer, and Jill Otake, in order of appointment) occupy a third of the fifteen. South Asian women (Cathy Bissoon, Indira Talwani, and Neomi Rao) have three seats. There are also three Chinese judges (Dolly Gee, Miranda Du, and Pamela Chen), with Du listed twice, being Vietnamese on her mother's side and ethnic Chinese on her father's side. Vietnamese women (Jacqueline Nguyen and Du) and Korean women (Lucy Koh and Jennifer Choe-Groves) hold two seats each, and there is one woman of Filipino ancestry (Lorna Schofield).

The appointments of women with particular Asian backgrounds are clearly not proportional to their percentages in the general population. For example, even though a third of the fifteen Asian women judges are of Japanese background, people of Japanese ancestry make up less than 5 percent of Asians in the United States.[2] Three of the Asian women judges of Japanese ancestry are from the District of Hawaii, which has a total population of about 1,420,500 that is about 38 percent Asian (534,600).[3] About a third of that 38 percent is of Japanese ancestry, exceeded within the Asian population only by those of Filipino ancestry.[4] Attorneys of Japanese ancestry make up 12.6 percent of Hawaii's bar, with women of Japanese ancestry occupying about 5.2 percent.[5]

When Kobayashi and I were appointed, Hawaii's senior senator was Daniel Inouye, who is of Japanese ancestry. With my own appointment, I had the sense that Senator Inouye was pleased at the thought that a child of a 442nd Infantry veteran would become an Article III judge. When Otake was appointed, Mazie Hirono, also of Japanese ancestry, not only was one of Hawaii's senators; she was on the Senate Judiciary Committee. Of course, Senators Inouye and Hirono have also championed non-Japanese candidates, including non-Asian candidates, so no one should conclude that they considered Japanese ethnicity a prerequisite for their support.

If people of Asian backgrounds were appointed in proportion to their percentages in the Asian population of the United States, there would be more judges of Chinese background, as individuals of Chinese background make up about 24 percent of the nation's Asian population.[6] Within the nation's total Asian population, Chinese are followed closely by Asian Indians. Filipinos and the "Other Asian" categories have more than 15 percent each. Vietnamese constitute more than 10 percent, and Koreans are close to 8 percent, with Japanese being more than 4 percent.[7]

Three of the fifteen Asian women judges I study, or about 20 percent, are of Chinese background. Gee is in California, where, according to the most recent census data I consulted, about 28 percent of the Asian population is of Chinese ancestry.[8] Du is in Nevada, where about 16 percent of the Asian population is Chinese and about 7 percent is Vietnamese (with Asians making up a little more than 8 percent of the state's total population).[9] Finally, Chen is in New York, where about 42 percent of the Asian population is of Chinese ancestry.[10] Especially for someone seeking to become a district judge, the racial makeup of the individual's state typically matters more than national figures for race. That is because, for most district courts, an individual needs to have the support of the senators from the applicant's state. Senators have considerable influence in recommendations to a district court, which, unlike a federal circuit court, operates entirely within a state's borders (although a few district courts, such as the district courts in Puerto Rico and the District of Columbia, are not within any state and therefore have no assigned senators). Senators may consider the political benefits to themselves of recommending to the president a member of a specific constituency that they focus on.

That there are not more judges of Chinese ancestry is notable not only because Chinese form the largest Asian group in the country but also because Chinese immigration to the United States preceded immigration from other parts of Asia. There was significant immigration from China in the late 1800s, as workers came to the United States to work on the transcontinental railroads.[11] The Chinese Exclusion Act of 1882 and its extension limited Chinese immigration for decades, but all exclusion acts were eventually repealed in 1943. Then, in the decades beginning in 1980 and 2010, there was significant immigration from China.[12]

Japanese immigration to the United States was at its height in the early 1900s,[13] especially in Hawaii, where Japanese men came to work in the sugarcane and pineapple fields. This length of time in the United States partly explains the number of Asian women who are Article III judges of Japanese ancestry. I, for example, would be considered *sansei*, meaning the third generation of my family in the United States (but the second generation of people born in the United States).

Koreans immigrated in significant numbers between the 1970s and around 2000, with peak numbers in the 1980s.[14] Vietnamese, South Asians, and Filipinos immigrated in significant numbers between the 1970s and around 2010, with Vietnamese peaking in the 1980s and South Asians and Filipinos peaking between 2000 and 2009.[15]

Talwani noted during her interview that South Asians were being appointed to Article III judgeships in numbers greater than might be expected, given how recent their significant immigration to the United States has been. As the statistics presented here indicate, people of Chinese ancestry are appointed in disappointingly low numbers, especially taking into account the fact that, of all Asian groups, Chinese have been in the United States in significant numbers for the longest time.

Of course, none of the Article III judges of Chinese ancestry that I profile in this book had the advantage of the long history of Chinese in the United States. Gee and Chen are the daughters of immigrants from China, and Du herself emigrated from Vietnam.

It bears noting that immigrants from India, the Philippines, and Trinidad came from English-speaking countries. English-language ability is far less common when immigrants arrive from China, Japan, Korea, or Vietnam. Bissoon, whose mother came from Trinidad, remarked that immigrants coming directly from India are often financially comfortable. Alternatively, as with Rao's parents, they arrive from India already well educated. These factors may have been advantages that have contributed to the number of South Asians (including men) appointed in recent years to the bench.

Five (Bissoon, Schofield, Talwani, Scholer, and Otake) of the fifteen Asian women judges I include here are of mixed race, with Bissoon having an Asian mother and a Latino father, Schofield and Scholer having Asian mothers and White fathers, and Talwani and Otake having White mothers and Asian fathers. Du is entirely Asian, but with a Vietnamese mother and an ethnically Chinese father.

The diversity among Asians makes it difficult to attribute a particular characteristic to a particular subset of the Asian community. What is clear is that race (and possibly, in some instances, ethnicity) likely played a role in the appointments of the fifteen judges. All Article III appointments are political, but rarely can one measure with precision how much weight to give to one specific factor. It is perhaps easiest to estimate that weight when the divergence between the general population and the makeup of the judiciary has become so stark that calls have gone out to add a particular demographic to the bench. Earlier in this book, I cited examples of California state and federal judges who pointed out the need for Asian judges. So far, I am not aware of widespread public calls for particular Asian ethnicities, but that could conceivably occur.

Something I found immensely interesting was how many of the fifteen judges were the children of immigrants. Eleven (Nguyen, Gee, Koh, Bissoon, Du, Schofield, Chen, Talwani, Choe-Groves, Scholer, and Rao) are the children of immigrants. Two (Nguyen and Du) of those eleven are themselves immigrants; they left homogeneously Asian Vietnam for a very diverse country. Schofield and Scholer had mothers who immigrated to the United States and fathers who were born in the United States.

Only four of us (Mollway, Matsumoto, Kobayashi, and Otake) were born to two parents born in the United States. These four also happen to be of Japanese ancestry. All four had one or more parents with graduate degrees. My father was a lawyer; Matsumoto's father was an architect and university professor; Kobayashi and Otake had fathers who were dentists; and Otake's mother returned to school and earned a master's degree. Higher education was in our family backgrounds. This was true for many of the judges with immigrant parents, but not all. For example, Bissoon was the first in her family to go to college, and Scholer was the first in her father's family to complete a college degree.

When so many members of the group share a feature as formative as having an immigrant parent, it is hard to overlook the significance of that feature. Nguyen recalled seeing how powerless her parents felt in the United States, and that greatly influenced her in empowering herself by becoming a lawyer. Parents are authority figures in most homes, after all, and immigrant children with better facility in English than their parents may see their parents' authority diminished outside the home. Gee expressly recognized the importance to her own development of seeing the difficulties that her parents faced as immigrants. She noted that helping her mother, who became a garment worker in the United States, navigate through life in this country inspired her to become a lawyer and to advocate for workers' rights. She also was influenced by a desire to honor her parents' sacrifices and struggles. Du recalls thinking of law as a profession that "gave voice" to people, particularly immigrants. Being an immigrant or the child of immigrants appears to have understandably had a huge impact on the career paths of many of these judges.

Choe-Groves recalled that even when she was very young her father asked her to review his patent applications before he submitted them to the in-house lawyer in the company where he worked. This impressed on her the importance of protecting one's own creations long before she formally studied intellectual property, but it also meant that her father trusted her to improve what he had written so that he would not be embarrassed.

The judges whose parents spoke English before arriving in the United States may have had a different experience from those whose parents did not arrive speaking English. Bissoon, Talwani, and Rao, for example, did not report needing to help their parents with language. Bissoon, however, recounted her blue-collar upbringing, and Rao has spoken about the inspiration provided her by her parents, who arrived in the United States with medical degrees but nearly penniless.

The reasons that their parents immigrated to this country may also have affected the judges. For some, their parents immigrated for economic opportunity, while Nguyen and Du were fleeing the aftermath of the Vietnam War and saw their parents' stature in the community change upon arrival in the United States. Chen's parents became stranded in the United States after the Communists defeated Chiang Kai-shek.

Some of the judges' parents who immigrated to the United States were the products of what has been called *hyper-selectivity*. This concept "takes into account the *dual* positive immigrant selectivity, in which an immigrant group boasts not only a higher percentage of college graduates compared with nonmigrants from their country of origin but also a higher percentage of college graduates compared with the general population in the host country."[16] Rao's parents, who both had medical degrees when they immigrated, come quickly to mind.

It appears to me that most of the judges who were the children of immigrants and saw their parents' vulnerabilities were focused on making sure that they were not as vulnerable as their parents had been.

Geography

The fifteen Article III judges in this book are concentrated for the most part in states with significant Asian populations. Three states—Hawaii, California, and New York—have multiple Asian women who are Article III judges.

The entire state of Hawaii is a single judicial district, so all three judges there (Mollway, Kobayashi, and Otake) sit on the same district court. This is not the same for New York or California.

Four of the fifteen Asian women sit in Article III positions on courts based in New York. Two of the New York judges (Matsumoto and Chen) are in the Eastern District of New York, while one (Schofield) is in the Southern District of New York. Matsumoto and Chen have been recently joined by Diane Gujarati, the seventeenth Asian woman to become an Article III judge. Choe-Groves sits on the Court of International Trade, which handles the entire country's international trade cases; it has its courthouse in New York City but can sit anywhere in the United States.

California is home to three Asian women who are Article III judges—one circuit judge (Nguyen on the Ninth Circuit, which includes Alaska, Arizona, California, Hawaii, Idaho, Montana, Nevada, Oregon, Washington, Guam, and the Northern Marianas), one judge (Gee) in the Central District of California, and one (Koh) in the Northern District of California.

Each of the other judges sits as the only Asian woman in her state (or, in the case of Rao, in her circuit) who is an Article III judge (Bissoon in the Western District of Pennsylvania, Du in the District of Nevada, Talwani in the District of Massachusetts, Scholer in the Northern District of Texas, and Rao on the DC Circuit).

That Hawaii, New York, and California have multiple Asian women Article III judges reflects their larger Asian populations. As already noted, about 38 percent of Hawaii's population is

Asian,[17] about 15 percent of California's population is Asian,[18] and about 8.5 percent of New York's population is Asian.[19]

Quite apart from the location of their courts, the places where the judges grew up are notable. Four judges spent parts of their youth in the South. Matsumoto says she stuck out as Asian while living as a child in North Carolina. Similarly, Koh, who was greatly influenced by her experiences in Mississippi, was one of only a few Asians as a child. Du's family settled for a while in Alabama, where Asians, not to mention Vietnamese, were scarce. Scholer went to school in Dallas and recalls with regret not wanting her mother to draw attention to herself by speaking Japanese.

The judges raised in the South were not alone in standing out in communities with few Asians. For instance, Schofield recalled not having a Filipino community around her in Indiana.

By contrast, those of us who grew up in communities with large Asian populations did not, as children, have the daily consciousness of sticking out because we were Asian, and seeing ourselves as judges may not have been as large a stretch as it may have been for others.

One additional point about geography bears mentioning. Judges are usually appointed to courts in locations in which they have practiced law. This is not a legal requirement, and occasionally judges are nominated to sit on courts that they have no prior connection to. In those instances, the bar association in the affected jurisdiction may object on the ground that there are competent candidates who are familiar with and known to local lawyers and judges. Otake's concern about being dubbed a "carpetbagger" in her candidacy was an offshoot of this phenomenon. Sometimes a court has several divisions, or what certain districts (like the District of New Jersey) call "vicinages." Du, for example, was originally assigned to the Las Vegas courthouse of the District of Nevada, with the understanding that she could later move to the Reno courthouse.

For the most part, the fifteen judges did not face major relocation when they became Article III judges. This geographical circumstance was a benefit that women in other professions do not always enjoy. Especially when women have spouses or partners with their own careers, having to relocate for a job can involve what has been called the *two-body problem*—the problem of whether the woman can feasibly relocate for her own advancement when the spouse or partner may lose career opportunities upon relocation.[20] When a man has a two-body problem, the woman may more commonly be expected to relocate than the other way around. Fortunately for the fifteen judges, this geographical concern did not hold them back.

Age

Most of the fifteen judges were appointed in their late forties or early fifties. Seven were appointed in their forties (Mollway, Nguyen, Koh, Du, Choe-Groves, Otake, and Rao), with four in their mid- to late forties and three in their early forties. Seven were appointed in their fifties (Matsumoto, Gee, Kobayashi, Bissoon, Schofield, Chen, and Talwani), and one judge (Scholer) was appointed in her early sixties.

This concentration of ages between forty-five and fifty-five is not unusual among Article III appointees in general. Presidents often seek nominees who are likely to serve for many years, extending the presidents' legacies. At the same time, most nominees have practiced long enough to have earned good reputations in the community and to pass muster when rated by the American Bar Association (ABA).

The age at which a judge is appointed may also be reflected in her family situation. Some of the judges (Gee and Chen) did not have children, but most of them did. Some of them had children who were relatively young at the time the judges took office. Some (Du and Otake) had helped raise stepchildren. Probably because of their ages when they applied to be Article III judges, none of the fifteen judges reported having gone through the nomination or confirmation process while pregnant or dealing with an infant. I do not, however, conclude from this that the judges would have refrained from applying if dealing with a pregnancy or an infant.

Judicial openings cannot always be foreseen, and an applicant must be ready to jump in to seize an opportunity. Kobayashi was pregnant when she applied to be a magistrate judge, for example.

Family Structure and Parents' Varied Professions

Six of the fifteen judges grew up as the oldest child (Kobayashi, Bissoon, Choe-Groves, Scholer, Otake, and Rao). Three judges were the youngest (Gee, Koh, and Chen). Five were the second child (Mollway, Matsumoto, Nguyen, Du, and Talwani). Schofield grew up as an only child. Birth order may have affected the judges' ambitions. When I interviewed her, Otake noted that being the oldest child led her to feel driven.

Matsumoto, Nguyen, and I were the only judges who grew up in families of more than three children. We were the first three Asian women to become Article III judges, and all of us were the second children in our families. I was born in 1950, the second of six; Matsumoto was born in 1955, the second of five; and Nguyen was born in 1965, the second of six. Larger families may have been more common decades ago (although Schofield, born in 1956, is an only child, and Scholer, born in 1957, was the elder of two siblings).

Bissoon's biological father was killed when she was only four years old; her mother then married someone she knew from Trinidad, who was the father figure in Bissoon's life. Schofield was raised by a single mother. Otake lost her father when she was twelve.

The judges' families had different professions, with varied incomes. I am the only one with a lawyer as a parent, although seeing my father regularly bring paperwork home actually made me think as a child that I did not want to be a lawyer. The most common profession among the parents of the fifteen judges was that of an educator. Matsumoto and Kobayashi described their mothers as teachers, and five judges (Matsumoto, Koh, Chen, Talwani, and Choe-Groves) had one or both parents teaching at the college level. Choe-Groves's father was a chemist at a private company and an avid inventor. Nguyen's and Du's parents, having fled Vietnam, went on to own their own businesses. Nguyen and Du were clearly influenced by the hardships their parents faced in the United States. Nguyen worked in her father's doughnut shop, and Du helped her father gather cardboard boxes for recycling. Choe-Groves's mother was another entrepreneurial parent who owned several businesses. Kobayashi and Otake had fathers who were dentists, and both of Rao's parents were physicians. Schofield's mother was a pharmacist. Nguyen's mother worked for a time as a dental assistant. Otake's mother was a nurse and then a social worker. While Gee's father became an aerospace engineer, Gee was greatly influenced by her mother, a garment worker, who wanted to ensure that her daughter avoided the hardships garment workers faced. Chen and I each had a parent who worked in the public sector, Chen's father with the Internal Revenue Service and my mother with the Hawaii Department of Labor. Koh's father was a businessman in insurance and real estate. Bissoon's stepfather was an auto glass installer, and her mother worked in retail once Bissoon headed off to college. Scholer's father had a career in sales.

Although every child is affected by family finances, what the judges focused on more than economic circumstances was the impact of parental attitudes. Nguyen, Kobayashi, Du, and Schofield recounted their parents' cautioning them against certain career paths. Du and Schofield talked about their somewhat rebellious responses. Scholer's mother was overtly opposed to Scholer's run for a state judgeship, coming around to supporting her only belatedly. Somehow, these judges overcame their parents' concerns in this regard.

Choe-Groves was encouraged by her mother to seek a judgeship, but for the most part, the judges did not report seeking judgeships based on advice from their parents. This is true even for me; my father, a lawyer, was not the impetus for my judicial application.

The range of family circumstances makes it difficult to identify a particular pattern in the judges' family backgrounds that contributed directly to their decisions to seek Article III judgeships. What seems most likely is that the contribution of those backgrounds was less direct, showing up in the judges' attitudes, which are discussed later in this book.

Political Affiliation

The fifteen judges were appointed by four presidents—two Democrats (William Clinton and Barack Obama) and two Republicans (George W. Bush and Donald Trump).

I was appointed by President Clinton, followed by Matsumoto, appointed by President George W. Bush. President Obama appointed the next ten Asian women (Nguyen, Gee, Koh, Kobayashi, Bissoon, Du, Schofield, Chen, Talwani, and Choe-Groves). President Trump appointed Scholer, Otake, and Rao (and more recently appointed Asian women who were not interviewed for this book).

Although it is sometimes assumed that a judge's political preferences match those of the president who nominated her, this is not always accurate. For example, Choe-Groves was appointed by Obama to fill a Republican seat on the Court of International Trade. Scholer, who ran as a Republican in a partisan judicial election in Texas, was nominated by Obama. She failed to get confirmed then, but later she was nominated by Trump and did get confirmed. A number of judges gave no hint of political affiliation in their Senate questionnaires, and it is hard to say that they were politically aligned with their appointing presidents, particularly because senators of opposing political parties may have influenced the nominations.

Canon 5 of the Code of Conduct for United States Judges, applicable to all Article III judges except Supreme Court justices and to all non–Article III federal judges, provides that a judge should refrain from political activity. Canon 5 includes under the umbrella of "political activity" endorsing or opposing candidates for political office, contributing to political organizations or candidates, and attending events sponsored by political organizations or candidates. The Article III judges who were former magistrate judges were governed by the Code while magistrate judges. Former assistant U.S. attorneys (AUSAs) were also limited in political activities by the Hatch Act. Factors such as these may have contributed to the answer of "none" given by some of the judges on their Senate Judiciary Committee questionnaires when asked about memberships in political parties and roles in campaigns.

Certainly some of the judges did have activities before they became judges that indicated political preferences. Besides the examples listed earlier, Rao was working in the Trump administration and indicated in her questionnaire that she had been a member of groups of lawyers supporting Republican candidates. This means that three judges (Choe-Groves, Scholer, and Rao) indicated Republican connections before they became judges. Five judges (Mollway, Koh, Du, Chen, and Talwani) noted on their questionnaires that in earlier years they had done some volunteer work for Democratic candidates for various state or federal offices. The other seven indicated no political memberships or activities before seeking Article III judgeships. Political connections are therefore not always a prerequisite for appointment, although they clearly did affect some appointments.

Type of Career

The fifteen judges were fairly evenly divided in coming from government jobs or private practice.

Eight went directly from state or federal government jobs to Article III judgeships. Three of the eight (Matsumoto, Kobayashi, and Bissoon) were federal magistrate judges right before becoming Article III judges. Two (Nguyen and Koh) were state court judges; Scholer had been a state court judge but was a private practitioner right before becoming an Article III judge. Two (Chen and Otake) came to the bench from positions as AUSAs, although notably four other judges (Matsumoto, Nguyen, Koh, and Schofield) had at one time been AUSAs. One (Rao) was a federal administrator.

Seven judges (Mollway, Gee, Du, Schofield, Talwani, Choe-Groves, and Scholer) went from private practice to Article III judgeships. However, it bears noting that some of these private practitioners (Schofield, Choe-Groves, and Scholer) had spent parts of their careers in government service, and Schofield had retired from practice before she was nominated.

Five of the judges had been judicial law clerks early in their careers. Gee, Bissoon, and Talwani clerked for federal district judges and then became federal district judges. Otake clerked for a state supreme court justice. Rao, now a federal circuit judge, clerked for a federal circuit judge and then for a U.S. Supreme Court justice. Several judges mentioned that their experiences as clerks gave them some familiarity with the job of a judge. Bissoon recalled thinking as a law clerk that a judge's job was very attractive.

Most of the judges came from litigation backgrounds. I include Gee and Talwani in this category. Although they were more familiar with arbitration than jury trial, they unquestionably practiced in a litigation context. With thirteen of the fifteen judges being trial judges, it makes sense that those who operated at the trial level would be interested in being on a trial court. Nguyen, at the circuit court level, had been a prosecutor and a trial judge. Only Rao, with her academic career and her position as the head of the Office of Information and Regulatory Affairs (OIRA), had no significant litigation experience. Notably, Rao sits on an appellate court, not a trial court. That makes a difference because appellate judges are reviewing decisions by trial judges, not making sometimes instantaneous rulings on what witnesses are allowed to say during trials.

Chris Kang from the Obama administration remarked that many senators expect or prefer candidates who come with prosecutorial experience or who worked in large corporate law firms. None of the fifteen judges had a significant criminal defense or nonprofit practice, although that scarcity is true of judicial nominees in general, not just of those who are Asian women. Nor did any of the fifteen judges spend a majority of her law practice primarily concentrating on scientific or technical issues, although several of them litigated intellectual property lawsuits that may well have required them to become familiar with such issues, particularly if the cases involved patent disputes or copyright issues relating to computer software.

Summarizing the Demographic Characteristics

The characteristic that stands out the most for me is the immigrant status of nearly three-quarters of the judges. I knew that some of them had immigrant parents, but until I studied the data, I had not realized how many of them had grown up with parents who were immigrants. This, coupled with statements by a number of them about how that affected them, is to me a critical thread among most of the members of the cohort.

I have not studied the family backgrounds of all the Asian men who have become Article III judges, but I suspect that within that group, the percentage of those with immigrant parents is equally high. The percentage may even be higher because Asian men were appointed years before I was, making it even likelier that they came from families without long backgrounds in the United States. It would surely be interesting to study the entire group of Article III judges with immigrant parents to trace the influence of this factor. There may be many Latino judges with immigrant parents, and, of course, White and African American judges may also have immigrant parents. Whether that influenced the members of those groups in the same way the Asian women were influenced is beyond the scope of what I discuss in this book.

The fifteen Asian women had varying ethnicities and grew up in various locations. While I have also looked at their ages, their family backgrounds, their political connections, and their legal careers, it is once again difficult to conclude that any factor influenced them in ways unique to Asian women. As the number of Asian women who become federal judges increases, more patterns may become obvious. I look forward to seeing those develop.

Attitudinal Factors

What is not captured in any discussion about demographic characteristics is the role of individual personalities. I noticed that certain attitudes kept recurring. I identified two in particular that are worth singling out, although I do not have enough information to conclude that they are unique to Asians, to women, to judges, or to Asian women who are judges.

Reliance on Encouragement

Many of the judges said that they did not consider applying for an Article III judgeship until others suggested they do so. They had to be invited to imagine themselves as Article III judges, which is particularly notable because many of them had legal practices that involved appearing before Article III judges.

I recognize, naturally, that any concern about not imagining oneself as a judge is by no means limited to women or to Asians. But women of color may have twice the difficulty seeing themselves in powerful positions. Chris Kang of the Obama administration notes that it might be harder for women of color to dream when they do not see many judges who look like them. Having talked to a great number of judicial candidates, he says that White male candidates not uncommonly talk about having wanted to be judges from the time they first read *To Kill a Mockingbird* as teenagers. By contrast, he says, women and minorities tend to wait until later in their careers to consider judgeships, thinking that they need longer résumés to be in the running.

When now-Chief Judge Padmanabhan Srikanth "Sri" Srinivasan of the DC Circuit spoke at the annual NAPABA convention in Kansas City, Missouri, on November 9, 2013, he told a joke that resonated with his audience. At the time, he had only recently been confirmed to a judgeship on the DC Circuit, and there was already buzz around him about a possible future Supreme Court appointment. I remember that he pronounced the crowd of Asian lawyers and judges (including himself) all failures because we were not doctors. The crowd laughed en masse, recognizing the trope that, in Asian families, the highest level of success is becoming a doctor. Part of that attitude lies in the assumed financial security of a career in medicine. Law is a second-best choice.

Srinivasan said at a separate event celebrating women in the law, "Everybody doubts their belonging and worthiness in some measure. I definitely did—and still do. This is just going to be a part of the thing when you're looking out in the world in which everyone isn't like you. It's natural to doubt whether you belong and whether you're worthy, but you do belong and you are worthy."[21]

Encouraging would-be applicants not to doubt their worth is exactly the message that many of the Asian women I interviewed had an express desire to convey. But for many of them, it was not a lesson they had themselves fully absorbed before becoming Article III judges. This is not to say that they thought of themselves as bad lawyers; of course that was not the case. No one applies for an Article III judgeship without thinking that she is good at what she does. The thought that seems to have infected many of these women is that they might not be seen as being good *enough*, or, even if they were good enough, that they were imposters or did not "belong," to use Srinivasan's word.

My own journey to an Article III judgeship began when some attorneys asked me if I was applying to fill an Article III vacancy. At the time, I was well into my career as a civil litigator and was giving no thought to seeking to fill a vacancy that I thought required political connections that I did not see myself as having. That anyone else had identified me as a candidate was surprising and validating.

Matsumoto reported that a sitting judge encouraged her to apply for an Article III position. Even then, she hesitated out of a sense of deference to possible candidates who were senior to her. It was only after another judge said that Article III vacancies were not always available and she might not get chosen anyway that she threw her hat into the ring.

Both Nguyen and Gee had been active in recruiting others for judicial positions without themselves becoming applicants until friends urged them to apply. Gee resisted applying for a very long time until her friend wore her down. When a Ninth Circuit position opened up, Gee and Nguyen encouraged each other to seek elevation to the Ninth Circuit. There was no attempt by either to elbow the other aside.

Koh and Scholer were encouraged by others to seek state court judgeships, which set them on paths that led to Article III judgeships, although Scholer said that becoming a judge was already in her heart. Chen and Schofield were encouraged by friends to seek Article III judgeships.

For her part, Du was so taken aback when Senator Harry Reid said he wanted to submit her name for an Article III position that she exclaimed that she was not qualified. She thought of herself as lacking the "pedigree" that predominated among the Article III judges who preceded her.

Otake was encouraged by Article III judges to consider an Article III judgeship, first in the Western District of Washington, then in the District of Hawaii.

The reliance on outside validation is familiar to me. But these same judges recognize that this self-effacing attitude did not actually serve them well, and they now encourage others to act more confidently.

Gee, for example, says that you should not "step in your own way," even though it is "extremely uncomfortable" to sell yourself. Chen urges Asian attorneys to see themselves as worthy "if you do a good job." Schofield counsels making an asset of anything that makes you different. In short, many of the judges display a consciousness that even though humility is a highly valued trait in many Asian cultures, it can be a detriment when taken to an extreme. When you add being a woman, it is not hard to see the problem, especially when what one is looking at is a federal judiciary that remains dominated by White men.

In that context, Choe-Groves was fortunate to have had a mother who encouraged her to seek a judgeship. This encouragement was intended to put forward an option that would allow her more control over her busy schedule as a mother and practitioner, but the idea had been planted. When Choe-Groves was approached about seeking a seat on the Court of International Trade, she was receptive.

Not all the judges indicated that it was encouragement by others that caused them to seek Article III judgeships. At first I thought that some of them had an inner confidence that not all of us had. In their interviews with me, none of the judges exhibited this in a form I interpreted as arrogance, but some of them seemed not to have needed a spark from outside themselves to cause them to apply to fill vacancies. However, after repeatedly reviewing the materials available to me, I concluded that what I initially saw as a difference in type is really only a difference in timing. Some of the judges may have thought on their own about seeking judgeships, but they then looked to others for advice, validation, and encouragement. It is not clear to me that, without validation and encouragement, they would have proceeded.

Some of the judges may have thought about seeking an Article III judgeship on their own simply because of the positions they were in when an Article III vacancy arose. For example, we can look at the three judges who applied for Article III positions while they were federal magistrate judges. A federal magistrate judge is part of a federal district court and works closely with district judges. It would be entirely natural for a federal magistrate judge to contemplate applying to fill a district judge vacancy. It is not at all surprising that Bissoon did not mention to me needing someone to suggest that, as a magistrate judge, she seek a district court judgeship when faced with a vacancy. But once she had that thought, she sought counsel from the district judge for whom she had clerked. That district judge encouraged her, even though he warned her that the odds might not be in her favor.

As a magistrate judge, Kobayashi received encouragement from the outset, but she never suggested to me that she had not herself mulled over possibly applying even before receiving encouragement. And although Matsumoto also reported receiving encouragement as a magistrate judge and hesitating, her hesitation was not founded on surprise, but rather on deference to more senior magistrate judges who might apply. I thus think that sometimes an applicant's position makes it natural to contemplate an Article III judgeship.

Having been a state court judge might similarly have made it easier to contemplate an Article III judgeship. As already noted, Nguyen was urged to seek a state court judgeship and then was urged to move from her state court position to a federal position, while Koh reported having been encouraged to seek a state court judgeship but did not indicate that she then needed to have a third party generate her interest in an Article III position. Scholer had been a state court judge from whom much was anticipated, so that when she sought an Article III judgeship, it seemed the inevitable outgrowth of what she had previously done. She did not need someone to suggest an Article III judgeship immediately before she applied; others had predicted such a move for her years earlier.

Talwani was in private practice when she learned that Senator Elizabeth Warren had issued an open invitation to applicants to fill a district court position. Senator Warren was clearly not limiting her options to those close to her or to some predetermined, preferred candidate. To Talwani, this meant she had a chance of being chosen. While Talwani did not report that someone else first introduced her to the idea that she herself should seek an Article III judgeship, she did have in her background lawyers known to her who had moved into judicial positions. In particular, she knew Marsha Berzon, who left the very kind of practice Talwani had to become a Ninth Circuit judge. Even if the idea of applying flowed naturally to Talwani from that background, she then turned to Steven Berzon for help.

Experience working with other judicial applicants sometimes might have contributed to the decision to seek a judgeship. Koh had worked on her county bar's vetting of applicants for state judgeships, and Rao had worked with federal judicial applicants. Their experiences may have helped them feel comfortable with the process. But that reaction was not universal. Nguyen and Gee, for example, had recruited judicial candidates, but even though they must have seen that they themselves would be competitive if they applied, it took pushes from outside for them to take that step.

Rao reported that her position as the administrator of the Office of Information and Regulatory Affairs (OIRA) put her in easy contact with Donald McGahn, who was then White House counsel in the Trump administration. After I interviewed Rao, I sought clarification as to whether she, McGahn, or someone else had initiated discussions about a possible Article III judgeship for her, but I was unable to obtain that information.[22]

I stress here that I am not saying that the need for encouragement is somehow unique to Asian women. Any applicant, of any ethnic background or gender, for an Article III judgeship is entering a complicated political process and needs and wants a great deal of support to succeed. But the number of Asian women who reported not having had the initial idea to apply come from themselves is worth noting. It may relate to the dearth of Asian women on the federal bench who could serve as role models, a situation that echoes Rosabeth Moss Kanter's study of how outsiders who join a group may be considered mere tokens until their number reaches a significant percentage in the group. Meera Deo, who studied women of color on law school faculties, noted that, in contrast to women of color, white men were "more direct about both their interest in leadership and pursuit of it." She noted that "they portray themselves as confident in their ability to do the job" and that academic institutions prioritize confidence, to the detriment of competent women who display less confidence.[23]

The depth of this lack of confidence was evident in the choices some of the fifteen judges made at a fairly early age, before they even went to law school. I, for example, opted out of pursuing a

PhD in English literature after reading that only a third of people with that degree ended up using it. I lacked the confidence that I would be in that top one-third. Schofield left her comparative literature studies upon realizing that people at the top of that field had grown up speaking more than one language, while she had only studied second languages. Choe-Groves, a talented pianist, saw herself as not being part of the elite group of performers in constant international demand. Undoubtedly, we told ourselves that we were being realistic, but these decisions reflect concern about not being good enough. At this point, it is to be hoped that the very existence of these fifteen judges may instill confidence in future applicants.

Indefatigable Nature

I became conscious that some of these judges had faced obstacles that echoed what other interviewees had faced. I began separating their reactions to these obstacles into separate categories, but by the end of the interviews, I found that what had seemed like differences were all of a piece. Not all the judges faced obstacles, but among those who did, once they had decided they wanted Article III judgeships, they were, each in her own way, indefatigable in seeking those judgeships. This sense of determination is a counterpoint to the lack of confidence discussed earlier. What may strengthen that determination is judicial applicants' knowledge, surely acquired by the time they are seeking federal judgeships, that they have earned respect within the legal profession.

Early hints of this indefatigable nature showed up in some of the judges' profiles even before they sought Article III judgeships. Nguyen reported that her father counseled her against majoring in English out of worry that those who spoke English at home would always have an advantage over her. Nguyen's response was that, by majoring in English, she would overcome any disadvantage in this regard. Du reported being "rebellious" in choosing to go to law school. Her parents' experiences made them distrustful of governmental institutions like courts, and they tried to discourage her. Schofield initially envisioned a career in comparative literature in spite of what she thought was her mother's preference that she study something likelier to be more practical in terms of earning a living. It was only after her mother died that Schofield switched to law, no longer feeling that she had to maintain independence from her mother's wishes and instead concluding that she did indeed need to be practical.

Scholer reported that when she ran for a state court seat, her mother was "completely unsupportive," thinking that it was unseemly to ask others for campaign contributions and to post signs advertising oneself. Scholer continued her campaign anyway. Her mother came around to supporting her, and Scholer won.

When I turn to the actual process of seeking Article III judgeships, I am impressed that two of the judges faced medical emergencies that they decided would not stop them. Schofield was in chemotherapy when Senator Chuck Schumer's committee notified her that Schumer wanted to submit her name to President Obama. She asked for a week to review her situation and ultimately decided that the chance might not come again and that she would go forward. Talwani had just submitted her application to Senator Elizabeth Warren's committee when she learned that her mother had suffered a ruptured brain aneurysm. She was interviewed by the committee not long after that, having had little in the way of preparation, but she was determined not to let the opportunity go.

Some of the judges had to deal with personal discomfort. Schofield, for example, after initial introductions from NAPABA, had to act as her own ambassador to the Filipino community, seeking support from organizations that understandably questioned why they should spend political capital on her when she had never previously helped them. Trying to win people over under those circumstances was uncomfortable, awkward, and difficult, but Schofield took on the task.

Otake reported worrying about being viewed as a "carpetbagger" by the Hawaii legal community, having spent most of her legal career in the Seattle area and having only recently returned to Hawaii when she applied. AUSAs are not themselves often the story, so inviting this kind of scrutiny must have been daunting.

Like most judicial applicants, the judges I interviewed experienced periods of inaction on their applications, followed by frantic running around on short notice. Gee sent her husband off ahead on their London honeymoon so she could attend a Rose Garden ceremony. Kobayashi flew from Honolulu to her Senate Judiciary Committee hearing in Washington, DC, just a few hours after she had gotten home from a workshop in Santa Fe. Scholer cut short a trip to Japan to attend a meeting in DC with Department of Justice attorneys, and later similarly had to interrupt a trip to Florida.

The most common obstacle was delay. Most of those delays related to political considerations that were not personal to the applicants. Some were caught in confirmation slowdowns that are typical when the president and the Senate majority are from different political parties. As a congressional session neared adjournment and an election loomed, applicants became particularly concerned about their fates. Some of the judges were questioned about specific cases or their ABA ratings. There was often little the applicants could do, but they stuck it out in the face of this uncertainty.

For two of the judges, the delays spanned the administrations of different presidents. Gee was nominated on May 27, 1999, by President Clinton. The Senate had a Republican majority at that time, and as the 2000 election neared, judicial nominees were not getting confirmed at all. Gee's nomination lapsed, something she doubtless anticipated when she had not been confirmed by the late summer of 2000. During the George W. Bush administration, Gee practiced law, apparently giving no further thought to a judgeship. She was persuaded to try again, and President Obama nominated her on August 6, 2009. She was confirmed less than five months later, on December 24, 2009. That she was willing to go through the process again is remarkable.

Scholer's experience went on even longer, beginning with an application in 2007 that did not result in a nomination. Even when she did get nominated, her nomination lapsed, and like Gee, Scholer was not immediately renominated. Instead, during the period after late 2007, she was focused on her state judgeship. Then, in mid-2014, she sought an Article III judgeship again. Two nominations ensued. The first, which did not proceed to confirmation, was by President Obama in 2016 to the Eastern District of Texas. The second was by President Trump to the Northern District of Texas in the fall of 2017. Scholer was confirmed in March 2018. The period from 2014 until 2018 was filled with uncertainties for Scholer, and her ability to survive them is notable.

Three of us faced significant controversy as we sought Article III judgeships. The controversies attached to me, Chen, and Rao were different in nature, and we therefore handled them differently.

It took me some time to get nominated, and then I waited thirty months from my first nomination in December 1995 until my confirmation in June 1998. Nominated by President Clinton, I faced opposition from the Republican majority in the Senate, whose members expressed concern that I was too liberal in my views. As evidence, they pointed to my position on the board of directors of the Hawaii chapter of the American Civil Liberties Union (ACLU), which had advocated on behalf of individuals seeking licenses for same-sex marriages. For the most part, I dealt with the controversy by trying to conduct business in as normal a fashion as I could in my private law practice. Of course, I noticed that, as pointed out by several politicians and by some of my friends and family members, almost all the Clinton nominees who were held up by the Republican Senate majority were women or minorities, and I was both. After I was finally confirmed, a Clinton judicial nominee who was White and from a state with two Republican senators marveled at my experience, given how quickly he had sailed through the Senate despite having had involvement with his local ACLU chapter.

The long wait affected my legal practice in many ways. It probably affected my income, although I was not calculating or considering that. In some ways, my wait was easier than what Gee and Scholer had to endure as they sought nominations from different presidents. I did not have to compete for a nomination more than once. Just getting a nomination is often exceedingly stressful. In other ways, my wait brought with it a greater impact on my career. Being a nominee means curtailing one's activities. I at first stopped appearing in federal district court. No one expects that of someone who is only an applicant for a nomination rather than an actual nominee, and, unlike a nominee, an applicant to be a nominee is not always identified publicly. After a substantial time, I returned to federal court. One of my federal cases was scheduled for trial, and all parties had consented to having the trial conducted by a magistrate judge. The magistrate judge consulted with the Administrative Office of the United States Courts about the propriety of presiding over a trial in which one party was represented by a nominee for a district judgeship. The magistrate judge anticipated seeking retention to another eight-year term, and if confirmed, I would be one of the judges voting on his retention request. He determined that he could preside.

For all of the extensive period during which I was a nominee, I was under scrutiny. Every day I faced questions about when I expected to be confirmed, often from federal judges who wondered if I had inside information about when the vacancy might be filled. They had a personal interest in the matter, as they were doing the work of the missing judge.

Although I knew I would withdraw if asked to do so by Hawaii's senators or the president, I did not think about withdrawing in the absence of such a request. Looking back, I think three things caused me to have this attitude. First, Senator Daniel Inouye never indicated that he was worried about whether he could see me through to confirmation. He knew much more than I did about my chances. Second, although I had been identified as supportive of advocates for same-sex marriage, it was not a matter I was speaking about or working on. Indeed, all nominees are counseled to keep a low profile. Third, I always remained amazed to have been nominated in the first place. Not only would it have been ungrateful and rude to dismiss that honor, but my amazement kept me from ever feeling entitled to a judgeship. That meant that if I had to, I would wait. I am not certain that just being patient qualifies as being indefatigable, but I do recall the difficulty of the combination of my long wait as a nominee and the limelight I faced.

The controversy Chen faced lent itself to a quicker and more direct solution. That any controversy was affecting her application was not a public matter, which allowed her to address it discreetly. Members of Senator Chuck Schumer's selection committee had concerns about a judge's critical comments concerning a particular case she had handled. She took the bold step of approaching the judge on the case for help. Chen hated having to advocate for herself, but the judge reacted by assuring her that he did not see her handling of that case as an impediment. It is easy to imagine the angst Chen must have had as she prepared to approach the judge, uncertain of how he would react. His reaction was a huge relief to her. Had he reacted negatively, not only would she probably not have been nominated, but she might have faced the awkwardness of thereafter appearing before that judge. She took a risk, and as it turned out, she progressed to nomination and then confirmation. Her controversy involved a single case, not a wide political difference. In her situation, a direct approach succeeded in a way that probably would not have been possible for me or for Rao.

Rao faced the most overt and vocal challenges of the three of us. She reacted by apologizing for statements she had made as a college student, pointing to her youth at the time, and saying that she would not express herself that way today. The internet has made statements from decades ago easy to locate. What once would have been difficult to unearth and might have been forgotten, even by Rao herself, was examined in detail, and Rao was asked to defend the resulting discoveries. What she walked back was primarily her tone, not the substance of what she had said, although she expressly took back a comment about "the dangerous feminist idealism which teaches women that they are equal."

One thing that may have helped Rao deal with the controversy was how short-lived it was. Less than two months elapsed between her nomination and her confirmation, and it was during that inter-val that most of the controversy played out. Still, the concerted attacks must have been personally difficult to absorb, especially outside the familiar academic context in which she could have spoken more freely and written a thorough explanation.

Rao told me that she knew what to expect from her earlier experience working with judicial candidates, but, of course, noth-ing focuses the mind more than being the one scrutinized. She was not a litigator and so did not have a litigator's experience of fight-ing off zealous opponents in what sometimes may be very conten-tious proceedings. At the same time, Rao may have been in faculty meetings that grew contentious, and she may have had robust back-and-forth discussions with other academics. Of course, a Senate Judiciary Committee hearing is not a setting in which any candidate can engage in free debate. Candidates are always coun-seled to try to avoid saying controversial things. No candidate has an advantage in that setting. But Rao did not go into her hearing unarmed or unprepared. She knew she would be questioned about her writings, and she had vocal supporters.

Sometimes a candidate anticipates a controversy that never materializes. Gee had expected her union lawyer background to be an impediment to her confirmation, but no such impediment materialized. In fact, Vincent Eng of NAPABA has noted that the union background was a plus when Gee was being encouraged to seek a Ninth Circuit position. Chen did not know whether she would be questioned about her sexual orientation; she was not.

Chris Kang thinks that being unflagging likely correlates with a candidate's assessment that her chance of ultimate success is good. The greater the chance of a positive outcome, the more relentlessly a candidate will pursue the judgeship. Few people will waste their time and energy on a hopeless cause.

I have no reason to think that the combined experiences of the judges I interviewed reflected more or less difficulty than the experiences of any group of fifteen Article III judges. Nor do I have any reason to think that the judges I interviewed exhibited greater tenacity. What is clear is that many of the judges I studied had to accept difficulties and opted to work single-mindedly to overcome them. In short, they had to want to be Article III judges enough to be indefatigable in addressing those difficulties. This indefatigable nature may be essential for success in many disparate endeavors beyond becoming Article III judges, as recognized by Angela Duckworth in her 2016 book *Grit: The Power of Passion and Perseverance*. Perseverance clearly played a role in many of my interviewees' stories.

Why Aren't These Other Asian Women Article III Judges?

Most nominees to Article III positions are ultimately confirmed. Of course, some have to be renominated by the same president or nominated by more than one president before getting confirmed, but the odds of getting confirmed once a person is nominated are good. I am therefore interested in looking at why more Asian women have not been nominated.

As I noted in the Introduction, I cannot pretend to do a comprehensive review of why particular Asian women who appear to be likely Article III candidates have not in fact been nominated. I cannot pretend even to present a statistically valid sample of such women. There is, after all, no comprehensive nationwide list of such women, and their interest or lack of interest in Article III positions is not contained in accessible public records. For the most part, to identify women to discuss in this section, I have relied on my own knowledge of such individuals and on information obtained from others knowledgeable about such individuals. I have been fortunate that a handful of them agreed to speak with me anonymously.

I look first at women who opted not to seek Article III judgeships, and then at women who applied but were not nominated. The first group is more interesting to me; the second group involves people with specific situations that may not be capable of generalization to the wider pool of potential applicants.

A number of factors appear to have influenced likely candidates into not seeking Article III judgeships.

The first factor is economics. Federal judges' pay has always been less than what a successful attorney could earn in private practice and also in tenured academic positions, but that gap has grown increasingly wide. Vincent Eng of NAPABA notes that leaving higher-paying positions in the law is particularly difficult for those with parents who emigrated from Asia and who did not themselves become wealthy. With Asian immigration including many recent immigrants, Eng says that immigrants' children may be the first generation in their families to have the chance to accumulate wealth. As these children reach the peak of their income-producing years, giving up that income to enter public service has no allure. This is an issue that transcends race and gender, of course, but Eng recognizes that some Asian candidates who have demurred when encouraged to seek judgeships have been responding to a strong cultural pull to continue in high-earning positions.[24]

Sometimes, of course, potential applicants have reason to think that they cannot pass the vetting process for an Article III judgeship. Putting aside issues of self-effacement, candidates may know about particular aspects of their résumés that may doom them. Eng says that especially when candidates have histories of drug use, they may decline to face questions by decision makers who are predisposed to reject them on that ground. There is no shortage of applicants without such histories who get preference. But not all presidents or senators consider past drug use automatically disqualifying. Some make distinctions when drug use was confined to student years. Others make allowances for marijuana use. But Eng says that he has seen candidates take themselves out of the running because of such considerations.

I have already discussed the comments by some of the judges I interviewed about their reticence in promoting themselves. Chris Kang told me that when he was in the Obama administration, he did not bother to encourage potential candidates who were unenthusiastic about seeking Article III judgeships. An applicant who was undecided or who held back would not get nominated. Some promising Asian women may have thus fallen by the wayside because of their own hesitation. Those who did apply may have had exactly the same reasons to hesitate, but they somehow overcame that feeling.

I talked with a small number of distinguished Asian women who did not apply for judgeships. Some of them were interviewed specifically for this analysis, while others I had talked to or knew about before I even conceived of studying Asian women in the context of federal judgeships. None agreed to be named, so I am avoiding giving so much of their biographies that they could be identified. They are from various jurisdictions.

One Asian woman (I will call her "Nonapplicant A" and will identify the others in a similar fashion) was very familiar with the process of becoming an Article III judge. Like some of the judges I interviewed, this woman had helped other applicants. A state court judge, she had been encouraged by NAPABA to seek an Article III judgeship herself but had declined. When I asked her why, she told me that she did not deem herself qualified. Based on my past interactions with this individual, I was taken aback by this answer. Nonapplicant A was articulate and knowledgeable, and her temperament was suitable for the bench. She sheepishly admitted that she had cautioned others against denigrating themselves when she encouraged them to apply. Still, she explained that it was her very familiarity with the process that gave her pause. She had seen candidates from more prestigious law schools than hers, with greater academic achievements, impressive judicial clerkships, and many exciting entries on their résumés. She thought she could not compete. I heard from several people that they had assured her that they would throw their support behind her if she threw her hat into the ring, but they had not succeeded in budging her. She was adamant that she would not apply.

Nonapplicant A's reference to academic records was particularly interesting. By the time they sought Article III positions, the fifteen Asian judges I have profiled had been out of school for a significant period and had amassed records as lawyers that were more revealing than their achievements as students. A prestigious law school may serve as a proxy for competence when an attorney is newly minted or is introduced to someone with little other basis for evaluating the attorney. By contrast, an applicant for an Article III position submits an enormous amount of information about herself to decision makers. These submissions far outweigh the name value of any law school. Of course, Nonapplicant A knew that, but she still viewed graduation from a prestigious law school as a kind of stamp of approval.

Among the fifteen judges I profile, Harvard Law School has three graduates (Mollway, Koh, and Bissoon). Three law schools, Georgetown, the University of California at Los Angeles (UCLA), and the former Boalt Hall at the University of California at Berkeley (now the UC Berkeley School of Law), have two each (Matsumoto and Chen from Georgetown, Nguyen and Gee from UCLA, and Du and Talwani from Berkeley). The other law schools have a single judge from the cohort—Kobayashi from Boston College, Schofield from New York University, Choe-Groves from Rutgers University followed by an LLM from Columbia University, Scholer from Cornell University, Otake from the University of Washington, and Rao from the University of Chicago. I myself do not think that Nonapplicant A's law school would have diminished her chances of becoming an Article III judge, but it was a factor she considered.

Nonapplicant B was an Asian woman with exactly the kind of résumé that Nonapplicant A said she herself lacked. Nonapplicant B had academic honors from a highly ranked law school, a federal judicial clerkship, and an impressive career that included service in a presidential administration and a position in academia. She was approached about an Article III appointment and was even interviewed by administration lawyers but ultimately decided not to proceed. At the time, people she knew questioned her decision, but she says she has no regrets. She says that she was accustomed to speaking her mind and worried that she would be unhappy about having to restrain herself if she were a judge. Indeed, she was conscious that past writings in which she had expressed opinions might have complicated her chances of being confirmed, although she said that was not her primary concern.

A major factor for her was that the court she was being encouraged to seek a seat on had a type of caseload that was not attractive to her. She says that she may have been too young at the time, and that, given her other career options, the particular position she was considering was simply not her dream job. She notes that she was not then appearing regularly in court.[25] She says, however, that right now she might be interested in a position on a different court. Few people have the luxury of being picky about which Article III court to sit on, but Nonapplicant B's résumé may make her that rare person.

Nonapplicant C was an Asian litigator who was encouraged by an Article III judge to seek an Article III position but declined to apply. At the time, she was focused on her young children and her elderly parents. She also had a geographic concern, as she would have had to relocate to be closer to the courthouse. Of course, many other applicants with her issues still go ahead and apply for Article III judgeships. Vacancies may not arise when or where it is convenient, or they may arise when one has aged out of being a likely contender. But Nonapplicant C concluded that the time was not right for her.

Sometimes it is political rather than personal considerations that can cause someone not to apply. Some years ago, I spoke to a state appellate judge who was seriously considering applying for a federal circuit judgeship. This Asian woman (Nonapplicant D) had a number of personal attributes that seemed likely to make her a prime candidate for nomination, and she was reviewing her probable competition in an informed manner. But Nonapplicant D was only attractive as a potential nominee to a particular political party, and that party was booted out of power. At that point, Nonapplicant D stopped thinking about an Article III appointment.

Political considerations can derail applicants in other ways. Nonapplicant E was a prominent Asian woman only recently appointed to a nonjudicial position when a judicial vacancy arose;

she did not seek a judgeship out of concern that doing so would be a slap in the face to politicians who had just helped her get her nonjudicial appointment. Nonapplicant F had a federal executive position that had been extremely hard to fill. The president at the time was concerned that if the woman became a federal judge, the executive position that he had labored so hard to fill would be nearly impossible to staff. The Asian woman was discouraged from seeking nomination to an Article III judgeship.

Nonapplicant G was an Asian woman who was a state court judge and who was encouraged to seek a federal court position. She weighed her options and instead decided to seek advancement within the state court system. She was successful in that regard. Although a federal appointment remains an option for her, it is now less likely that she will leave the state court bench.

Nonapplicant G was far from the only Asian woman I knew who was an elected state court judge and appeared to be a good candidate for an Article III judgeship. The experience of running for election and courting voters made these women acutely conscious that any remark they made might be fatal not only to their chances in state court elections but also to potential federal nominations. They tended to be exceedingly circumspect, and I was not surprised that these prime candidates declined to be interviewed or identified by me.

It is difficult to compare these women to the Article III judges I interviewed. The Article III judges doubtless refrained from sharing certain things with me, but they all spoke from the vantage point of their lifetime appointments. There are surely many reasons that Asian women do not apply for Article III judgeships, but for some of them, the reason they have not applied is that they do not feel qualified or that they do not think they will be selected. They have taken themselves out of the running. Others simply do not want to be Article III judges at all. Some are thinking about possibly applying but so far are not committed to wanting Article III judgeships. For this last group, the experience of the Asian women who are Article III judges teaches that unless you are among the fortunate few who sail through nomination and confirmation, you must want the job if you expect to survive the kind of pitfalls that applicants all too often encounter.

Women Who Applied but Were Not Nominated

While most nominees succeed in getting confirmed, most applicants do not end up getting nominated. A nominee, while sometimes facing opposition from advocates and politicians, is not competing with another individual to fill a particular seat. By contrast, applicants seeking a nomination may have a host of competitors. Asian women applicants are as susceptible as others to failing to get nominated. Although some of the Article III judges I interviewed were singled out for consideration (e.g., Du and Choe-Groves), most of us went through an application process that put us in competition with numerous other applicants. Other Asian women may well have been among those candidates with whom we and other judges competed.

It is difficult to identify unsuccessful Asian women applicants. Applications are not public, and applicants frequently keep their actions private so as not to prejudice themselves in their existing jobs if they end up remaining in them.

One Asian woman who was on a short list for an Article III position was an experienced state trial judge before whom hundreds of attorneys had appeared. One of those attorneys had gone on to hold a powerful political position, and he had a long memory. He had been unhappy with the judge's performance when he appeared before her years earlier, and he used his position to ensure that she was not selected from the short list. This was frustrating and hurtful for the applicant, but she had no way to overcome the obstacle. Even if she thought that the objector's reaction was ill founded or affected by her sex, the objector thought he was acting reasonably. He was likely unconscious of the influence, if any, of the applicant's gender. Whatever steps the applicant may have taken to disabuse him of his view were unsuccessful.

As with any group, some Asian women applicants are simply not qualified but do not recognize that at the start. They may lack the credentials to become Article III judges. Sometimes they advance far in the nomination process before their failings are recognized. If their applications somehow become public in the meantime, this can be damaging to their careers, and they may decide not to reapply even when they have later gained the necessary credentials. I have seen this occur.

Even when applicants are qualified, they may not be able to match competitors' political connections. An Article III nomination is political, and presidents and senators are often influenced by such connections.

And there are times when a stellar candidate may simply be out of luck. The candidate may not be the ideal age from a president's point of view or may be handling a politically sensitive case at the very time she is applying. Timing is critical in any Article III nomination, and a nominating decision sometimes has nothing to do with whether an applicant is Asian or a woman. Many of the judges I interviewed noted the part that luck played in their appointments, referring to needing the stars to align or for lightning to strike. Their recognition of their good fortune is akin to what Malcolm Gladwell, in his 2008 book *Outliers: The Story of Success*, noted had been essential to the success of certain high achievers.

Sometimes race and sex are indeed in issue in a way that may disfavor an Asian woman. For example, decision makers could be focused on filling a vacancy on a particular court with an African American judge. In the District of Hawaii, Asian women of Japanese background (Kobayashi and Otake) occupy two of the four active district judgeships, and I, myself of Japanese ancestry, am serving in the same district as a senior district judge. Putting aside the temporary judgeship issue I discussed earlier, it may be that the person selected to fill the next vacancy in the District of Hawaii will not be a Japanese American woman. I do not, of course, mean to discourage Japanese American women in Hawaii from applying. I have no crystal ball, and a Japanese American woman could indeed be nominated. My point is only that candidates have to accept that they may have limited control over certain aspects of the political process.

Conclusion

By mid-2019, fifteen Asian women were Article III judges. This is a far cry from my lonely years as the only Asian woman to be an Article III judge between 1998 and 2008, when Matsumoto became the second Asian woman to become an Article III judge. Each of the Asian women in the cohort has her own story about becoming an Article III judge.

The Asian category encompasses considerable diversity, but one recurring theme is the effect of being an immigrant or the child of an immigrant. Three-quarters of the judges examined in this book were the children of immigrants, and seeing the difficulties their parents faced after arriving in the United States left a huge imprint on many of these women that inspired them to become lawyers and then judges.

The judges' personal traits present another interesting aspect. Many of them recognized that they and other Asian women had hindered themselves by being reluctant to put themselves forward. But once the members of the fifteen decided to put themselves forward, they were all in, tireless in pursuit of their goal. They did not let difficulties derail them. And face difficulties they did—sometimes medical, sometimes political, sometimes personal.

While Asian women remain underrepresented in the federal judiciary, my hope is that their stories and the themes I have discussed will serve as a guide for future applicants seeking to join the ranks of Article III judges. I am not confining my hope to Asian women. We learn from each other's stories. I do not think self-effacement is limited to Asian women. Nor do I think the relentless pursuit of one's goal is required only for Asian women. I have learned a great deal by studying these judges, and I hope that the lessons they impart will be absorbed by others.

Acknowledgments

I am grateful to Duke's Bloch Judicial Institute for providing me with the scholarship that permitted me to participate in the program and with a stimulating environment in which to learn and to write.

A great many people helped me. All the students in Duke's judicial studies program were sitting judges, and two of the judges in particular were unending sources of support for me throughout the program—my roommate Molly Huskey, the chief judge of the Idaho Court of Appeals; and Marina Garcia Marmolejo, a district judge on the U.S. District Court for the Southern District of Texas. My thesis advisor, Mitu Gulati, at the time a member of Duke's faculty, provided invaluable advice and encouragement and patiently responded to my inquiries long after I had completed the Duke program.

During this book's preparation, Colleen Brost, Matthew Ezer, Joni Gross, Darsie Ing-Dodson, Kenneth May, and Keiko Rose provided comments, encouragement, and help (sometimes with much-needed technological advice). I am grateful for their patience and support, and for their ability to join me in laughing along the way. Shannon Lashbrook, Renee Kiyabu, and Pete Gayatinea of the Ninth Circuit's library assisted me in locating resources and in determining what was available.

And, of course, I am grateful to the judges who agreed to be interviewed, as well as to Vincent Eng and Chris Kang for their interviews. The women whose anonymous interviews are discussed in part 3 also provided invaluable insights. Judges

Anthony Ishii, Ramona V. Manglona, Brenda Rhoades, and Frances Tydingco-Gatewood kindly responded to my inquiries for brief biographical information. A conversation with Karen Narasaki led to an important revision. Finally, Jasper Chang, the editor of this book, has patiently guided me through the process by which my thesis was transformed into this book. He somehow saw value in my manuscript from the outset and helped me in countless ways to make the text clearer, often by asking questions. Without complaining to me, he put up with what must have seemed to him to be my never-ending revisions.

This book would not exist without all the help I received.

Notes

Introduction

1. A master of laws degree, or LLM, is a degree available to someone who already has a juris doctor, or JD, which is the degree earned when one graduates from law school. The anomaly of getting a master's degree after getting a doctoral degree results from the history of law degrees. What is now a JD was formerly referred to as a bachelor of laws degree, or LLB. Law schools switched to the JD terminology as better reflecting the status of a law degree as obtained after someone already has a bachelor's degree, but the schools kept the LLM designation.

2. Brenda Rhoades, email to the author, July 11, 2019.

3. Jennifer L. Thurston, "Black Robes, White Judges: The Lack of Diversity on the Magistrate Judge Bench," *Law and Contemporary Problems* 82 (2019): 63–102.

4. Frances Tydingco-Gatewood, emails to the author, June 23, 2019, and June 24, 2019.

5. Ramona V. Manglona, emails to the author, June 23, 2019.

Part I. Context

1. "Population Estimates," QuickFacts, U.S. Census Bureau, accessed February 28, 2020, https://www.census.gov/quickfacts/fact/table/US/PST045218#PST045218 (data on website updated over time, so will differ by date); "Population and Housing Estimates," U.S. Census, https://www.census.gov/population/estimates/nation/intfile2-1.txt (data no

longer available at this website; readers are referred to http://www.data
.census.gov). Some data may be available at http://www.data.census
.gov, but if that website is difficult to navigate, historical data may also
be found at http://www2.census.gov and at https//www.statista.com/
statistics/183489/population-of-the-us-by-ethnicity-since-2000.

2. "ACS Demographic & Housing Estimates," U.S. Census Bureau,
accessed February 28, 2020, https://data.census.gov/cedsci/all?q=gender
%20and%20race%202018&hidePreview=false&tid=ACSDP1Y2018
.DP05&y=2018, table DP05.

3. "American FactFinder," U.S. Census Bureau, accessed February 27,
2020, https://factfinder.census.gov/faces/tableservices/jsf/pages/
productview.xhtml?pid=PEP_2018_PEPALL5N&prodType=table,
table for July 1, 2018 (website decommissioned; readers are referred to
http://www.data.census.gov).

4. "American FactFinder," U.S. Census Bureau, accessed February 27,
2020, https://factfinder.census.gov/faces/tableservices/jsf/pages/
productview.xhtml?src=bkmk# (website decommissioned; readers are
referred to http://www.data.census.gov). I use *Latino* and *Latina* for
two reasons. First, those terms avoid any confusion as to whether individuals such as Brazilian Portuguese Americans are included (they are).
Second, when speaking about women, *Latina* is shorter than *Hispanic
women*. The Federal Judicial Center (FJC), however, uses *Hispanic* in
its demographic information about Article III judges. Census counts
treat *Latino* and *Hispanic* as interchangeable and refer to Whites as
non-Hispanic or non-Latino Whites.

5. "The State of Diversity and Inclusion in the Legal Profession,"
Institute for Inclusion in the Legal Profession, 2014, http://www
.theiilp.com/Resources/Documents/IILP_2014_Final.pdf, 17, table 1;
"Household Data Annual Averages: 11. Employed Persons by Detailed
Occupation, Sex, Race, and Hispanic or Latino Ethnicity," U.S.
Bureau of Labor Statistics, accessed July 3, 2019, https://www.bls.gov/
cps/cpsaat11.htm.

6. "Florence Ellinwood Allen," Federal Judicial Center, accessed May 4,
2021, https://www.fjc.gov/history/judges/allen-florence-ellinwood. See
also Phyllis Kravitch, "Women in the Legal Profession: The Past 100
Years," *Mississippi Law Journal* 69 (1999): 64.

7. "History from 1919–1927," Women's Bar Association of District of Columbia, accessed May 4, 2021, https://www.wbadc.org/history #From_1917-1927.

8. "Genevieve Rose Cline," Federal Judicial Center, accessed May 4, 2021, https://www.fjc.gov/history/judges/cline-genevieve-rose.

9. "Burnita Shelton Matthews," Federal Judicial Center, accessed May 4, 2021, https://www.fjc.gov/history/judges/matthews-burnita-shelton. See also Kravitch, "Women in the Legal Profession," 60–61.

10. Andrew Westney, "Native Judges Still Looking for Room on Federal Bench," Law 360, accessed October 4, 2019, https://www.law360.com/articles/1204970/native-judges-still-looking-for-room-on-federal-bench.

11. "American Indian Judges on the Federal Courts," Federal Judicial Center, accessed April 28, 2021, https://www.fjc.gov/history/judges/search/american-indian. The FJC's American Indian category does not include Native Hawaiians, who are included in the Pacific Islander category.

12. "African American Judges on the Federal Courts," Federal Judicial Center, accessed July 5, 2019, https://www.fjc.gov/history/judges/search/african-american.

13. "African American Judges." William Henry Hastie became "the first black judge in the entire federal system" when, in 1937, he was appointed to the non–Article III U.S. District Court for the District of the Virgin Islands. David B. Wilkins, "Testing the Resources of the Law: John Robinson Wilkins, Berkeley Law, and the Limits of Law and Development," YouTube video, 1:10:11, August 22, 2019, https://www.youtube.com/watch?v=GXqB3EaHV5Y&feature=youtube.

14. "1979: The Year Women Changed the Judiciary," Administrative Office of the U.S. Courts, accessed May 4, 2021, https://www.uscourts.gov/news/1979-year-women-changed-judiciary.

15. "1979."

16. "Biographical Directory of Article III Federal Judges, 1789–Present," Federal Judicial Center, accessed July 1, 2019, https://www.fjc.gov/history/judges.

17. "Biographical Directory."

18. "Hispanic Judges on the Federal Courts," Federal Judicial Center, accessed July 1, 2019, https://www.fjc.gov/history/judges/search/hispanic.

19. "Hispanic Judges."

20. "Hispanic Judges."

21. "Hispanic Judges."

22. "Hispanic Judges."

23. "Hispanic Judges."

24. "Asian American Judges on the Federal Courts," Federal Judicial Center, accessed July 18, 2019, https://www.fjc.gov/history/judges/search/asian-american.

25. "Asian American Judges."

26. "The Court of Claims, 1855–1982," Federal Judicial Center, accessed February 19, 2020, https://www.fjc.gov/history/courts/court-claims-1855-1982. The trial level of the old Court of Claims became today's Court of Federal Claims, which is not an Article III court.

27. "Asian American Judges."

28. "Asian American Judges."

29. "Asian American Judges." This statistic includes Walter Meheula Heen, who had a January 1981 recess appointment to the District of Hawaii but was never confirmed by the Senate. His service ended in December 1981. The figure of thirty does not include judges confirmed after July 2019, including Patrick Bumatay, who, on December 10, 2019, became the first Filipino federal appellate judge when he was confirmed to the Ninth Circuit.

30. "Asian American Judges."

31. "Diversity on the Bench," Federal Judicial Center, accessed July 3, 2019, https://www.fjc.gov/history/judges/diversity-bench.

32. A senior judge is someone who, having qualified to do so by a combination of age and years as an Article III judge, opts to assume a status that allows that judge, if the judge so chooses, to moderate the judge's workload while still functioning as a judge at the same pay. See 28 U.S.C. § 371.

33. Igor Bobic and Alexis Arnold, "Trump's Largely White and Male Appellate Judges, in One Photo," HuffPost, August 5, 2019, https://www.huffpost.com/entry/trump-judges-white-male-nominees_n_5d484719e4b0acb57fd05ec3.

34. Melissa Nann Burke, Robert Snell, and Jonathan Oosting, "Trump Picks First Black Female Judge Nominee as He Tries to Fill Mich.

Vacancies," *Detroit News*, March 8, 2019, https://www.detroitnews
.com/story/news/politics/2019/03/08/trump-nominates-first-black
-woman-judge-federal-bench-michigan/3105805002.

35. "African American Judges on the Federal Courts," Federal Judicial
Center, accessed February 19, 2020, https://www.fjc.gov/history/judges/
search/african-american. It has since been revised.

36. Carl W. Tobias, "Appointing Lesbian, Gay, Bisexual, Transgender and
Queer Judges in the Trump Administration," *Washington University
Law Review Online* 96 (June 2018): 15n18. See also "LGBT Article III
Judges," Minority Corporate Counsel Association, last updated May 7,
2020, https://www.mcca.com/resources/reports/federal-judiciary/lgbt
-judges.

37. Tobias, "Appointing Lesbian," 15.

38. "African American Judges."

39. "This Is the First Time Our Judicial Pool Has Been This Diverse,"
White House, June 28, 2016, https://obamawhitehouse.archives.gov/
share/first-time-our-judicial-pool-has-been-diverse; "LGBT Article III Judges."

40. "LGBT Article III Judges."

41. "LGBT Article III Judges."

42. "Women Judges on the Federal Courts," Federal Judicial Center,
accessed September 1, 2019, https://www.fjc.gov/history/judges/search/
women. See also Samantha Allen, "Trump Nominates His First Out-
LGBT Judge. Will He Match Obama's 11?," Daily Beast, August 25,
2018, https://www.thedailybeast.com/trump-nominates-his-first-out
-lgbt-judge-will-he-match-obamas-11.

43. Patrick Gregory, "Openly Gay Prosecutor Could Again Be Trump
Appeals Court Pick," *U.S. Law Week*, June 12, 2019, https://www
.bloomberglaw.com/document/X165I4ROoooooo?bna_news_filter=us
-law-week&jcsearch=BNA%25200000016b4c34d4f0a36b4d748b850000
#jcite. See also "Asian American Judges on the Federal Courts," Fed-
eral Judicial Center, accessed May 4, 2021, https://www.fjc.gov/history/
judges/search/asian-american-judges.

44. "History of the Federal Judiciary" and "Biographical Directory of Article III Federal Judges," Federal Judicial Center, accessed July 10, 2019,
https://www.fjc.gov/history/judges/search/advanced-search.

45. Danielle Root, Jake Faleschini, and Grace Oyenubi, "Building a More Inclusive Federal Judiciary," Center for American Progress, October 3, 2019, https://www.americanprogress.org/issues/courts/reports/2019/10/03/475359/building-inclusive-federal-judiciary.

46. National Asian Pacific American Bar Association Judiciary Committee, *Asian Pacific American Judges* (annual convention handout), November 7, 2019.

47. See, for example, the discussion of Neomi Rao's confirmation later in this book.

48. See, for example, Ethan Bronner, *Battle for Justice: How the Bork Nomination Shook America* (New York: W. W. Norton, 1989); Paul Collins Jr. and Lori Ringhand, *Supreme Court Confirmation Hearings and Constitutional Change* (Cambridge: Cambridge University Press, 2013); John Danforth, *Resurrection: The Confirmation of Clarence Thomas* (New York: Viking, 1994); Dion Farganis and Justin Wedeking, *Supreme Court Confirmation Hearings in the U.S. Senate: Reconsidering the Charade* (Ann Arbor: University of Michigan Press, 2014); Jeannie Suk Gerson, "Understanding the Partisanship of Brett Kavanaugh's Confirmation Hearings," *New Yorker*, September 12, 2018, https://www.newyorker.com/news/our-columnists/understanding-the-partisanship-of-brett-kavanaughs-confirmation-hearings; Wil Haygood, *Showdown: Thurgood Marshall and the Supreme Court Nomination That Changed America* (New York: Vintage, 2015); Mollie Hemingway and Carrie Severino, *Justice on Trial: The Kavanaugh Confirmation and the Future of the Supreme Court* (Washington, D.C.: Regency, 2019); Carl Hulse, *Confirmation Bias: Inside Washington's War on the Supreme Court, from Scalia's Death to Justice Kavanaugh* (New York: HarperCollins, 2019); Ruth Marcus, *Supreme Ambition: Brett Kavanaugh and the Conservative Takeover* (New York: Simon & Schuster, 2019); Robin Pogrebin and Kate Kelly, *The Education of Brett Kavanaugh: An Investigation* (London: Portfolio Penguin, 2019); Jane Mayer and Jill Abramson, *Strange Justice: The Selling of Clarence Thomas* (Los Angeles: Graymalkin Media, 1994); Mark Silverstein, *Judicious Choices: The New Politics of Supreme Court Confirmations* (New York: W. W. Norton, 1994); Paul Simon, *Advice and Consent: Clarence Thomas, Robert Bork and the Intriguing History of the Supreme Court's Nomination Battles* (Washington, D.C.:

National Press, 1992); Norman Vieira and Leonard Gross, *Supreme Court Appointments: Judge Bork and the Politicization of Senate Confirmations* (Carbondale: Southern Illinois University Press, 1998); and Benjamin Wittes, *Confirmation Wars: Preserving Independent Courts in Angry Times* (Lanham, Md.: Rowman & Littlefield, 2006).

49. See, for example, Ilya Shapiro, *Supreme Disorder: Judicial Nominations and the Politics of America's Highest Court* (New York: Simon & Schuster, 2020).

50. For a discussion that does not focus on the Supreme Court, see Sheldon Goldman, *Picking Federal Judges: Lower Court Selection from Roosevelt through Reagan* (New Haven, Conn.: Yale University Press, 1999). In *Shortlisted: Women in the Shadows of the Supreme Court* (New York: New York University Press, 2020), Hannah Brenner Johnson and Renee Knake Jefferson examine women who were considered for the U.S. Supreme Court but were not appointed.

51. See, for example, A. J. Stichman, Kimberly Hassell, and Carol Archbold, "Strength in Numbers? A Test of Kanter's Theory of Tokenism," *Journal of Criminal Justice* 38 (2010): 633–639; and Lynn Zimmer, "Tokenism and Women in the Workplace: The Limits of Gender-Neutral Theory," *Social Problems* 35 (1988): 64–77.

52. See, for example, Patricia Lewis and Ruth Simpson, "Kanter Revisited: Gender, Power, and (In)Visibility," *International Journal of Management Reviews* 14, no. 2 (2011): 141–158.

53. See, for example, Janice Yoder and Lynne Berendsen, "Outsider within the Firehouse: African American and White Women Firefighters," *Psychology of Women Quarterly* 25 (2001): 27–36. See also Devon Carbado and Mitu Gulati, "Working Identity," *Cornell Law Review* 85 (2000): 1259–1308; and Devon Carbado and Mitu Gulati, *Acting White? Rethinking Race in "Post-racial" America* (Oxford: Oxford University Press, 2013).

54. See, for example, Suzanne Homer and Lois Schwartz, "Admitted but Not Accepted: Outsiders Take an Inside Look at Law School," *Berkeley Women's Law Journal* 5 (1990): 1–74; and David Wilkins, "The New Social Engineers in the Age of Obama: Black Corporate Lawyers and the Making of the First Black President," *Howard Law Journal* 53 (2010): 557–644.

55. Relevant to my study is the considerable scholarship in which writers have tracked diversity on the bench. See, for example, Sheldon Goldman and Matthew Saronson, "Clinton's Nontraditional Judges: Creating a More Representative Bench," *Judicature* 78 (1994): 68–73. See also Sheldon Goldman, "The Judicial Confirmation Crisis and the Clinton Presidency," *Presidential Studies Quarterly* 28, no. 4 (1998): 838–844. In 2002, Judge (and future Supreme Court Justice) Sonia Sotomayor asked what it would mean "to have more women and people of color on the bench." Sonia Sotomayor, "A Latina Judge's Voice," *Berkeley La Raza Law Journal* 13 (2002): 90. Years later, Jonathan Stubbs, noting the continuing overrepresentation of White males in the federal judiciary, asked, "What are the long-term costs to American society and the prospects of a representative American democracy where overwhelmingly the socioeconomic and political leadership is drawn principally from one gender, race, and socioeconomic status minority group?" Jonathan K. Stubbs, "A Demographic Snapshot of America's Federal Judiciary: A Prima Facie Case for Change," *NAACA News*, February 2011, 4, https://scholarship.richmond.edu/cgi/viewcontent.cgi ?article=1074&context=law-faculty-publications. Stubbs was pessimistic that change was likely in the foreseeable future. He noted that the U.S. population was majority female, but even Obama, who appointed a record number of women to the federal bench, still appointed mostly male judges (58 percent). Jonathan K. Stubbs, "A Demographic History of Federal Judicial Appointments by Sex and Race: 1789–2016," *Berkeley La Raza Law Journal* 26 (2016): 92.

56. Examples are found in Pat K. Chew and Robert E. Kelley, "Myth of the Color-Blind Judge: An Empirical Analysis of Racial Harassment Cases," *Washington University Law Review* 86 (2009): 1117–1166; Harry T. Edwards, "A Tribute to Leon Higginbotham, Jr.: Race and the Judiciary," *Yale Law & Policy Review* 30 (2002): 327, 329–330; Sherrilyn A. Ifill, "Racial Diversity on the Bench: Beyond Role Models and Public Confidence," *Washington & Lee Law Review* 57 (2000): 494; Jennifer Peresie, "Female Judges Matter: Gender and Collegial Decision-making in the Federal Appellate Courts," *Yale Law Journal* 114, no. 7 (2005): 1759–1790; Maya Sen, "Diversity, Qualification, and Ideology: How Female and Minority Judges Have Changed or Not Changed

over Time," *Wisconsin Law Review* 2 (2017): 367–399; Sylvia R. Lazos, "Only Skin Deep: The Cost of Partisan Politics on Minority Diversity of the Federal Bench: Why Care Whether Judges Look 'like America' If, Because of Politics, a 'Voice of Color' Has Become a 'Whisper of Color'?," *Indiana Law Journal* 83, no. 4 (2008): 1425; and Russell Wheeler, "Changing Backgrounds of U.S. District Judges: Causes and Possible Implications," *Judicature* 93 (2010): 140–149.

57. Amber Fricke and Angela Onwuachi-Wittig, "Do Female 'Firsts' Still Matter? Why They Do for Female Judges of Color," *Michigan State Law Review* 2012 (2012): 1542–1543.

58. Fricke and Onwuachi-Wittig, 1541.

59. Fricke and Onwuachi-Wittig, 1542. See also Carlton W. Reeves, "Defending the Judiciary: A Call for Justice, Truth, and Diversity on the Bench," prepared remarks upon receiving the Thomas Jefferson Foundation Medal in Law, April 11, 2019 (available at https://assets .documentcloud.org/documents/5836481/Thomas-Jefferson-Award -Speech-April-2019.pdf).

60. For example, on July 30, 2020, Senator Josh Hawley said on the floor of the Senate that he would vote only for Supreme Court nominees who have explicitly stated that *Roe v. Wade* was wrongly decided. See "Hawley Draws Hard Line on Supreme Court Nominees, Abortion," AP News, July 30, 2020, https://apnews.com/3d30cbf74fa39a01ef1746357eab5ebd. For a report on Leonard Leo's influence on President Donald Trump's judicial appointments, see Robert O'Harrow Jr. and Shawn Boburg, "A Conservative Activist's Behind-the-Scenes Campaign to Remake the Nation's Courts," *Washington Post*, May 21, 2019, https:// www.washingtonpost.com/graphics/2019/investigations/leonard-leo -federalists-society-courts/. On the other side of the political spectrum, the Alliance for Justice has a "Building the Bench" program that in no way eschews ideology. Others have advocated that senators' selection committees, which purport to be nonpolitical and merit-based, should be scrapped because they tend to have members who are prosecutors and corporate lawyers who recommend candidates like themselves. See Brian Fallon and Christopher Kang, "Biden Must Prioritize the Courts If Elected," *Data for Progress* (blog), July 30, 2020, https://www .dataforprogress.org/blog/biden-must-prioritize-the-courts-if-elected.

61. Eric Chung, Samuel Dong, Xiaonan April Hu, Christine Kwon, and
    Goodwin Liu, Yale Law School, and National Asian Pacific American
    Bar Association, *A Portrait of Asian Americans in the Law*, 2017, https://
    www.apaportraitproject.org. This paper was followed by a study about
    law school enrollment trends, particularly among Asian students,
    which Justice Liu also co-authored. Miranda Li, Phillip Yao, and
    Goodwin Liu, "Who's Going to Law School? Trends in Law School
    Enrollment since the Great Recession," *University of California Davis
    Law Review* 54 (2020): 613–662.
62. Chung et al., *Portrait of Asian Americans in the Law*, 24.
63. Chung et al., 25.
64. Chung et al., 25.
65. See National Asian Pacific American Bar Association Judiciary
    Committee, *Asian American Judges: Article III/Article IV/DC Courts*,
    November 7, 2019; and National Asian Pacific American Bar Associa-
    tion National Convention 2016, *Pearls of Wisdom from APA "Firsts" on
    the Bench*, accessed May 4, 2021 at https://cdn.ymaws.com/www.napaba
    .org/resource/resmgr/2016_napaba_con/CLE_Materials/CLE_501.pdf.
66. Edward M. Chen, "The Judiciary, Diversity, and Justice for All," *Asian
    American Law Journal* 10, no. 1 (2003): 130.
67. Chen, 128–129 (footnotes omitted).
68. Ming W. Chin, "Fairness or Bias: A Symposium on Racial and Ethnic
    Composition and Attitudes in the Judiciary," *Asian American Law
    Journal* 4 (1997): 194.
69. Pat K. Chew and Luke T. Kelley-Chew, "The Missing Minority
    Judges," *Journal of Gender, Race & Justice* 14 (2010): 180.
70. Josh Hsu, "Asian American Judges: Identity, Their Narratives, and
    Diversity on the Bench," *Asian Pacific American Law Journal* 11
    (2006): 93.

Part II. The Asian Women Article III Judges

1. See the Federal Judicial Center website, https://www.fjc.gov.
2. "Ratings of Article III and Article IV Judicial Nominees," American
   Bar Association, accessed May 4, 2021, https://www.americanbar.org/
   groups/committees/federal_judiciary/ratings.

3. When the committee gives a unanimous, substantial majority, or majority "not qualified" rating, the ABA may explain that rating to the Senate Judiciary Committee. See, for example, Ariane de Vogue and Alex Rogers, "'Not Qualified' Rating and Accusation from American Bar Association Moves Trump Nominee to Tears," CNN, October 30, 2019, https://www.cnn.com/2019/10/30/politics/american-bar -association-nominees-vandyke/index.html; and Debra Cassens Weiss, "GOP Senators Clash over ABA during Hearing for Judicial Nominee Rated 'Not Qualified,'" *ABA Journal*, September 26, 2019, http:// www.abajournal.com/news/article/gop-senators-criticize-aba-ratings -during-hearing-for-nominee-rated-not-qualified.

4. National Asian Pacific American Bar Association, *2015 Year in Review, Partnerships: American Bar Association*, 22, accessed May 4, 2021, https:// cdn.ymaws.com/www.napaba.org/resource/resmgr/Year-in-Review/ NAPABA_2015_in_Review.pdf ("NAPABA also worked with the ABA to address its judicial ratings of women and people of color."); see also Maya Sen, "How Judicial Qualification Ratings May Disadvantage Minority and Female Candidates," *Journal of Law and Courts* 2, no. 1 (2014): 33–66. The ABA has also sometimes been accused of being "biased against conservatives." Carrie Severino, "The ABA Has Outdone Itself Rating Lawrence VanDyke 'Not Qualified,'" *National Review*, October 30, 2019, https://www.nationalreview.com/bench-memos/the -aba-has-outdone-itself-rating-lawrence-vandyke-not-qualified.

5. Lee Rawles, "Its Ratings System under Fire, ABA Stresses Importance of Federal Judicial Candidate Evaluations," *ABA Journal*, January 1, 2018, https://www.abajournal.com/magazine/article/federal_judicial _candidate_evaluations.

6. Charlie Savage, "Biden Won't Restore Bar Association's Role in Vetting Judges," *New York Times*, February 5, 2021, https://www.nytimes.com/ 2021/02/05/us/politics/biden-american-bar-assoication-judges.html.

7. Vincent Eng, interview with the author by telephone, October 24, 2019.

8. Chris Kang, interview with the author by telephone, November 21, 2019.

9. "Mollway, Susan Oki," Federal Judicial Center, accessed May 4, 2021, https://www.fjc.gov/history/judges/mollway-susan-oki. This and subsequent FJC biographies have been edited lightly for style.

10. In 2007, George H. Wu of the Central District of California succeeded another Asian Article III judge, Ronald S. W. Lew, who had taken senior status.

11. The position of chief judge of a lower federal court differs from the position of the chief justice of the U.S. Supreme Court. One becomes the chief judge of a lower court by virtue of seniority, provided that one is below the age of sixty-five when one's term begins and one does not serve after turning seventy. The term of a chief judge is usually limited to seven years, but some courts provide for shorter terms by agreement, and some chief judges serve longer than seven years because there is no eligible judge to step in. See 28 U.S.C. § 45 (for chief circuit judges); and 28 U.S.C. § 136 (for chief district judges).

12. I took my husband's name in 1973, which was years before I entered law school. I kept that name after we got divorced in 2006, not only because I had used it my entire legal career, but also because keeping it avoided yet another change that our son would have to get used to.

13. Ratings of Article III Judicial Nominees, 104th Congress, accessed May 4, 2021, https://www.americanbar.org/content/dam/aba/migrated/2011_build/federal_judiciary/ratings104.pdf.

14. Ratings of Article III Judicial Nominees, 105th Congress, accessed May 4, 2021, https://www.americanbar.org/content/dam/aba/migrated/2011_build/federal_judiciary/ratings105.pdf.

15. "Roll Call Vote 105th Congress—2nd Session," U.S. Senate, accessed May 4, 2021, https://www.senate.gov/legislative/LIS/roll_call_lists/roll_call_vote_cfm.cfm?congress=105&session=2&vote=00166.

16. "Roll Call Vote 105th Congress—2nd Session."

17. "Matsumoto, Kiyo A.," Federal Judicial Center, accessed May 4, 2021, https://www.fjc.gov/history/judges/matsumoto-kiyo.

18. Kiyo A. Matsumoto, interviewed by the author by telephone on September 5, 2019, augmented by email to the author dated February 21, 2020.

19. Anthony Ishii, email to the author dated October 17, 2019, concerning his parents (I had prior knowledge about Judges Tashima and Takasugi).

20. "The George Matsumoto Prize," North Carolina Modernist, accessed May 4, 2021, http://www.ncmodernist.org/matsumotoprize.htm.

21. "Judge Kiyo Matsumoto Delivers 11th Annual Korematsu Lecture," *NYU News*, March 17, 2010, https://www.law.nyu.edu/news/KOREMATSU_MATSUMOTO.

22. Ratings of Article III Judicial Nominees, 110th Congress, accessed May 4, 2021, https://www.americanbar.org/content/dam/aba/migrated/2011_build/federal_judiciary/ratings110.pdf.

23. "Confirmation Hearings on Federal Appointments," U.S. Congress, Serial No. J-110-8, June 11, 2008, https://www.congress.gov/110/chrg/shrg48894/CHRG-110shrg48894.htm.

24. "PN1458—Kiyo A. Matsumoto—the Judiciary," Congress.gov, accessed May 4, 2021, https://www.congress.gov/nomination/110th-congress/1458?s=1&r=5.

25. "Korematsu Lecture."

26. "Nguyen, Jacqueline Hong-Ngoc," Federal Judicial Center, accessed May 4, 2021, https://www.fjc.gov/history/judges/nguyen-jacqueline-hong-ngoc.

27. Jacqueline Hong-Ngoc Nguyen, interviewed by the author by telephone on September 10, 2019, augmented by emails to the author on November 12, 2020.

28. "Voices of America: Enhancing Diversity on the Bench—Judge Jacqueline Nguyen," L.A. Progressive, April 26, 2010, https://www.laprogressive.com/voices-america-enhancing-diversity-bench-2.

29. Barack Obama Scholars Program, "Jacqueline Nguyen," Occidental College, accessed May 4, 2021, https://obamascholars.oxy.edu/person/jacqueline-nguyen.

30. Robert Greene, "Davis Names Assistant U.S. Attorney Jacqueline Nguyen to Fill Vacancy on Los Angeles Superior Court," *Metropolitan News-Enterprise*, August 14, 2002, http://www.metnews.com/articles/nguyo81402.htm.

31. Ratings of Article III Judicial Nominees, 111th Congress, accessed May 4, 2021, https://www.americanbar.org/content/dam/aba/migrated/2011_build/federal_judiciary/ratings111.pdf.

32. https://www.congress.gov/nomination/111th-congress/841.

33. Ratings of Article III Judicial Nominees, 112th Congress, accessed May 4, 2021, https://www.americanbar.org/content/dam/aba/uncategorized/2011/ratings112.pdf.

34. Alexa Vaughn, "Obama Taps L.A. Federal Judge Nguyen for 9th Circuit," *L.A. Times*, September 23, 2011, https://www.latimes.com/politics/la-xpm-2011-sep-23-la-pn-nguyen-9thcircuit-20110923-story.html.

35. "On the Nomination PN985: Jacqueline H. Nguyen, of California, to Be United States Circuit Judge for the Ninth Circuit," GovTrack, May 7, 2012, https://www.govtrack.us/congress/votes/112-2012/s88.

36. Casey Tolan, "How Jacqueline Nguyen Went from a Vietnamese Refugee to a Potential Supreme Court Nominee," Splinter News, February 18, 2016, https://splinternews.com/how-jacqueline-nguyen-went-from-a-vietnamese-refugee-to-1793854865.

37. Lydia Wheeler, "Clinton's Court Shortlist Emerges," *Hill*, July 30, 2016, https://thehill.com/regulation/court-battles/289643-clintons-court-shortlist-emerges.

38. "Gee, Dolly Maizie," Federal Judicial Center, accessed May 4, 2021, https://www.fjc.gov/history/judges/gee-dolly-maizie.

39. In-person interview conducted by the author on July 22, 2019, at the Davenport Grand Hotel, Spokane, Washington (during the 2019 Ninth Circuit Conference), augmented by subsequent email exchanges on July 23, 2019, September 3, 2019, November 21, 2019, March 3, 2020, and March 4, 2020. There is an interesting segment on Gee in the NAPABA Inspirational Video Series (available at https://www.youtube.com/watch?v=yAaFQVltOxE).

40. Ratings of Article III Judicial Nominees, 106th Congress, accessed May 4, 2021, https://www.americanbar.org/content/dam/aba/migrated/2011_build/federal_judiciary/ratings106.pdf.

41. "Remarks on the Observance of Asian/Pacific American Heritage Month," May 25, 2000, https://www.govinfo.gov/content/pkg/PPP-2000-book1/html/PPP-2000-book1-doc-pg1025.htm. The five Asian judges that President Clinton was referring to were Denny Chin, appointed to the Southern District of New York in 1994; George King, appointed to the Central District of California in 1995; Atsushi Wallace Tashima, elevated from the Central District of California to the Ninth Circuit in 1996; Anthony Ishii, appointed to the Eastern District of California in 1997; and me, appointed to the District of Hawaii in 1998.

42. "Remarks by President William J. Clinton at Asian Pacific American Institute for Congressional Studies Dinner," *American Presidency Project*, May 25, 2000, https://www.presidency.ucsb.edu/documents/remarks-the-observance-asianpacific-american-heritage-month.

43. Ratings of Article III Judicial Nominees, 111th Congress, accessed May 4, 2021, https://www.americanbar.org/content/dam/aba/migrated/2011_build/federal_judiciary/ratings111.pdf.

44. Transcript of Senate Judiciary Committee hearing on September 23, 2009 (available at https://www.congress.gov/111/chrg/shrg62345/CHRG-111shrg62345.htm), 974.

45. "Koh, Lucy Haeran," Federal Judicial Center, accessed May 4, 2021, https://www.fjc.gov/history/judges/koh-lucy-haeran.

46. Herbert Choy preceded Koh as the first Article III judge of Korean ancestry, but he sat on the Ninth Circuit, not a district court.

47. Lucy Haeran Koh, interviewed by the author by telephone on September 9, 2019, augmented by emails to the author on September 12, 2019, and February 25, 2020.

48. Davey Alba, "The Meme-Worthy Judge of Silicon Valley's Titans," Wired, April 21, 2015, https://www.wired.com/2015/04/lucy-koh.

49. Lucy Koh, "Combatting Inequality," in *Harvard Law School's Handbook and Directory for Law Students and Lawyers Seeking Public Service Work*, 1995–1996, 26.

50. Philip Lee, "The Griswold 9 and Student Activism for Faculty Diversity at Harvard Law School in the Early 1990s," *Harvard Journal of Racial and Ethnic Justice* 27 (2011): 49–96.

51. Lee, 80.

52. Ratings of Article III Judicial Nominees, 111th Congress, accessed May 4, 2021, https://www.americanbar.org/content/dam/aba/migrated/2011_build/federal_judicary/ratings111.pdf.

53. "Roll Call Vote 111th Congress—2nd Session," U.S. Senate, June 7, 2010, https://www.senate.gov/legislative/LIS/roll_call_lists/roll_call_vote_cfm.cfm?congress=111&session=2&vote=00178.

54. Kerry Kassam, "Judging the Judges: Who Are the Most Cited New Jurists on the Federal Bench?," *Above the Law*, April 23, 2015, https://abovethelaw.com/2015/04/judging-the-judges-who-are-the-most-cited-new-jurists-on-the-federal-bench.

55. Ratings of Article III Judicial Nominees, 114th Congress, accessed May 4, 2021, https://www.americanbar.org/content/dam/aba/uncategorized/GAO/WebRatingChart114.pdf.

56. Howard Mintz, "White House Expected to Nominate High-Profile Silicon Valley–Based Judge Lucy Koh to Federal Appeals Court," *Mercury News*, February 1, 2016, https://www.mercurynews.com/2016/02/01/white-house-expected-to-nominate-high-profile-silicon-valley-based-judge-lucy-koh-to-federal-appeals-court ("legal experts say Koh should not pack her office just yet, given likely Senate Republican resistance to any of the president's picks for the 9th Circuit on the eve of an election"). Although in the past it was not unusual for judicial nominations to slow as an election neared, a number of President Trump's judicial nominees were sped through the confirmation process as the 2020 presidential election neared. This was the case not just on lower federal courts. Aided by the Senate majority leader, Republican Mitch McConnell from Kentucky, Amy Coney Barrett was confirmed to the U.S. Supreme Court within weeks after Justice Ruth Bader Ginsburg died, and just days before the 2020 election.

57. Lydia Wheeler, "Clinton's Court Shortlist Emerges," *Hill*, July 30, 2016, https://thehill.com/regulation/court-battles/289643-clintons-court-shortlist-emerges.

58. Wheeler.

59. Demand Justice, "Demand Justice's Supreme Court Shortlist," accessed May 4, 2021, https://demandjustice.org/supreme-court-shortlist.

60. Demand Justice, "About Us," accessed May 4, 2021, https://demandjustice.org/about.

61. Koh may have been disqualified from inclusion because she was a former partner at a large law firm. See Brian Fallon and Christopher Kang, "No More Corporate Lawyers on the Federal Bench: The Next Democratic President Should Try Nominating Judges Who Haven't Been Partners at Big Law Firms," *Atlantic*, August 21, 2019, https://www.theatlantic.com/ideas/archive/2019/08/no-more-corporate-judges/596383.

62. "Kobayashi, Leslie Emi," Federal Judicial Center, accessed May 4, 2021, https://www.fjc.gov/history/judges/kobayashi-leslie-emi.

63. Leslie Emi Kobayashi, interviewed by the author in person in Kobayashi's chambers in Honolulu, Hawaii, August 2, 2019, augmented by a telephone conversation on September 12, 2019.

64. Ken Kobayashi, "Dignity Key for Kobayashi," *Honolulu Star Advertiser*, December 27, 2010, https://www.staradvertiser.com/2010/12/27/hawaii -news/dignity-key-for-kobayashi.

65. Kobayashi.

66. Kobayashi.

67. Ratings of Article III Judicial Nominees, 111th Congress, accessed May 4, 2021, https://www.americanbar.org/content/dam/aba/migrated/ 2011_build/federal_judiciary/ratings111.pdf.

68. Carlton W. Reeves, "Defending the Judiciary: A Call for Justice, Truth, and Diversity on the Bench (Footnotes Omitted)," prepared remarks upon receiving the Thomas Jefferson Foundation Medal in Law, April 11, 2019 (available at https://assets.documentcloud.org/documents/5836481/Thomas -Jefferson-Award-Speech-April-2019.pdf). The "two senators" that Reeves refers to were Richard Durbin of Illinois and Jon Kyl of Arizona.

69. "PN1656—Leslie E. Kobayashi—the Judiciary," Congress.gov, accessed May 4, 2021, https://www.congress.gov/nomination/111th-congress/ 1656?q=%7B%E2%80%9Csearch%E2%80%9D%3A%E2%80%9C5310 %227D&s=3&r=6.

70. "Kobayashi and Chang Confirmed by Senate," *Asian American Press*, December 23, 2010, https://aapress.com/government/kobayashi-and -chang-confirmed-by-senate.

71. In 2012, Edmond Chang of the Northern District of Illinois noted in an email to Asian judges that he had just sworn in his colleague, John Lee. He wondered whether that was the first time an Asian Article III judge had sworn in another Asian Article III judge. I told him that had already occurred in 2010 in the District of Hawaii.

72. Kerry Kassam, "Judging the Judges: Who Are the Most Cited New Jurists on the Federal Bench?," *Above the Law*, April 23, 2015, https:// abovethelaw.com/2015/04/judging-the-judges-who-are-the-most-cited -new-jurists-on-the-federal-bench.

73. *Kamakana v. City and County of Honolulu*, Civ. No. 00-729, 2002 WL 32255355 (D. Haw. November 25, 2002), *affirmed*, 447 F.3d 1172 (9th Cir. 2006).

74. See Pub. L. No. 101-650 (December 1, 1990). See also "U.S. District Courts: Authorized Temporary Judgeships," United States Courts, accessed May 4, 2021, https://www.uscourts.gov/sites/default/files/district-temporary-judgeships_0.pdf.

75. To illustrate, if the judge who initially fills a judgeship created as a temporary judgeship serves as an active judge for twenty years, and the position expires five years after that judge's confirmation, the judge is unaffected and may serve as long as she chooses. However, if the position expires at the end of five years and the judge dies or steps down at six years, the position cannot be filled. Expiration dates can be extended, and the District of Hawaii has had repeated extensions, including an extension that expired after the date I took senior status in late 2015. Because the vacancy I created by taking senior status arose while the temporary judgeship was still in effect, my position could be filled at any time. That is, the operative date is the date the vacancy is created, not the date the vacancy is filled. A vacancy created before the expiration date may be filled at any time. For that reason, Jill Otake could fill my position in 2018, the vacancy having been created in 2015, before the extension of the temporary judgeship had expired.

76. See Pub. L. No. 116-6 (February 15, 2019). See also "Chronological History of Authorized Judgeships in U.S. District Courts," United States Courts, accessed May 4, 2021, https://www.uscourts.gov/sites/default/files/districtchronol19.pdf.

77. "Bissoon, Cathy," Federal Judicial Center, accessed May 4, 2021, https://www.fjc.gov/history/judges/bissoon-cathy.

78. Cathy Bissoon, interviewed by the author by telephone on September 19, 2019, augmented by emails to the author dated September 20, 2019, September 8, 2020, and November 10, 2020.

79. See 28 U.S.C. § 636(c).

80. Ratings of Article III Judicial Nominees, 111th Congress, accessed May 4, 2021, https://www.americanbar.org/content/dam/aba/migrated/2011_build/federal_judiciary/ratings111.pdf.

81. Ratings of Article III Judicial Nominees, 112th Congress, accessed May 4, 2021, https://www.americanbar.org/content/dam/aba/uncategorized/2011/ratings112.pdf.

82. "On the Nomination PN11: Cathy Bissoon, of Pennsylvania, to Be United States District Judge for the Western District of Pennsylvania," GovTrack, accessed May 4, 2021, https://www.govtrack.us/congress/votes/112-2011/s166.

83. "Du, Miranda Mai," Federal Judicial Center, accessed May 4, 2021, https://www.fjc.gov/history/judges/du-miranda-mai (the FJC website leaves blank the end date for Du's law firm membership, but the author has added an end date of 2012 to correspond to Du's commission as a judge).

84. Miranda Mai Du, interviewed by the author by telephone on September 26, 2019, augmented by emails to the author on October 17, 2019, September 10, 2020, and November 5, 2020.

85. Ratings of Article III Judicial Nominees, 112th Congress, accessed May 4, 2021, https://www.americanbar.org/content/dam/aba/uncategorized/2011/ratings112.pdf.

86. The rating was possibly related to a case that Du discussed in her Senate Judiciary Committee questionnaire. There was a discovery sanction issued against her client in the case, which was ultimately dismissed on jurisdictional grounds. Du also recalls that during her FBI background check, she was asked why she had not disclosed an order that had issued in another case she had worked on that capped any damage award as a sanction for a failure to provide discovery relating to damages. Du says that she had not considered the case to be covered by an inquiry about actions taken against her personally.

87. "Roll Call Vote 112th Congress 2nd Session," U.S. Senate, March 28, 2012, https://www.senate.gov/legislative/LIS/roll_call_lists/roll_call_vote_cfm.cfm?congress=112&session=2&vote=00061.

88. "Schofield, Lorna Gail," Federal Judicial Center, accessed May 4, 2021, https://www.fjc.gov/history/judges/schofield-lorna-gail.

89. Lorna Gail Schofield, interviewed by the author by telephone on October 9, 2019, augmented by an email to the author on February 23, 2020.

90. Cristina D. C. Pastor, "First Fil-Am Federal Judge Lorna Schofield: 'I Had No Filipino Consciousness Growing Up,'" *USA Inquirer*, February 24, 2018, https://usa.inquirer.net/10419/first-fil-federal-judge-lorna-schofield-no-filipino-consciousness-growing.

91. Ratings of Article III Judicial Nominees, 112th Congress, accessed May 4, 2021, https://www.americanbar.org/content/dam/aba/uncategorized/2011/ratings112.pdf.

92. Joseph Pimental, "Lorna Schofield, One of National Law Journal's 50 Most Influential Minority Lawyers and Nominee for Federal District Court Judge, Southern District of NY," *Asian Journal*, January 28, 2012, https://www.asianjournal.com/usa/newyork-newjersey/lorna-schofield-one-of-national-law-journals-50-most-influential-minority-lawyers-and-nominee-for-federal-district-court-judge-southern-district-of-ny.

93. "PN1556, Lorna G. Schofield, the Judiciary," Congress.gov, accessed May 4, 2021, https://www.congress.gov/nomination/112th-congress/1556.

94. "Chen, Pamela Ki Mai," Federal Judicial Center, accessed May 4, 2021, https://www.fjc.gov/history/judges/chen-pamela-ki-mai.

95. Pamela Ki Mai Chen, interviewed by the author by telephone on August 29, 2019, augmented by emails to the author on September 6, 2019, and October 7, 2020.

96. As noted at the start of part 2, NAPABA was also questioning the ABA about this very matter.

97. Ratings of Article III Judicial Nominees, 112th Congress, accessed May 4, 2021, https://www.americanbar.org/content/dam/aba/uncategorized/2011/ratings112.pdf.

98. Ratings of Article III Judicial Nominees, 113th Congress, accessed May 4, 2021, https://www.americanbar.org/content/dam/aba/uncategorized/GAO/WebRatingChart.pdf.

99. "PN11, Pamela Ki Mai Chen, the Judiciary," Congress.gov, accessed October 2, 2020, https://www.congress.gov/nomination/113th-congress/11?s7&r=23.

100. "Talwani, Indira," Federal Judicial Center, accessed May 4, 2021, https://www.fjc.gov/history/judges/talwani-indira.

101. Indira Talwani, interviewed by the author by telephone on October 7, 2019, augmented by emails to the author on February 23, 2020, and February 24, 2020. She declined to provide a photograph of herself for inclusion in this book.

102. Berzon was a nominee at the same time I was. We knew each other, and I was conscious that she and I were both facing delays in getting confirmed.

103. "Judicial Nominations," Committee on the Judiciary, accessed May 4, 2021, http://www.judiciary.senate.gov/nominations/judicial/?Keyword= Talwani.

104. Ratings of Article III Judicial Nominees, 113th Congress, accessed May 4, 2021, https://www.americanbar.org/content/dam/aba/ uncategorized/GAO/WebRatingChart.pdf.

105. Paul Kane, "Reid, Democrats Trigger 'Nuclear' Option; Eliminate Most Filibusters on Nominees," *Washington Post*, November 21, 2013, https:// www.washingtonpost.com/politics/senate-poised-to-limit-filibusters-in -party-line-vote-that-would-alter-centuries-of-precedent/2013/11/21/ d065cfe8-52b6-11e3-9fe0-fd2ca728e67c_story.html.

106. Ratings of Article III Judicial Nominees, 113th Congress, accessed May 4, 2021, https://www.americanbar.org/content/dam/aba/ uncategorized/GAO/WebRatingChart.pdf.

107. "On the Nomination PN1220: Indira Talwani, of Massachusetts, to Be United States District Judge for the District of Massachusetts," Gov-Track, May 8, 2014, https://www.govtrack.us/congress/votes/113-2014/s137.

108. "Groves, Jennifer Choe," Federal Judicial Center, accessed May 4, 2021, https://www.fjc.gov/history/judges/groves-jennifer-choe.

109. Jennifer Choe-Groves, interviewed by the author by telephone on September 12, 2019, augmented by emails to the author on October 17, 2019, and October 20, 2020.

110. Patrick Folliard, "Spotlighting: Taking the Next Step," *Diversity & the Bar*, May/June 2010, reprinted at https://www.mcca.com/mcca-article/ spotlighting-may-june-2010.

111. Folliard.

112. 28 U.S.C. § 251. For a critique of this statutory provision, see Adam J. Rappaport, "The Court of International Trade's Political Party Diversity Requirement: Unconstitutional under Any Separation of Powers Theory," *University of Chicago Law Review* 68 (2001): 1429–1458.

113. Ratings of Article III Judicial Nominees, 114th Congress, accessed May 4, 2021, https://www.americanbar.org/content/dam/aba/ uncategorized/GAO/WebRatingChart114.pdf.

114. The most Choe-Groves could say was that her "best guess" was that the minority rating was related to her lack of appearances before the Court of International Trade.

115. "Scholer, Karen Gren," Federal Judicial Center, accessed May 4, 2021, https://www.fjc.gov/history/judges/scholer-karen-gren.

116. James Ho took a seat on the Fifth Circuit a few months before Scholer did, to become the first Asian Article III judge in the Fifth Circuit.

117. Scholer was one of a group of judges nominated by President Obama who did not get confirmed, but then were nominated by President Trump. That group includes Scholer's colleague in the Northern District of Texas, James Wesley Hendrix. Another Asian woman, Diane Gujarati, was nominated by Obama for a seat in the Eastern District of New York, did not get confirmed, then was nominated by Trump for a seat in the same district, was not confirmed, was renominated by Trump in 2019, and was confirmed in 2020.

118. Karen Gren Scholer, interviewed by the author by telephone on October 14, 2019, augmented by emails to the author on the same day and on November 10, 2020, and by a telephone conversation on March 10, 2020.

119. Scholer's given name of "Gren" is a shortened, Americanized version of her father's Polish family surname.

120. Selwyn Crawford, "High Profile: A Perfect Fit, Asian American Woman 'Just Feels Right' on the District Court Bench," *Dallas Morning News*, April 21, 2002, 3F. This article was given to me by Scholer, who did not indicate that anything in the article was incorrect.

121. Crawford, 3F.

122. Crawford, 3F.

123. Crawford, 3F.

124. Much of this detail comes from remarks by Judge Amos Mazzant III of the Eastern District of Texas in July 2018, at Scholer's investiture. Scholer provided me with a copy of Mazzant's remarks to ensure that I would have an accurate account of dates and other details.

125. John Council, "A Decade Later, Texas Finally Sees Its First Asian-American U.S. District Judge," Law.com, Texas Lawyer, May 1, 2018, https://www.law.com/texaslawyer/2018/05/01/a-decade-later-texas-finally-sees-its-first-asian-american-u-s-district-judge.

126. Ratings of Article III Judicial Nominees, 114th Congress, accessed May 4, 2021, https://www.americanbar.org/content/dam/aba/uncategorized/GAO/WebRatingChart114.pdf.

127. Ratings of Article III Judicial Nominees, 115th Congress, accessed May 4, 2021, https://www.americanbar.org/content/dam/aba/uncategorized/GAO/Web%20rating%20Chart%20Trump%20115.pdf.

128. Roll Call Vote 115th Congress—2nd Session, U.S. Senate, March 5, 2018, https://www.senate.gov/legislative/LIS/roll_call_lists/roll_call_vote_cfm.cfm?congress=115&session=2&vote=00046.

129. Council, "Decade Later."

130. The Susan Lucci remark is also recounted in Council, "Decade Later," which says that Scholer's husband described her as "the Susan Lucci of Texas federal judges." For any reader unfamiliar with Susan Lucci, I note here that she was an actress who played Erica Kane on *All My Children*, an ABC soap opera. Lucci became famous for being repeatedly nominated for an Emmy without winning until she finally won, in 1999, after eighteen tries.

131. "Otake, Jill Aiko," Federal Judicial Center, accessed May 4, 2021, https://www.fjc.gov/history/judges/otake-jill-aiko.

132. Jill Aiko Otake, interviewed by the author in Otake's chambers in Honolulu, Hawaii, on July 19, 2019, augmented by emails to the author dated September 6, 2019, by a telephone conversation on September 12, 2019, and by emails to the author on February 21, March 5, March 21, September 15, and October 6, 2020.

133. See Nick Grube, "Hawaii Federal Judge Nomination Offers Glimpse of Partisan Dealmaking," Civil Beat, March 7, 2018, https://www.civilbeat.org/2018/03/hawaii-federal-judge-nomination-offers-glimpse-of-partisan-dealmaking.

134. Harsh Voruganti, "Jill Otake—Nominee for the U.S. District Court for the District of Hawaii," *Vetting Room*, February 27, 2018, https://www.vettingroom.org/2018/02/27/jill-otake.

135. Voruganti.

136. Voruganti.

137. Ratings of Article III Judicial Nominees, 115th Congress, accessed May 4, 2021, https://www.americanbar.org/content/dam/aba/uncategorized/GAO/WebRatingChart115.pdf.

138. "Senate Floor Activity—Wednesday, August 1, 2018," U.S. Senate, accessed May 4, 2021, https://www.senate.gov/legislative/LIS/floor_activity/2018/08_01_2018_Senate_Floor.htm.

139. "Rao, Neomi Jehangir," Federal Judicial Center, accessed May 4, 2021, https://www.fjc.gov/history/judges/rao-neomi-jehangir.

140. Neomi Jehangir Rao, interviewed by the author by telephone on October 2, 2019.

141. "Statement of Neomi Rao, United States Homeland Security and Government Affairs Committee Hearing on the Nomination of Neomi Rao to Be the Administrator of the Office of Information and Regulatory Affairs, Office of Management and Budget," Senate Homeland Security and Governmental Affairs Committee, June 7, 2017, https://www.hsgac.senate.gov/imo/media/doc/Prepared%20Statement-Rao-2017-06-07.pdf.

142. Neomi Rao, "Submission, Silence, Mediocrity," *Yale Free Press*, November 1993, accessed May 4, 2021, at https://www.documentcloud.org/documents/5684271-Rao-Submission-Silence-Mediocracy.html.

143. An unofficial transcript of Rao's hearing before the Senate Judiciary Committee, held on February 5, 2019, was made available online by Bloomberg Government, "Senate Judiciary Committee Hearing on Pending Nominations, Sked Final," February 7, 2019, 22, http://www.bgov.com.

144. Bloomberg Government, 22.

145. Neomi Rao and Luis Roth, "Separate, but More Than Equal: From Admissions to Ethnic Deans, a Look at Minorities at Yale," *Yale Free Press*, accessed May 4, 2021, at https://assets.documentcloud.org/documents/5684269/Rao-Separate-but-More-Than-Equal.pdf. (I could not find a copy of this bearing a publication year, but the article identifies Rao as a junior, so it was apparently written during the 1993–1994 academic year.)

146. Rao and Roth.

147. Rao and Roth.

148. Rao and Roth.

149. See, for example, letter dated February 11, 2019, from In Our Own Voice: National Black Women's Reproductive Justice Agenda, National Asian Pacific American Women's Forum, and National Latina Institute for Reproductive Health to Senator Lindsay Graham and Senator Dianne Feinstein (citing Rao's article and stating that Rao "consistently expressed views in her writing throughout college and in her

20s that demonstrate hostility toward communities of color"), https://
www.napawf.org/our-work/content/2019/2/11/letter-of-opposition-by
-reproductive-justice-groups-to-neomi-raos-confirmation.

150. Neomi Rao, "How the Diversity Game Is Played," *Washington Times*,
July 17, 1994, WLNR 236705 (1994), https://afj.org/wp-content/
uploads/2019/12/07-How-the-Diversity-Game-is-Played.pdf.

151. Rao, 6.

152. Rao, 6.

153. Harsh Voruganti, "Neomi Rao—Nominee to the U.S. Court of
Appeals for the D.C. Circuit," *Vetting Room*, February 11, 2019, https://
vettingroom.org/2019/02/11/neomi-rao.

154. See, for example, Shane Croucher, "Who Is Neomi Rao? Trump
Nominee to Replace Brett Kavanaugh Wrote Controversial Date
Rape Column in College," *Newsweek*, January 15, 2019, https://www
.newsweek.com/trump-neomi-rao-brett-kavanaugh-date-rape-column
-1291483; and Sarah Jones, "Why Kavanaugh Replacement Neomi
Rao Is So Controversial," *New York Magazine*, March 14, 2019, http://
nymag.com/intelligencer/2019/03/neomi-rao-controversial.html.

155. Remarks by President Trump at Diwali Ceremonial Lighting of the
Diya, White House, November 13, 2019, https://in.usembassy.gov/
remarks-by-president-trump-at-diwali-ceremonial-lighting-of-the
-diya-at-the-white-house/.

156. "NAPABA Applauds Nomination of Neomi Rao to D.C. Circuit,"
NAPABA, November 14, 2018, https://www.napaba.org/page/neomi
_rao_dccircuit_nomination.

157. Ratings of Article III Judicial Nominees, 116th Congress, accessed
May 4, 2021, https://www.americanbar.org/content/dam/aba/
administrative/government_affairs_office/webratingchart-trump116
.pdf?logActivity=true.

158. Neomi Rao, "Shades of Gray," *Yale Herald*, October 14, 1994, accessed
May 4, 2021, at https://afj.org/wp-content/uploads/2019/12/02-Shades
-of-Gray.pdf.

159. Bloomberg Government, "Senate Judiciary Committee Hearing."

160. Neomi Rao, "The Feminist Dilemma," *Yale Free Press*, April 1993,
https://www.afj.org/wp-content/uploads/2019/12/02-The-Feminist
-Dilemma.pdf.

161. Rao.

162. Bloomberg Government, "Senate Judiciary Committee Hearing."

163. Letter from Neomi Rao to Senators Lindsey Graham and Dianne
    Feinstein, February 11, 2019, https://www.judiciary.senate.gov/imo/
    media/doc/Letter%20from%20N.%20Rao%20to%20SJC.pdf.

164. Neomi Rao, "Substantive Dignity—Dwarf-Throwing, Burqa Bans,
    and Welfare Rights," *Volokh Conspiracy*, May 18, 2011, http://volokh
    .com/2011/05/18/substantive-dignity-dwarf-throwing-burqa-bans-and
    -welfare-rights.

165. Rao. This is not Rao's only discussion of this topic. See also, for exam-
    ple, Neomi Rao, "Three Concepts of Dignity in Constitutional Law,"
    Notre Dame Law Review 86 (2011): 183–271.

166. Ann E. Marimow and Seung Min Kim, "Justice Thomas Working
    behind the Scenes to Boost Trump's Court Nominee," *Washington Post*,
    February 28, 2019, https://www.washingtonpost.com/powerpost/trumps
    -court-nominee-overcomes-gop-concerns-secures-panels-backing/
    2019/02/28/fa33bc86-3adc-11e9-aaae-69364b2ed137_story.html.

167. Marimow and Kim.

168. See, for example, Alliance for Justice, "Neomi Rao: United States
    Court of Appeals for the Washington D.C. Circuit," accessed May 4,
    2021, https://www.afj.org/nominee/neomi-rao; Carrie N. Baker, "10
    Reasons Feminists Are Wary of Neomi Rao," *Ms.*, February 11, 2019,
    https://msmagazine.com/2019/02/11/10-reasons-feminists-wary-neomi
    -rao; Marcela Howell, Sung Yeon Choimorrow, and Jessica Gonzalez-
    Rojas, "Neomi Rao Will Not Protect Rights of Women of Color," *Hill*,
    February 15, 2019, https://thehill.com/opinion/judiciary/430077-neomi
    -rao-will-not-protect-rights-of-women-of-color; Theresa Lau, "Five
    Things You Should Know about D.C. Circuit Nominee Neomi Rao,"
    National Women's Law Center, February 14, 2019, https://nwlc.org/
    blog/five-things-you-should-know-about-d-c-circuit-nominee-neomi
    -rao; and Ephrat Livri, "To Understand Trump Judicial Pick Neomi
    Rao, Consider Her Writing on Dwarf-Tossing," Quartz, November 29,
    2018, https://qz.com/1477549/to-understand-trump-judicial-pick
    -neomi-rao-consider-her-writing-on-dwarf-tossing.

169. See, for example, Elizabeth Slattery, "4 Key Issues in Neomi Rao's
    Judicial Confirmation Hearing," Heritage Foundation, February 6,

2019, https://www.heritage.org/courts/commentary/4-key-issues
-neomi-raos-judicial-confirmation-hearing; Jonathan S. Tobin, "The
Battle over Neomi Rao Is the Latest in the Judicial Wars: Republicans
Must Stand up to Democrats' Attempt to Damage a Rising Legal
Star," *National Review*, February 6, 2019; https://www.nationalreview
.com/2019/02/neomi-rao-nomination-democrats-try-to-damage-rising
-legal-star; and Shoshana Weissmann, "Neomi Rao Was Right about
Dwarf Tossing, Dignity, and Consent. She Deserves to Be a Federal
Judge: A Defense of Brett Kavanaugh's Nominated Replacement on
the D.C. Circuit," *Reason*, November 26, 2018, https://reason.com/
2018/11/26/neomi-rao-was-right-about-dwarf-tossing. For a discussion
about what one commentator calls a "schism" between libertarians and
the conservative right, as highlighted by reactions to Rao's nomination,
see Daniel Horowitz, "The Fight over Judicial Nominee Neomi Rao
Reveals a Big Schism on the Right," *Conservative Review*, February 26, 2019, https://www.conservativereview.com/news/fight-judicial
-nominee-neomi-rao-reveals-big-schism-right.

170. "PN247, Neomi J. Rao, the Judiciary," Congress.gov, accessed May 4,
2021, https://www.congress.gov/nomination/116th-congress/247.

171. "PN247."

172. "Indian-American Neomi Rao Sworn in as Judge of Powerful
U.S. Court," *Hindu Business Line*, March 21, 2019, https://www
.thehindubusinessline.com/news/world/indian-american-neomi-rao
-sworn-in-as-judge-of-powerful-us-court/article26597495.ece.

173. Amy Howe, "Trump Releases New List of Potential Supreme Court
Nominees," *SCOTUSblog*, May 9, 2020, https://www.scotusblog.com/
2020/trump-releases-new-list-of-potential-supreme-court-nominees.

174. "Pacold, Martha Maria," Federal Judicial Center, accessed May 4, 2021,
https://www.fjc.gov/history/judges/pacold-martha-maria.

175. "Gujarati, Diane," Federal Judicial Center, accessed May 4, 2021, https://
www.fjc.gov/history/judges/gujarati-diane.

176. "Current Judicial Vacancies," U.S. Courts, accessed January 4, 2021,
https://www.uscourts.gov/judges-judgeships/judicial-vacancies/current
-judicial-vacancies.

Part III. Analyzing the Data

1. See Cynthia Grant Bowman, "Women in the Legal Profession from the 1920s to the 1970s: What Can We Learn from Their Experience about Law and Social Change?," *Maine Law Review* 61 (2009): 2–25; and Stacy Caplow and Shira A. Scheindlin, "'Portrait of a Lady': The Woman Lawyer in the 1980s," *NYU Law Review* 35 (1990): 391–446.

2. "Asian Alone by Selected Groups, Asian Japanese," U.S. Census Bureau, accessed March 2, 2020, https://data.census.gov/cedsci/table?q=asian%20japanese&tid=ACSDT1Y2018.C02015&t=Asian.

3. "ACS Demographic and Housing Estimates," U.S. Census Bureau, accessed March 2, 2020, https://data.census.gov/cedsci/table?q=hawaii&g=0400000US15&tid=ACSDP1Y2018.DP05.

4. "ACS Demographic and Housing Estimates."

5. "2019 Bar Statistics and Summaries," Hawaii State Bar Association, accessed May 4, 2021, https://hsba.org/images/hsba/HSBA/Annual%20Statistics%20Results/2019_Bar_Statistics_and_Summaries.pdf.

6. "Asian Alone by Selected Groups, Asian Japanese."

7. "American FactFinder: ACS Demographic and Housing Estimates, 2013–2017 American Community Survey 5-Year Estimates, DP05," U.S. Census Bureau, accessed March 2, 2020, https://factfinder.census.gov/faces/tableservices/jsf/pages/productview.xhtml?src=bkmk. The FactFinder page has been decommissioned, and the U.S. Census Bureau now refers the public to https://www.data.census.gov. One site that includes this data is "2013-2017 ACS 5-Year Estimates," accessed May 4, 2021, https://www.census.gov/programs-surveys/acs/technical-documentation/table-and-geography-changes/2017/5-year.html.

8. "Asian Alone by Selected Groups, Asian Chinese California," U.S. Census Bureau, accessed March 2, 2020, https://data.census.gov/cedsci/table?q=asian%20chinese%20california&g=0400000US06&tid=ACSDT1Y2018.C02015&t=Asian.

9. "Asian Alone by Selected Groups, Asian Chinese Nevada," U.S. Census Bureau, accessed March 16, 2020 https://data.census.gov/cedsci/table?q=asian%20chinese%20nevada&g=0400000US32&tid=ACSDT1Y2018.C02015&t=Asian.

10. "Asian Alone by Selected Groups, Asian Chinese New York," U.S. Census Bureau, accessed March 2, 2020, https://data.census.gov/cedsci/table?q=asian%20chinese%20new%20york&g=0400000US36&tid=ACSDT1Y2018.C02015&t=Asian.

11. U.S. Department of Homeland Security Office of Immigration Statistics, *2017 Yearbook of Immigration Statistics*, 2017, https://www.dhs.gov/immigration-statistics/yearbook/2017, tables 1 and 2. The yearbook provides information about persons obtaining lawful permanent resident status, which I use as a rough approximation of when significant immigration occurred.

12. Office of Immigration Statistics, tables 1 and 2.

13. Office of Immigration Statistics, tables 1 and 2.

14. Office of Immigration Statistics, tables 1 and 2.

15. Office of Immigration Statistics, tables 1 and 2.

16. Min Zhou and Jennifer Lee, "Hyper-selectivity and the Remaking of Culture: Understanding the Asian American Achievement Paradox," *Asian American Journal of Psychology*, 8, no. 1 (2017): 7 (emphasis in original). Zhou and Lee add, "The opposite of hyper-selectivity is hypo-selectivity, which refers to an immigrant group's dual negative selectivity—having a lower percentage of college graduates compared with their compatriots in the country of origin and to the general population in the host country" (7–8).

17. "Hawaii, Annual Estimates of the Resident Population: April 1, 2020, to July 1, 2019," U.S. Census Bureau, accessed March 2, 2020, https://data.census.gov/cedsci/table?q=hawaii&g=0400000US15&tid=ACSDP1Y2018.DP05.

18. "ACS Demographic and Housing Estimates, California," U.S. Census Bureau, accessed March 2, 2020, https://data.census.gov/cedsci/table?q=california&g=0400000US06&tid=ACSDP1Y2018.DP05.

19. "ACS Demographic and Housing Estimates, New York," U.S. Census Bureau, accessed March 2, 2020, https://data.census.gov/cedsci/table?q=new%20york&g=0400000US36&tid=ACSDP1Y2018.DP05.

20. Meera Deo, *Unequal Profession: Race and Gender in Legal Academia* (Redwood City, Calif.: Stanford University Press, 2019), 26–29. An interesting historical adjunct to Deo's study is Herma Kay Hill's

Paving the Way: The First American Women Law Professors (Oakland: University of California Press, 2021).

21. Ann Marimow, "Merrick Garland Passes Gavel to Sri Srinivasan to Lead Influential Appeals Court," *Washington Post*, February 13, 2020, https://www.washingtonpost.com/local/legal-issues/merrick-garland -passes-gavel-to-sri-srinavasan-to-lead-influential-appeals-court/ 2020/02/13/2bb5e316-4e77-11ea-b721-9f4cdc90bc1c-story.html.

22. Neomi Rao, email to the author, October 17, 2019.

23. Deo, 116-117.

24. Financial concerns are not unique to would-be judges. Deo reports the same issue for lawyers who leave law firms to join law school faculties. Deo, 21.

25. I have often thought that it is people who are engrossed in litigation who may be most interested in switching roles in the courtroom from being an advocate to controlling the decisions issued. Nonapplicant B was not such a person.

Bibliography

Helpful Internet Sources

American Bar Association (https://www.americanbar.org for judicial nominee ratings)

Bloomberg Government (https://www.bgov.com)

Congress.gov (https://congress.gov for nominations and transcripts)

Federal Judicial Center (https://www.fjc.gov)

GovTrack (https://www.govtrack.us/congress/votes)

National Asian Pacific American Bar Association (https://www.napaba.org)

Senate Committee on the Judiciary (https://www.judiciary.senate.gov)

U.S. Bureau of Labor Statistics (https://bls.gov)

U.S. Government Printing Office (https://www.govinfo.gov)

U.S. Senate (https://www.senate.gov for vote records)

Books, Articles, and Records

Alba, Davey. "The Meme-Worthy Judge of Silicon Valley's Titans." Wired, April 21, 2015. https://www.wired.com/2015/04/lucy-koh.

Allen, Samantha. "Trump Nominates His First Out-LGBT Judge. Will He Match Obama's 11?" Daily Beast, August 25, 2018. https://www.thedailybeast.com/trump-nominates-his-first-out-lgbt-judge-will-he-match-obamas-11.

Alliance for Justice. "Neomi Rao: United States Court of Appeals for the Washington D.C. Circuit." Accessed May 4, 2021. https://www.afj.org/nominee/neomi-rao.

Asian American Press. "Kobayashi and Chang Confirmed by Senate." December 23, 2010. https://aapress.com/government/kobayashi-and -chang-confirmed-by-senate.

Associated Press. "Hawley Draws Hard Line on Supreme Court Nominees, Abortion." AP News, July 30, 2010. https://apnews.com/ 3d30cbf74fa39a01ef1746357eab5ebd.

Baker. Carrie N. "10 Reasons Feminists Are Wary of Neomi Rao." *Ms.*, February 11, 2019. https://msmagazine.com/2019/02/11/10-reasons-feminists -wary-neomi-rao.

Barack Obama Scholars Program. "Jacqueline Nguyen." Occidental College. Accessed May 4, 2021. https://obamascholars.oxy.edu/person/jacqueline -nguyen.

Bobic, Igor, and Alexis Arnold. "Trump's Largely White and Male Appellate Judges, in One Photo." HuffPost, August 5, 2019. https:// www.huffpost.com/entry/trump-judges-white-male-nominees_n _5d484719e4b0acb57fd05ec3.

Bowman, Cynthia Grant. "Women in the Legal Profession from the 1920s to the 1970s: What Can We Learn from Their Experience about Law and Social Change?" *Maine Law Review* 61 (2009): 2–25.

Bronner, Ethan. *Battle for Justice: How the Bork Nomination Shook America.* New York: W. W. Norton, 1989.

Burke, Melissa Nann Burke, Robert Snell, and Jonathan Oosting. "Trump Picks First Black Female Judge Nominee as He Tries to Fill Mich. Vacancies." *Detroit News*, March 8, 2019. https://www.detroitnews.com/ story/news/politics/2019/03/08/trump-nominates-first-black-woman -judge-federal-bench-michigan/3105805002.

Caplow, Stacy, and Shira A. Scheindlin. "'Portrait of a Lady': The Woman Lawyer in the 1980s." *NYU Law Review* 35 (1990): 391–446.

Carbado, Devon, and Mitu Gulati. *Acting White? Rethinking Race in "Postracial" America.* Oxford: Oxford University Press, 2013.

———. "Working Identity." *Cornell Law Review* 85 (2000): 1259–1308.

Chen, Edward M. "The Judiciary, Diversity, and Justice for All." *Asian American Law Journal* 10, no. 1 (January 2003): 127–142.

Chew, Pat K., and Luke T. Kelley-Chew. "The Missing Minority Judges." *Journal of Gender, Race & Justice* 14 (2010): 179–198.

Chew, Pat K., and Robert E. Kelley. "Myth of the Color-Blind Judge: An Empirical Analysis of Racial Harassment Cases." *Washington University Law Review* 86 (2009): 1117–1166.

Chin, Ming W. "Fairness or Bias: A Symposium on Racial and Ethnic Composition and Attitudes in the Judiciary." *Asian American Law Journal* 4 (1997): 181–194.

Chung, Eric, Samuel Dong, Xiaonan April Hu, Christine Kwon, and Goodwin Liu, Yale Law School, and National Asian Pacific American Bar Association. *A Portrait of Asian Americans in the Law.* 2017. https://www.apaportraitproject.org.

Collins, Paul, Jr., and Lori Ringhand. *Supreme Court Confirmation Hearings and Constitutional Change.* Cambridge: Cambridge University Press, 2013.

Council, John. "A Decade Later, Texas Finally Sees Its First Asian-American U.S. District Judge." Law.com, Texas Lawyer, May 1, 2018. https://www.law.com/texaslawyer/2018/05/01/a-decade-later-texas-finally-sees-its-first-asian-american-u-s-district-judge.

Crawford, Selwyn. "High Profile: A Perfect Fit, Asian American Woman 'Just Feels Right' on the District Court Bench." *Dallas Morning News,* April 21, 2002, 3F.

Croucher, Shane. "Who Is Neomi Rao? Trump Nominee to Replace Brett Kavanaugh Wrote Controversial Date Rape Column in College." *Newsweek,* January 15, 2019. https://www.newsweek.com/trump-neomi-rao-brett-kavanaugh-date-rape-column-1291483.

Danforth, John. *Resurrection: The Confirmation of Clarence Thomas.* New York: Viking, 1994.

Demand Justice. "Demand Justice's Supreme Court Shortlist." Accessed May 4, 2021. https://demandjustice.org/supreme-court-shortlist.

Deo, Meera E. *Unequal Profession: Race and Gender in Legal Academia.* Redwood City, Calif.: Stanford University Press, 2019.

de Vogue, Ariane, and Alex Rogers. "'Not Qualified' Rating and Accusation from American Bar Association Moves Trump Nominee to Tears." CNN, October 30, 2019. https://www.cnn.com/2019/10/30/politics/american-bar-association-nominees-vandyke/index.html.

Duckworth, Angela. *Grit: The Power of Passion and Perseverance.* New York: Simon & Schuster, 2016.

Edwards, Harry T. "A Tribute to Leon Higginbotham, Jr.: Race and the Judiciary." *Yale Law & Policy Review* 30 (2002): 325–330.

Fallon, Brian, and Christopher Kang. "Biden Must Prioritize the Courts If Elected." *Data for Progress* (blog), July 30, 2020. https://www.dataforprogress.org/blog/biden-must-prioritize-the-courts-if-elected.

———. "No More Corporate Lawyers on the Federal Bench: The Next Democratic President Should Try Nominating Judges Who Haven't Been Partners at Big Law Firms." *Atlantic*, August 21, 2019. https://www.theatlantic.com/ideas/archive/2019/08/no-more-corporate-judges/596383.

Farganis, Dion, and Justin Wedeking. *Supreme Court Confirmation Hearings in the U.S. Senate: Reconsidering the Charade.* Ann Arbor: University of Michigan Press, 2014.

Folliard, Patrick. "Spotlighting: Taking the Next Step." *Diversity & the Bar*, May/June 2010. Reprinted at https://www.mcca.com/mcca-article/spotlighting-may-june-2010.

Fricke, Amber, and Angela Onwuachi-Wittig. "Do Female 'Firsts' Still Matter? Why They Do for Female Judges of Color." *Michigan State Law Review* 2012 (2012): 1529–1554.

Gerson, Jeannie Suk. "Understanding the Partisanship of Brett Kavanaugh's Confirmation Hearings." *New Yorker*, September 12, 2018. https://www.newyorker.com/news/our-columnists/understanding-the-partisanship-of-brett-kavanaughs-confirmation-hearings.

Gladwell, Malcolm. *Outliers: The Story of Success.* New York: Little, Brown, 2008.

Goldman, Sheldon. "The Judicial Confirmation Crisis and the Clinton Presidency." *Presidential Studies Quarterly* 28, no. 4 (1998): 838–844.

———. *Picking Federal Judges: Lower Court Selection from Roosevelt through Reagan.* New Haven, Conn.: Yale University Press, 1999.

Goldman, Sheldon, and Matthew Saronson. "Clinton's Nontraditional Judges: Creating a More Representative Bench." *Judicature* 78 (1994): 68–73.

Greene, Robert. "Davis Names Assistant U.S. Attorney Jacqueline Nguyen to Fill Vacancy on Los Angeles Superior Court." *Metropolitan News-Enterprise*, August 14, 2002. http://www.metnews.com/articles/nguyo81402.htm.

Gregory, Patrick. "Openly Gay Prosecutor Could Again Be Trump Appeals Court Pick." *U.S. Law Week*, June 12, 2019. https://www.bloomberglaw .com/document/X165I4ROo00000?bna_news_filter=us-law-week& jcsearch=BNA%25200000016b4c34d4f0a36b4d748b850000#jcite.

Grube, Nick. "Hawaii Federal Judge Nomination Offers Glimpse of Partisan Dealmaking." Civil Beat, March 7, 2018. https://www.civilbeat.org/ 2018/03/hawaii-federal-judge-nomination-offers-glimpse-of-partisan -dealmaking.

Hawaii State Bar Association. "2019 Bar Statistics & Summaries." Accessed May 4, 2021. https://hsba.org/images/hsba/HSBA/Annual%20Statistics %20Results/2019_Bar_Statistics_and_Summaries.pdf.

Haygood, Wil. *Showdown: Thurgood Marshall and the Supreme Court Nomination That Changed America*. New York: Vintage, 2015.

Hemingway, Mollie, and Carrie Severino. *Justice on Trial: The Kavanaugh Confirmation and the Future of the Supreme Court*. Washington, D.C.: Regency, 2019.

Hill, Herma Kay. *Paving the Way: The First American Women Law Professors*. Oakland: University of California Press, 2021.

Hindu Business Line. "Indian-American Neomi Rao Sworn in as Judge of Powerful U.S. Court." March 21, 2019. https://www.thehindubusinessline .com/news/world/indian-american-neomi-rao-sworn-in-as-judge-of -powerful-us-court/article26597495.ece.

Homer, Suzanne, and Lois Schwartz. "Admitted but Not Accepted: Outsiders Take an Inside Look at Law School." *Berkeley Women's Law Journal* 5 (1990): 1–74.

Horowitz, Daniel. "The Fight over Judicial Nominee Neomi Rao Reveals a Big Schism on the Right." *Conservative Review*, February 26, 2019. https://www.conservativereview.com/news/fight-judicial-nominee -neomi-rao-reveals-big-schism-right.

Howe, Amy. "Trump Releases New List of Potential Supreme Court Nominees." *SCOTUSblog*, September 9, 2020. https://www.scotusblog.com/ 2020/09/trump-releases-new-list-of-potential-supreme-court-nominees.

Howell, Marcella, Sung Yeon Choimorrow, and Jessica Gonzalez-Rojas. "Neomi Rao Will Not Protect Rights of Women of Color." *Hill*, February 15, 2019. https://thehill.com/opinion/judiciary/430077-neomi-rao -will-not-protect-rights-of-women-of-color.

Hsu, Josh. "Asian American Judges: Identity, Their Narratives, and Diversity on the Bench." *Asian Pacific American Law Journal* 11 (2006): 92–119.

Hulse, Carl. *Confirmation Bias: Inside Washington's War on the Supreme Court, from Scalia's Death to Justice Kavanaugh.* New York: HarperCollins, 2019.

Ifill, Sherrilyn A. "Racial Diversity on the Bench: Beyond Role Models and Public Confidence." *Washington and Lee Law Review* 57 (2000): 405–495.

Institute for Inclusion in the Legal Profession. "The State of Diversity and Inclusion in the Legal Profession." ILP Report 2014. https://theiilp .wildapricot.org/Resources/Documents/IILP_2014_Final.pdf.

Johnson, Hannah Brenner, and Renee Knake Jefferson. *Shortlisted: Women in the Shadows of the Supreme Court.* New York: New York University Press, 2020.

Jones, Sarah. "Why Kavanaugh Replacement Neomi Rao Is So Controversial." *New York Magazine*, March 14, 2019. http://nymag.com/ intelligencer/2019/03/neomi-rao-controversial.html.

Kane, Paul. "Reid, Democrats Trigger 'Nuclear' Option; Eliminate Most Filibusters on Nominees." *Washington Post*, November 21, 2013. https://www .washingtonpost.com/politics/senate-poised-to-limit-filibusters-in-party -line-vote-that-would-alter-centuries-of-precedent/2013/11/21/d065cfe8 -52b6-11e3-9fe0-fd2ca728e67c_story.html.

Kanter, Rosabeth Moss. *Men and Women of the Corporation.* New York: Basic Books, 1977.

Kassam, Kerry. "Judging the Judges: Who Are the Most Cited New Jurists on the Federal Bench?" *Above the Law*, April 23, 2015. https:// abovethelaw.com/2015/04/judging-the-judges-who-are-the-most-cited -new-jurists-on-the-federal-bench.

Kobayashi, Ken. "Dignity Key for Kobayashi." *Honolulu Star Advertiser*, December 27, 2010. https://www.staradvertiser.com/2010/12/27/hawaii -news/dignity-key-for-kobayashi.

Koh, Lucy. "Combatting Inequality." In *Harvard Law School's Handbook and Directory for Law Students and Lawyers Seeking Public Service Work.* 1995–1996.

Kravitch, Phyllis. "Women in the Legal Profession: The Past 100 Years." *Mississippi Law Journal* 69 (1999): 57–71.

L.A. Progressive. "Voices of America: Enhancing Diversity on the Bench—Judge Jacqueline Nguyen." April 26, 2010. https://www .laprogressive.com/voices-america-enhancing-diversity-bench-2.

Lau, Theresa. "Five Things You Should Know about D.C. Circuit Nominee Neomi Rao." National Women's Law Center, February 14, 2019. https://nwlc.org/blog/five-things-you-should-know-about-d-c-circuit-nominee-neomi-rao.

Lazos, Sylvia R. "Only Skin Deep: The Cost of Partisan Politics on Minority Diversity of the Federal Bench: Why Care Whether Judges Look 'like America' If, Because of Politics, a 'Voice of Color' Has Become a 'Whisper of Color'?" *Indiana Law Journal* 83, no. 4 (2008):1423–1479.

Lee, Philip. "The Griswold 9 and Student Activism for Faculty Diversity at Harvard Law School in the Early 1990s." *Harvard Journal of Racial and Ethnic Justice* 27 (2011): 49–96.

Lewis, Patricia, and Ruth Simpson. "Kanter Revisited: Gender, Power, and (In)Visibility." *International Journal of Management Reviews* 14, no. 2 (2011): 141–158.

Li, Miranda, Phillip Yao, and Goodwin Liu. "Who's Going to Law School? Trends in Law School Enrollment since the Great Recession." *University of California Davis Law Review* 54 (2020): 613–662.

Livri, Ephrat. "To Understand Trump Judicial Pick Neomi Rao, Consider Her Writing on Dwarf-Tossing." Quartz, November 29, 2018. https://qz.com/1477549/to-understand-trump-judicial-pick-neomi-rao-consider-her-writing-on-dwarf-tossing.

Marcus, Ruth. *Supreme Ambition: Brett Kavanaugh and the Conservative Takeover*. New York: Simon & Schuster, 2019.

Marimow, Ann. "Merrick Garland Passes Gavel to Sri Srinivasan to Lead Influential Appeals Court." *Washington Post*, February 13, 2020. https://www.washingtonpost.com/local/legal-issues/merrick-garland-passes-gavel-to-sri-srinivasan-to-lead-influential-appeals-court/2020/02/13/2bb5e316-4e77-11ea-b721-9f4cdc90bc1c_story.html.

Marimow, Ann E., and Seung Min Kim. "Justice Thomas Working behind the Scenes to Boost Trump's Court Nominee." *Washington Post*, February 28, 2019. https://www.washingtonpost.com/powerpost/trumps-court-nominee-overcomes-gop-concerns-secures-panels-backing/2019/02/28/fa33bc86-3adc-11e9-aaae-69364b2ed137_story.html.

Mayer, Jane, and Jill Abramson. *Strange Justice: The Selling of Clarence Thomas*. Los Angeles: Graymalkin Media, 1994.

Mintz, Howard. "White House Expected to Nominate High-Profile Silicon Valley–Based Judge Lucy Koh to Federal Appeals Court." *Mercury News*, February 1, 2016. https://www.mercurynews.com/2016/02/01/white-house-expected-to-nominate-high-profile-silicon-valley-based-judge-lucy-koh-to-federal-appeals-court.

Minority Corporate Counsel Association. "LGBT Article III Judges." Last updated May 7, 2020. https://www.mcca.com/resources/reports/federal-judiciary/lgbt-judges.

National Asian Pacific American Bar Association. *2015 Year in Review, Partnerships: American Bar Association*. 2015. https://cdn.ymaws.com/www.napaba.org/resource/resmgr/Year-in-Review/NAPABA_2015_Year-in-Review.pdf.

National Asian Pacific American Bar Association Judiciary Committee. *Asian Pacific American Judges*. Annual conference handout, November 7, 2019.

National Asian Pacific American Bar Association National Convention 2016. *Pearls of Wisdom from APA "Firsts" on the Bench*. Accessed May 4, 2021. https://cdn.ymaws.com/www.napaba.org/resource/resmgr/2016_napaba_con/CLE_Materials/CLE_501.pdf.

North Carolina Modernist. "The George Matsumoto Prize." Accessed May 4, 2021. http://www.ncmodernist.org/matsumotoprize.htm.

NYU News. "Judge Kiyo Matsumoto Delivers 11th Annual Korematsu Lecture." March 17, 2010. https://www.law.nyu.edu/news/KOREMATSU_MATSUMOTO.

O'Harrow, Robert, Jr., and Shawn Boburg. "A Conservative Activist's Behind-the-Scenes Campaign to Remake the Nation's Courts." *Washington Post*, May 21, 2019, https://www.washingtonpost.com/graphics/2019/investigations/leonard-leo-federalists-society-courts/.

Pastor, Cristina D. C. "First Fil-Am Federal Judge Lorna Schofield: 'I Had No Filipino Consciousness Growing Up.'" *USA Inquirer*, February 24, 2018. https://usa.inquirer.net/10419/first-fil-federal-judge-lorna-schofield-no-filipino-consciousness-growing.

Peresie, Jennifer. "Female Judges Matter: Gender and Collegial Decision-making in the Federal Appellate Courts." *Yale Law Journal* 114, no. 7 (2005): 1759–1790.

Pimental, Joseph. "Lorna Schofield, One of National Law Journal's 50 Most Influential Minority Lawyers and Nominee for Federal District Court

Judge, Southern District of NY." *Asian Journal*, January 28, 2012. https://
www.asianjournal.com/usa/newyork-newjersey/lorna-schofield-one
-of-national-law-journals-50-most-influential-minority-lawyers-and
-nominee-for-federal-district-court-judge-southern-district-of-ny.

Pogrebin, Robin, and Kate Kelly. *The Education of Brett Kavanaugh: An
Investigation*. London: Portfolio Penguin, 2019.

Rao, Neomi. "The Feminist Dilemma." *Yale Free Press*, April 1993. https://
www.afj.org/wp-content/uploads/2019/12/02-The-Feminist-Dilemma.pdf.

———. "How the Diversity Game Is Played." *Washington Times*, July 17,
1994, WLNR 236705. https://afj.org/wp-content/uploads/2019/12/07
-How-the-Diversity-Game-is-Played.pdf.

———. "Shades of Gray." *Yale Herald*, October 14, 1994. Accessed May 4, 2021,
at https://afj.org/wp-content/uploads/2019/12/01-Shades-of-Gray.pdf.

———. "Submission, Silence, Mediocrity." *Yale Free Press*, November 1993.
Accessed May 4, 2021, at https://www.documentcloud.org/documents/
5684271-Rao-Submission-Silence-Mediocracy.html.

———. "Substantive Dignity—Dwarf-Throwing, Burqa Bans, and Welfare
Rights." *Volokh Conspiracy*, May 18, 2011. http://volokh.com/2011/05/18/
substantive-dignity-dwarf-throwing-burqa-bans-and-welfare-rights.

———. "Three Concepts of Dignity in Constitutional Law." *Notre Dame
Law Review* 86 (2011): 183–271.

Rao, Neomi, and Luis Roth. "Separate, but More Than Equal: From Admissions to Ethnic Deans, a Look at Minorities at Yale." *Yale Free Press*,
1993–1994.

Rappaport, Adam J. "The Court of International Trade's Political Party
Diversity Requirement: Unconstitutional under Any Separation of Powers Theory." *University of Chicago Law Review* 68, no. 4 (2001): 1429–1458.

Rawles, Lee. "Its Ratings System under Fire, ABA Stresses Importance
of Federal Judicial Candidate Evaluations." *ABA Journal*, January
2018. https://www.abajournal.com/magazine/article/federal_judicial
_candidate_evaluations.

Reeves, Carlton W. "Defending the Judiciary: A Call for Justice, Truth,
and Diversity on the Bench." Prepared Remarks upon Receiving the
Thomas Jefferson Foundation Medal in Law, April 11, 2019. https://
assets.documentcloud.org/documents/5836481/Thomas-Jefferson-Award
-Speech-April-2019.pdf.

Root, Danielle, Jake Faleschini, and Grace Oyenubi. "Building a More
   Inclusive Federal Judiciary." Center for American Progress, October 3,
   2019. https://www.americanprogress.org/issues/courts/reports/2019/10/
   03/475359/building-inclusive-federal-judiciary.

Savage, Charlie. "Biden Won't Restore Bar Association's Role in Vetting
   Judges." *New York Times*, February 5, 2021. https://www.nytimes.com/
   2021/02/05/us/politics/biden-american-bar-association-judges.html.

Sen, Maya. "Diversity, Qualification, and Ideology: How Female and
   Minority Judges Have Changed or Not Changed over Time." *Wisconsin
   Law Review* 2 (2017): 367–399.

———. "How Judicial Qualification Ratings May Disadvantage Minority
   and Female Candidates." *Journal of Law and Courts* 2, no. 1 (2014): 33–66.

Severino, Carrie. "The ABA Has Outdone Itself Rating Lawrence Van-
   Dyke 'Not Qualified.'" *National Review*, October 30, 2019. https://www
   .nationalreview.com/bench-memos/the-aba-has-outdone-itself-rating
   -lawrence-vandyke-not-qualified.

Shapiro, Ilya. *Supreme Disorder: Judicial Nominations and the Politics of America's Highest Court.* New York: Simon & Schuster, 2020.

Silverstein, Mark. *Judicious Choices: The New Politics of Supreme Court Confirmations.* New York: W. W. Norton, 1994.

Simon, Paul. *Advice and Consent: Clarence Thomas, Robert Bork, and the
   Intriguing History of the Supreme Court's Nomination Battles.* Washington,
   D.C.: National Press, 1992.

Slattery, Elizabeth. "4 Key Issues in Neomi Rao's Judicial Confirmation Hearing." Heritage Foundation, February 6, 2019. https://www.heritage.org/
   courts/commentary/4-key-issues-neomi-raos-judicial-confirmation-hearing.

Sotomayor, Sonia. "A Latina Judge's Voice." *Berkeley La Raza Law Journal* 13
   (2002): 87–94.

Stichman, A. J., Kimberly Hassell, and Carol Archbold. "Strength in
   Numbers? A Test of Kanter's Theory of Tokenism." *Journal of Criminal
   Justice* 38 (2010): 633–639.

Stubbs, Jonathan K. "A Demographic History of Federal Judicial Appointments by Sex and Race: 1789–2016." *Berkeley La Raza Law Journal* 26
   (2016): 92–128.

———. "A Demographic Snapshot of America's Federal Judiciary:
   A Prima Facie Case for Change." *NAACA News*, February 2011.

https://scholarship.richmond.edu/cgi/viewcontent.cgi?article=1074&
context=law-faculty-publications.

Thurston, Jennifer. "Black Robes, White Judges: The Lack of Diversity on the Magistrate Judge Bench." *Law and Contemporary Problems* 82 (2019): 63–102.

Tobias, Carl W. "Appointing Lesbian, Gay, Bisexual, Transgender and Queer Judges in the Trump Administration." *Washington University Law Review Online* 96 (June 2008): 11–22.

Tobin, Jonathan S. "The Battle over Neomi Rao Is the Latest in the Judicial Wars: Republicans Must Stand up to Democrats' Attempt to Damage a Rising Legal Star." *National Review*, February 6, 2019. https://www.nationalreview.com/2019/02/neomi-rao-nomination-democrats-try-to-damage-rising-legal-star.

Tolan, Casey. "How Jacqueline Nguyen Went from a Vietnamese Refugee to a Potential Supreme Court Nominee." Splinter News, February 18, 2016. https://splinternews.com/how-jacqueline-nguyen-went-from-a-vietnamese-refugee-to-1793854865.

U.S. Department of Homeland Security Office of Immigration Statistics. *2017 Yearbook of Immigration Statistics*. 2017. https://www.dhs.gov/immigration-statistics/yearbook/2017.

Vaughn, Alexa. "Obama Taps L.A. Federal Judge Nguyen for 9th Circuit." *L.A. Times*, September 23, 2011. https://www.latimes.com/politics/la-xpm-2011-sep-23-la-pn-nguyen-9thcircuit-20110923-story.html.

Vieira, Norman, and Leonard Gross. *Supreme Court Appointments: Judge Bork and the Politicization of Senate Confirmations*. Carbondale: Southern Illinois University Press, 1998.

Voruganti, Harsh. "Jill Otake—Nominee for the U.S. District Court for the District of Hawaii." *Vetting Room*, February 27, 2018. https://www.vettingroom.org/2018/02/27/jill-otake.

———. "Neomi Rao—Nominee to the U.S. Court of Appeals for the D.C. Circuit." *Vetting Room*, February 11, 2019. https://vettingroom.org/2019/02/11/neomi-rao.

Weiss, Debra Cassens. "GOP Senators Clash over ABA during Hearing for Judicial Nominee Rated 'Not Qualified.'" *ABA Journal*, September 26, 2019. http://www.abajournal.com/news/article/gop-senators-criticize-aba-ratings-during-hearing-for-nominee-rated-not-qualified.

Weissmann, Shosana. "Neomi Rao Was Right about Dwarf Tossing, Dignity, and Consent. She Deserves to Be a Federal Judge: A Defense of Brett Kavanaugh's Nominated Replacement on the D.C. Circuit." *Reason*, November 26, 2018. https://reason.com/2018/11/26/neomi-rao -was-right-about-dwarf-tossing.

Westney, Andrew. "Native Judges Still Looking for Room on Federal Bench." Law 360, October 4, 2019. https://www.law360.com/articles/ 1204970/native-judges-still-looking-for-room-on-federal-bench.

Wheeler, Lydia. "Clinton's Court Shortlist Emerges." *Hill*, July 30, 2016. https://thehill.com/regulation/court-battles/289643-clintons-court -shortlist-emerges.

Wheeler, Russell. "Changing Backgrounds of U.S. District Judges: Causes and Possible Implications." *Judicature* 93, no. 4 (2010): 140–149.

White House. "This Is the First Time Our Judicial Pool Has Been This Diverse." June 28, 2016. https://obamawhitehouse.archives.gov/share/first -time-our-judicial-pool-has-been-diverse.

Wilkins, David. "The New Social Engineers in the Age of Obama: Black Corporate Lawyers and the Making of the First Black President." *Howard Law Journal* 53 (2010): 557–644.

———. "Testing the Resources of the Law: John Robinson Wilkins, Berkeley Law, and the Limits of Law and Development." YouTube video, 1:10:11, August 22, 2019. https://www.youtube.com/watch?v= GXqB3EaHV5Y&feature=youtube.

Wittes, Benjamin. *Confirmation Wars: Preserving Independent Courts in Angry Times*. Lanham, Md.: Rowman & Littlefield, 2006.

Women's Bar Association of District of Columbia. "History from 1919–1927." https://www.wbadc.org/history#From1917-1927.

Yoder, Janice, and Lynne Berendsen. "Outsider within the Firehouse: African American and White Women Firefighters." *Psychology of Women Quarterly* 25, no. 1 (2001): 27–36.

Zhou, Min, and Lee, Jennifer. "Hyper-selectivity and the Remaking of Culture: Understanding the Asian American Achievement Paradox." *Asian American Journal of Psychology* 8, no. 1 (2017): 7–15.

Zimmer, Lynn. "Tokenism and Women in the Workplace: The Limits of Gender-Neutral Theory." *Social Problems* 35 (1988): 64–77.

Index

Abraham, Spencer, 36, 39, 40
Acheson, Eleanor, 37, 62
Acoba, Simeon R., Jr., 143
Administrative Office of U.S. Courts, 190
African Americans: judges, 12–13, 14, 16;
  population of, 11
age of judges, 173–174
Akaka, Daniel, 34, 35, 79
Alejandro, Nitza Quinones, 16
Allen, Florence Ellinwood, 11
Alliance for Justice, 38, 215n60
American Bar Association, 119; judicial
  nominee ratings of, 23, 24–25, 106, 108,
  173, 188. *See individual judges' profiles for
  individual ratings*
American Civil Liberties Union,
  36–37, 41, 43, 81, 189
American Judicature Society, 79
Antonin Scalia Law School, George
  Mason University, 151
Arizona, District of, 12
Article III, U.S. Constitution, 1–2
Ashcroft, John, 37
Asian, use of term, 3–4
Asian American, use of term, 3–4
Asian American Bar Association, Texas,
  136
Asian American Bar Association of New
  York, 46, 48, 106, 112, 115
Asian American Justice Center, 83, 106
Asian Indians. *See* South Asian
  Americans

Asian Pacific American Bar Association
  of Silicon Valley, 72
  Asians: number of federal judges,
  14–15, 16; population of, 11, 165
assistant U.S. attorney, 45, 48, 53, 71, 103,
  111, 112, 141, 142, 146, 176, 177, 188
attitudes of judges, 180–193

bachelor of laws degree, 207n1
bankruptcy judges, 2, 122
Barrett, Amy Coney, 152
Batts, Deborah, 16
Bennett, Mark, 144
Berzon, Marsha, 118, 119, 184, 226n102
Berzon, Stephen, 119, 184
Bharara, Preet, 46
Biden, Joseph, 25, 81, 158, 160
Bidong Island, 95
biracial Asian women judges, 88, 102, 118,
  131, 140, 168
birth order, 140, 174
Bissoon, Cathy, 14, 165, 168, 169, 170, 171,
  173, 174, 175, 176, 177, 178, 183–184, 197;
  profile of, 87–93
Blackburn, Marsha, 152
boat people, 95
Bork, Robert, 18
Boston College Law School, 77, 197
Boxer, Barbara, 61, 64, 65, 72, 73
Brodie, Margo, 112
Brown, Ada Elene, 12, 15
Brownback, Sam, 46

Hakka Chinese dialect, 96
hapa haole, 140
Hardiman, Thomas, 90
Harris, Kamala, 153
*Harvard Civil Rights-Civil Liberties Law
Review*, 37
Harvard Law School, 33, 70, 87, 197
Harvard University, 70
Hastie, William Henry, 209n13
Hatch, Orrin, 62
Hatch Act, 176
Hawaii: Asian bar in, 166; District of, 1,
31, 77, 139, 140, 165, 182, 201; population
of, 20, 165, 171
Hawley, Josh, 155, 215n60
Heen, Walter Meheula, 210n29
Heller, Dean, 98
Hirono, Mazie, 84, 85, 143, 144, 145, 166
Hispanic, use of term, 208n4
Ho, James, 127, 228n116
housing discrimination, 44, 60
Hsu, Josh, 22
Humetawa, Diane, 12
Hutchison, Kay Bailey, 40, 133, 134
hyper-selectivity, 170, 235, 248

Ikuta, Sandra Segal, 23
Illinois, Northern District of, 5, 16, 83, 158
immigration: from China, 59, 111, 167, 168;
effect of timing, 163; effect on judges,
169–171, 179, 202; from Japan, 32, 43, 78,
131, 140, 167, 168; from Korea, 69, 124,
167, 168; from the Philippines, 102, 167,
168; from South Asia, 88, 118, 148, 167,
168, 170; from Trinidad, 88, 168; from
Vietnam, 50–51, 95–96, 167, 168
indefatigable nature of judges, 186–193
Indian Americans. *See* South Asian
Americans
Indian diaspora, 88
Inouye, Daniel K., 34, 35, 39, 79, 82, 166,
190
internment camps, Japanese American,
32, 43
Ishii, Anthony, 43

Japanese American Citizens' League, 43
Japanese Americans: internment of,
32, 43; population of; women federal
judges, 31–48, 77–86, 130–38, 139–146,
165, 166, 169
Japanese language, 32, 78, 131, 172
JD, 207n1
Johnson, Karen Gren, 122, 134. *See* Scholer, Karen Gren
Johnson, Mark, 122
Judaism, 148
judges' parents, summary of professions
of, 169, 174–175
judicial salary, 195
Juilliard School, 124
juris doctor degree, 207n1

Kang, Chris, 27, 29, 74, 80, 99, 120, 164,
180, 192, 195
Kanter, Rosabeth Moss, 19, 20, 185
Kashiwa, Shiro, 14
Kavanaugh, Brett, 18, 151
KAYA: Filipino Americans for Progress,
106
Kearse, Amalya, 12
Kelley, Angel, 160
Kelley-Chew, Luke T., 22
Kennedy, Edward, 71
Kerry, John, 120
Kim, Wan, 127
King, Rodney, 70
Kobayashi, Leslie Emi, 99, 142, 165, 166,
169, 171, 173, 174, 175, 176, 177, 184, 188,
197, 201; profile of, 77–86
Koh, Lucy Haeran, 165, 169, 171, 172,
173, 174, 175, 176, 177, 182, 184, 185, 197;
profile of, 68–76; student activities
contrasted with activities by Rao,
Neomi, 149
Korean Americans: population of, 166;
women federal judges, 68–76, 123–129,
165
Korean language, 124
Korematsu, Fred, 43
Kyl, Jon, 127

About the Author

SUSAN OKI MOLLWAY has been a federal judge in the District of Hawaii for over twenty years, serving as the chief judge of the district from 2009 to 2015. Before entering the judiciary, she graduated cum laude from Harvard Law School in Cambridge, Massachusetts, then worked as a civil litigator. She later earned an LLM from Duke University in Durham, North Carolina.